An Injury to All

The Unmaking of the British Working Class

Ewan Gibbs

VERSO
London • New York

First published by Verso 2026

The manufacturer's authorized representative in the EU
for product safety (GPSR) is LOGOS EUROPE, 9 rue
Nicolas Poussin, 17000, La Rochelle, France
contact@logoseurope.eu

1 3 5 7 9 10 8 6 4 2

Verso
UK: 6 Meard Street, London W1F 0EG
US: 207 East 32nd Street, New York, NY 10016
versobooks.com

Verso is the imprint of New Left Books

ISBN-13: 978-1-80429-649-3
ISBN-13: 978-1-80429-651-6 (UK EBK)
ISBN-13: 978-1-80429-652-3 (US EBK)

British Library Cataloguing in Publication Data
A catalogue record for this book is available from the British Library

Library of Congress Cataloging-in-Publication Data
A catalog record for this book is available from the Library of Congress

Typeset in Sabon LT by Hewer Text UK Ltd, Edinburgh
Printed and bound by CPI Group (UK) Ltd, Croydon CR0 4YY

Contents

Abbreviations

ACAS	Advisory, Conciliation and Arbitration Service
APEX	Association of Professional, Executive, Clerical and Computer Staff
BEA	British Electricity Authority
BNP	British National Party
CPGB	Communist Party of Great Britain
EETPU	Electrical, Electronic, Telecommunications and Plumbing Union
ETU	Electrical Trades Union
FBU	Fire Brigades Union
IMF	International Monetary Fund
MRC	Modern Records Centre
NAECI	National Agreement for the Engineering Construction Industry
NAFF	National Association for Freedom
NALGO	National and Local Government Officers' Association
NCB	National Coal Board
NDLS	National Dock Labour Scheme
NMMS	National Mining Museum of Scotland
NUM	National Union of Mineworkers
NUMSA	National Union of Mineworkers Scottish Area
RMT	National Union of Rail, Maritime and Transport Workers
SCEBTA	Scottish Colliery Enginemen, Boilermen and Tradesmen's Association
SSHA	Scottish Special Housing Association

SSP	Scottish Socialist Party
TGWU	Transport and General Workers' Union
TNA	The National Archives, Kew
TUC	Trades Union Congress
UKIP	United Kingdom Independence Party

Introduction

The Unmaking of the British Working Class

Jimmy Hood was a twenty-year-old mining engineer when Auchlochan colliery in Coalburn, South Lanarkshire, succumbed to the closure programme of the National Coal Board (NCB). It was 1968, and Jimmy weighed up his options: he could retrain for the steel works, become an expat engineer in post-colonial Zambia or earn 'mega money' down south in booming Nottinghamshire. He plumped for Nottinghamshire.[1]

Like other Midlands coalfield villages, Ollerton was a haven of employment and prosperity. Jimmy was given a new house for his family at discounted rent. Mining 'coward's coal', which came much easier than the meagre rewards of the dank, dangerous seams in Lanarkshire, he earned almost one and a half times as much as he had at Auchlochan. Ollerton was one of the most productive pits in Europe, supplying vast new power stations that lined the River Trent. The area had been christened 'Megawatt Valley' owing to its place at the centre of Britain's electricity supply.

At Ollerton, Jimmy found himself in a new, cosmopolitan environment. As well as fellow Scots and men from elsewhere in Britain, miners from Eastern Europe and the Commonwealth swelled the workforce. Workers from South Wales brought their tradition of marching jazz bands to Nottinghamshire.[2] Scots and Geordies founded their own social clubs, but miners and their families also congregated together at the huge Miners' Welfare, which was boastfully known locally as 'the Palladium of the North'.

As a young boy, Jimmy had been whirled around the family living room by his mother as she celebrated Labour's electoral gains in Scotland's industrial constituencies. Finally, they had seen the backs of the hated Tories! At least locally. Such memories were the foundation of lifelong commitments. Jimmy took part in the 1972 miners' strike for wage improvements alongside his workmates, acting as a mobile 'flying picket'. Two years later, he was active in another successful strike which ushered in the Three-Day Week and triggered the defeat of Edward Heath's Conservative government at the February 1974 general election. Eventually, he became one of the leaders of his coalfield's striking miners during the defining year-long struggle with Margaret Thatcher's Conservatives over the future of coal mining in the country.

Unlike Jimmy, most miners in Nottinghamshire refused to join the 1984–85 strike. His local parliamentary constituency, Sherwood, had voted Conservative in the previous general election and would return an increased Tory majority in 1987.[3] Ollerton was a major flashpoint during the first phase of the strike. David Jones, a young miner from Yorkshire, was killed while picketing the pit.[4] Jimmy experienced the intimidation and violence meted out by members of the strike-breaking majority in Nottinghamshire when his car was vandalised and his garage set on fire. He even received intimidating anonymised phone calls from people falsely claiming to have kidnapped his young daughter.[5]

Defeat and the miners' return to work marked the beginning of the end of the world that had made Jimmy Hood. Ollerton mined its last coal a decade later. By then, Jimmy had moved back to Scotland. He became one of the last coal miners to become a Labour MP as Member for Clydesdale in his old South Lanarkshire stomping ground. On the backbenches at Westminster, Jimmy chaired the European Scrutiny Committee and voted against his own party's Iraq War. He lost his seat in 2015 to a newly potent political challenge: Scottish nationalism.[6] On doorsteps across ex-council housing estates and new-build privately owned schemes, Scottish National Party activists persuaded disaffected voters that they better represented social solidarity and egalitarianism than a Labour Party yoked to the British state and the concerns of an increasingly divergent English electorate.[7]

Jimmy passed away two years later.

The British working class lost its place at the centre of the national imagination during the late twentieth century. In a structural sense, a large proportion of the workforce continues to be employed in manual or routine non-manual jobs. Nevertheless, politically and culturally they have been a diminishing presence since the 1960s. Just as Edward Thompson wrote a classic study of the 'making' of the nineteenth-century English working class, I want to trace how the post–Second World War working class was 'unmade' across England, Scotland and Wales.[8] Cataclysmic episodes such as the 1984–85 miners' strike and the rapid transfer of council housing to private ownership under Thatcher's Right to Buy scheme are important parts of this story. So too are processes that unravelled over several decades: the grinding experience of industrial job losses, shifting voting patterns and momentous changes in how tens of millions of people thought about themselves and their position in society.

The unmaking is not a 'who done it', or an exercise in finger-pointing at folk villains from above or below, be they strike-breakers, newly propertied homeowners or even 'disenfranchised' British National Party (BNP) voters. All of these characters, and many more, will feature in the chapters which follow.

There were two pertinent trends in the unmaking of the British working class as it was present in mid-twentieth-century Britain: the decline of manufacturing jobs and the 'de-organisation' of workplaces. By 'de-organisation' I mean the diminishing importance of unionised workers in the British economy. Trade union organisation continued expanding in Britain into the 1970s even as industrial employment fell. There were significant gains among service-sector workers, particularly in the public sector, where remaining trade union strength primarily lies today. Union membership peaked in 1979 at above 13 million, more than half of the total workforce. It has since fallen beneath one-quarter. This drop-off is partially explained by the privatisation of nationalised industries and by practices such as bogus self-employment in sectors like lorry driving and construction. It also reflects the failure of trade unions to make much headway in the private service sector which now dominates employment in Britain, though in recent years there have been signs that this could change. As we shall see, however, de-organisation was above all the result of class struggle waged by employers, with important support from Conservative and Labour politicians.

It is against this backdrop that alternative political affiliations have reshaped working-class political outlooks, with advances made by the far right, Conservatism and Scottish nationalism. Gone is the shared investment in the British labour movement which structured working-class consciousness in the period that historian Eric Hobsbawm described as labour's 'forward march'.[9] For Hobsbawm, rising working-class confidence from the 1870s to the mid-twentieth century was imbued with the growth of heavy industry, trade unions and the Labour Party. A sense of common identification was grounded in a national popular culture in Victorian and Edwardian Britain which included newspaper readership, music halls and association football.[10] Shared ways of life and ways of thinking formed the basis for associational bonds and organisation across regional and national distinctions. A practically oriented politics of workplace trade unionism generated the solidarity proclaimed on labour movement banners, perhaps most enduringly the slogan that 'an injury to one is an injury to all'.

This was the making of the British working class that features in this book. In this vanished era, the British population was overwhelmingly composed of manual waged workers and their dependants. More than a century of intense economic change had concentrated the workforce into towns and cities, or else into distinctive industrial villages defined by coal mining or textiles production. Employment in manufacturing, mining, rail or dock transport was pivotal for how the working class came to understand itself and how it was understood by outsiders. Overwhelmingly, this population was also propertyless, depending on its wages to pay rent to private landlords.[11] Major industrial disputes from the 1880s to the 1910s had taken on an increasingly national character as unions were formed on the docks and among gas workers, railwaymen and coal miners. These had political implications, as they tested historical affiliations to the Liberal Party among a trade union movement no longer confined to a minority of comparatively privileged skilled trades. In turn, these developments encouraged support for independent working-class political representation through the Labour Party.

While it arose from conflict between workers and both Conservative and Liberal governments, Labour was built on a Liberal inheritance, committed to free trade and preserving Britain's place at the heart of a liberalised world economic order, as well as to imperialism and British nationhood. Labour matured within the politics of empire. A formative moment was its entry into the coalition government during the First World War, marking both a new standing for the labour movement in national politics and a new phase of collaboration with the emergent military-industrial complex. Dissenting anti-imperialist voices were generally sidelined, as the Labour Party, usually with the backing of its trade union allies, pursued policies that protected capital's political and economic interests within the formal and informal empire.[12] In later decades this continued, as Labour governments then managed Britain's retreat from empire and accommodation within a US-dominated world system.[13]

In the context of Second World War demands on industrial production and military mobilisation, unions and Labour Party politicians attained an unprecedented level of prestige and recognition following the formation of another coalition government in 1940. Economic planning and British national self-sufficiency displaced liberalism as the dominant focus of labour movement political economy. The 1945–51 Labour government included figures who remain lauded in the Labour Party and trade union movement today, such as Nye Bevan, the former South Wales miner and radical socialist; Ernest Bevin, a lorry driver from the South West of England and long-running general secretary of the Transport and General Workers' Union; and Herbert Morrison, the former London municipal authority member who was central to the design of nationalised enterprises. Each of these men came from manual working-class families and rose through their involvement in the labour movement. Despite significant personal and political differences between them, when they were at their most influential in government, Bevan, Bevin and Morrison also shared a commitment to the contours of 'Labourism': support for an industrially and politically integrated labour movement and a language and politics which privileged the 'national interest', as well as anti-communism and hawkish positioning on foreign policy.

In the post-war decades, affiliated trade unions devolved political business to the Parliamentary Labour Party, which in office was expected to wield the powers of an unreformed British state to deliver incremental gains for the labour movement. Ralph Miliband characterised Labourism as a politics of class collaboration and parliamentary cretinism.[14] For other New Left intellectuals such as Tom Nairn, Labourism was a disastrous accommodation with 'the mindless complacency of British bourgeois society'.[15] The tensions Labourism managed, ranging from worker dissatisfaction with union compromises and the shortcomings of Labour governments to conflicts between paternalistic local councillors and their municipal tenants, demonstrated the limitations of a form of politics which ultimately succumbed to latent brittleness.

The British working class at the apogee of Labourism was also defined by a distinctively *national* orientation. As David Edgerton's history of twentieth-century Britain underlines, the Labour Party was crucial in developing a vision of a post-imperial national-industrial economy centring on productivity growth and technological change, but also on the strategic importance of the energy production and manufacturing sectors.[16] In this worldview, a more productive economy was equated with material rewards and doing away with drudgery. Trade union politics were animated by creating the conditions for less work and higher wages. British workers were employed by the NCB and the British Electricity Authority. They travelled aboard British Rail trains and were cared for by the National Health Service, in services staffed by fellow unionised workers. Even in peacetime, male workers outside of specifically designated reserved occupations were expected to perform national service from the 1940s to the early 1960s.

The unmaking of the British working class would proceed through the dislocation of this form of Britishness. Industrial nationhood, along with its structure of publicly owned enterprises and government coordination of other sectors, fell into abeyance in the late twentieth century as more liberalised flows of capital and goods once again prospered. National identity stopped reverberating through coal mining, steelmaking or even aeroplane and car production. These sensibilities had their articulations on the left and from below, as well as from above and broadly on the right. Britishness and a centralised state became less appealing and increasingly seen as synonymous with rather than an alternative to empire. This was most visible in growing support for both devolution and independence in Scotland, and to a lesser extent Wales.

From the 1940s to the 1970s, uniquely in its history, the Labour Party had consistently won the majority of votes cast by manual workers, who were more likely than ever before or since to be a member of a trade union affiliated to the party.[17] Labour governments took major steps to intentionally unmake the worlds that had once made men like Bevan, Bevin and Morrison. Slum clearances demolished ageing miners' rows and city tenements. The number of railwaymen, coal miners and dockers plummeted as technological and industrial change fundamentally and purposively reshaped Britain's economy. Social and cultural habits changed too – 'privatism' was closely associated with 'affluence' in sociological debates over Britain's changing working class during the 1960s.[18] Communal activities like going to the cinema or attending football matches declined, in favour of home-centred leisure and growing television ownership. Increasing suburbanisation encouraged a disconnect between the workplace, the home and socialising.

The Labourist imagination struggled to make sense of changes which came to reverse the processes that had originally spurred the development of British working-class politics. By the late 1960s, manufacturing employment was past its peak and the changes that had already been visible in localised forms within the coalfields, port cities and cotton towns for a decade became a marked feature of national economic life. The bonds and assumptions which had underpinned the reality and understanding of a shared British working-class political interest declined as trade union membership then shrank from the early 1980s onwards.[19] Remaining trade union organisation also changed, matching a recomposed working class. It became more concentrated among women and an increasingly multicultural workforce employed in public services.[20] In the longer term, Labourism was no longer able to explain the direction of society or reflect, structure and mobilise evolving working-class constituencies. Workers and their families in turn became more liable to view the Labour Party as part of an alien state or 'the establishment' and less likely to see a labour movement as their 'side'.

Associational attachments formed through trade union organisation and their links to the Labour Party were pivotal to the form of British class-conscious politics. These formalised relationships were always founded on the more quotidian habits of the workgroup, the daily routines of family life, and how working-class people spent their evenings and weekends. In the late 1970s, Eric Hobsbawm influentially argued that it was the undoing of those circumstances which halted labour's 'forward march'. His explanations rested on the consciousness of workers themselves: they were no longer solidaristic but instead selfishly motivated to opportunistically use their power against Labour governments and public-service users, weakening the bonds of solidarity through which the welfare state had been constructed.[21]

This book outlines an alternative perspective. The unmaking of the British working class unfolded over a significantly longer period, extending into the late twentieth and early twenty-first centuries. Deindustrialisation may have conditioned the unmaking, but only in shaping the terrain. It was the de-organisation of the workforce at the behest of hostile governments and employers which was crucial in achieving the unmaking of a once powerful British working class. Alternative economic identities, as homeowners or self-employed entrepreneurs, but also appeals from xenophobic politics on the right, gained ground as class consciousness dissipated. In turn, these alternative orientations reshaped Labour Party politics, visible most fully in New Labour's disavowal of class and embrace of 'globalisation' in the 1990s.

The disappearance of the working class as a felt, hoped-for and called-on agent of societal change animates this book. Historian Selina Todd has described this shift as the degeneration of 'the people', the constituency of manual workers who exercised a dominant role in the mid-twentieth-century national imagination, into the denigrated 'dispossessed' of low-paid 'flexible' workers and benefit claimants who were branded the 'underclass' in the 1990s and 2000s.[22] Todd's foil is a valuable one, reinforced by her insistence on the long continuities in experiences of hierarchies and power imbalances in shaping the lives of working-class people.[23] If the deferential culture of trade unionism and the Labour Party has subsided, the deference demanded by employers has grown in the lives of precariously employed workers answerable to petty tyrants such as call-centre supervisors, Amazon warehouse managers and, in the case of Deliveroo riders and Uber drivers, even the algorithms which dictate their working lives.

I am a historian of coal mining and of work in the energy industries, along with deindustrialisation and factory closures. My research emphasises oral history, focusing on how working-class people recall the workplace, the home and family life. Some of the chapters that follow draw primarily on interviews I have recorded and work in archives, especially chapters 1 and 3, while others are more reliant on my reading of the press and published material. Gender, nationality and race are all central components for understanding how class was understood and reimagined in Britain. Edward Thompson limited his study of the 'making' of the working class to England, acknowledging the distinctiveness of early Scottish and Welsh labour histories.[24] Similarly, I have excluded Northern Ireland from this book. The British working class was defined by overlaps between organised workers and the Labour Party, as explored below, which explicitly excluded the six counties. Ulster's history requires a separate study of working-class politics. By contrast, Irish immigrants and their descendants, both Catholic and Protestant, appear in this book as important participants in the making and unmaking of the British working class.

Our story begins in the 1960s, when manufacturing employment peaked, Labour governments were becoming normalised and trade unions enjoyed a standing in public life they have never since matched. Not coincidentally, this was also the period when left-wing intellectuals advanced the most influential critiques of Labourism and the limitations of British working-class consciousness.[25] From this crest came the great unmaking, followed by the re-emergence of class in political discourses since the 2010s on a fundamentally altered political basis.

The unmaking of the British working class was directed and enforced from above, ideologically but also using the weapons of economic and physical force, including strike-breaking police operations and the scarring experience of impoverishment brought through workplace closures and dole queues. Yet these fundamental shifts in daily life were also navigated and made sense of from below, on terms which eroded a formerly strongly felt class affiliation. Defeat and despondency were obviously central to this process. So was the undermining of the economic and politically unifying features of nationhood, along with the recasting of the meaning of work, home and community.

Workers and their families emerge in the stories that follow – through their own words – not as objects but as subjects of history. They themselves contributed to burying a version of class politics, but they did so in the context of a profoundly unequal society marred by the concentration of power. This book prioritises episodes of strife and conflict because they powerfully reveal the fissures of social relationships under strain. These, however, are integrated within a longer duration of evolving relationships which eroded the living significance of class as a dominant means of understanding British society. Class has potently re-emerged in British political discourse in the 2010s and 2020s, on the right as well as the left, but on terms often highly detached from the material conditions or collective mobilisation of workers. Any positive agenda for a revived class politics will need to gain ground in the collective imagination of tens of millions of workers and their families to draw a recognised constituency together by defining its likenesses as well as its enemies. The stories told in this book demonstrate that, to borrow another line from Edward Thompson, the British working class was present at its own unmaking.[26] This is their history.

1

The New Working Class: 'Leave Your Picks Behind Ye'

'Stafford was certainly a prosperous town,' recalled Ken Rochester when I spoke to him in 2022. Ken is an octogenarian who still speaks with a trace of a Northumberland accent almost seventy years after his family left England's Great Northern coalfield for the West Midlands.[1] His father was a miner who grabbed the chance of a better future as Britain's newly publicly owned coal industry moved southwards. The National Coal Board (NCB) was offering ambitious young men security and advancement if, in the words of Durham coal miner and folk singer Jock Purdon, they were happy to 'leave your picks behind ye'.[2] Traditional tools for old-fashioned coal gathering would not be needed in the new world of mechanised, publicly owned mining and privatised living which Staffordshire promised.

This chapter explores the changing society that brought Ken and his family to the Midlands. Depictions of post-war 'affluence' often focus on the car worker and light-engineering manufacturing.[3] Yet the construction of an increasingly electrified society was also crucial to Britain's new political and economic order. Ginormous nationalised enterprises offered workers higher living standards and less drudgery in return for their embrace of rationalisation, efficiency and bureaucratic hierarchy.

In the 1960s, a workplace revolt of rising expectations challenged this Labourist edifice from within. Inflation and wage controls threw assumptions of shared interests between Labour governments and organised workers into doubt. After the formation of a new Conservative government headed by

Edward Heath in 1970, there was a crescendo of industrial mobilisation that culminated in national power and coal disputes which quite literally put the lights out across the country. These were class conflicts driven by the material advancement of prior decades.

Labourism, however, emerged reinforced by these disturbances. Workers who were crucial to supplying the material basis for more comfortable lives demanded that their own rewards and economic security become a matter of national priority. Miners and electricity workers mobilised within a national-industrial economy which granted unions a place at the table, and they were comparatively successful in achieving their ends. The working class came out of this period significantly changed, but not yet unmade.

New worlds of labour

Jock Purdon narrated the story of the miners who moved from the North East of England to Yorkshire and the Midlands. His anthem, 'Farewell to Cotia', commemorates the rundown of employment at his own workplace, Harraton (Nova Scotia) colliery on Wearside, which closed in 1965. For Purdon, the mass departure from the Durham coalfields was a forced exodus which came at a high social and cultural cost. Durham was central to the British coalfield imaginary as the home of the Big Meeting (also known as the Durham Miners' Gala), a major annual gathering of miners and their families dating back to the Victorian era which was hosted by the Durham Miners' Association. By tradition, the leader of the Labour Party addressed the Big Meeting, symbolising the contribution of the miners to the broader working-class movement and the symbiosis of coal mining and Labourist politics.[4] In Purdon's mournful homage to this now fading world, everything from union organisation to beer (in the form of Newcastle's distinctive brown ale) will be different in the new collieries and villages to the south:

Ye brave bold lads of Cotia
The time is drawing thus
Ye'll have tae change your banner, lads,
And join the exodus
But leave your cares behind ye
Your future has been planned
And off ye go tae Nottingham
Tae Robens' promised land[5]

Purdon closely associated the planned migration of the colliers and their families with Lord Alf Robens, who became the chairman of the NCB in 1961 and oversaw a dramatic reconstruction of the industry. Robens' life was a microcosm of the forward march of British labour. He served as a full-time official with the Union of Shop, Distributive and Allied Workers before becoming a Labour MP for the Durham coalfield constituency of Wansbeck at the landslide 1945 election. Robens was briefly the Minister of Labour and National Service and continued to act as a frontbench spokesman after Labour's defeat in 1951. With his ambitions for party leadership stalled through Hugh Gaitskell's success in the contest to replace Clement Attlee, Robens aptly instead became chairman of the NCB, one of the large new nationalised industries established by the government that he had served as a minister in.[6]

An Edwardian or even a Victorian observer would have recognised large parts of the British coal mining industry when it was brought into public ownership in 1947, establishing the Board as one of the world's biggest enterprises. Collieries with origins in the nineteenth century remained commonplace. They often had relatively small workforces – a couple of hundred men, or even fewer – and relied on labour-intensive manual methods such as the 'pillar and stoop' technique, by which pillars of coal were left in place while miners used pickaxes and shovels to gather coal around them. Employment was still concentrated in the older mining regions of South Wales and Scotland's Central Belt as well as in Durham, alongside the more recently developed English 'Central Coalfields' of South Yorkshire and the Midlands.

Robens embraced the NCB's ethos of gigantism and efficiency. The Board's workforce peaked at around 700,000 in the mid-1950s, when coal was still king of energy generation. Britain had experienced episodic and costly fuel shortages during the decade following the Second World War.[7] Governments pursued policies which aimed to maximise production levels. Coal Board and electricity-industry officials remained haunted by the cold winter of 1947, when shortages of coal contributed to blackouts which left homes dark and hampered crucial industrial production.[8] In this context, the miners were a precious resource, and the Board was anxious to retain men on its rolls. They enjoyed relatively high wages by the standards of British male industrial workers.

A few short years later, in the early 1960s, the mining workforce entered a sharp decline. By the time Robens was succeeded by his deputy, Derek Ezra, in 1971, the number of miners had more than halved, with total coal employment having fallen to around 300,000.[9] The industry looked very different too. Mining had been consolidated in large new mechanised 'superpits' reliant on vast mechanical systems for coal cutting, conveying and ventilation. By the early 1970s, coal had lost its long-held place as the cornerstone of energy generation as oil became Britain's premier fuel source. Coal had been permanently displaced, successively losing out to hydrocarbon competitors in land and seaborne transport, home heating and industrial production.[10] The one key expanding market coal still enjoyed was electricity, which exercised a determining influence on the working life of miners and the place of the organised working class in Britain's national economy. From 1950 to 1980, power station coal consumption increased from an annual burn of 33 to 90 million tonnes. Electricity generation rose from a relatively minor portion of British coal sales, amounting to just 15 per cent of coal burned in Britain, to become *the* coal market, accounting for over two-thirds of NCB production by the late 1970s.[11]

A place of opportunity

In 1954, Ken Rochester and his family arrived in Rugeley on the outskirts of Stafford to join a purpose-built community for the mining and electricity industries. The Rochesters were allocated to a new home on the large Pear Tree housing estate where miners and their families from South Wales, Northern England and Scotland relocated and lived alongside former German prisoners of war, Ukrainians and Poles. Life in Rugeley was better than it had been in Northumberland. Ken's father found work at Lea Hall colliery, a modern, highly productive new pit which was dug by the NCB for the purpose of supplying the new 'Rugeley A' power station, which had been developed by the recently nationalised electricity generator. Lea Hall was a place of opportunity. At his new pit, Ken's father was able to climb up the managerial hierarchy. There were jobs for all, including 'plenty of work for women'. Ken's aunt and mother both found work in expanding local consumer goods factories, each supplementing their household's income.[12] The dual incomes sustained by married women's labour were essential to sustaining rising living standards.

Rugeley was at the centre of a national economic transformation which was closely associated with material improvements in working-class life. Britain remained an industrial economy and a country of manual workers where families were sustained by the earnings of men and women like Ken's father and mother, an increasing portion of whom were labouring in evolving technological environments. The first power station at Rugeley was a cutting-edge engineering achievement. During the early 1960s, Rugeley A was home to the world's largest cooling tower. It pioneered innovative dry-cooling technology which became a source of pride in the local press. The *Birmingham Post* described it hopefully as 'a thing of massive beauty' but conceded that detractors saw this new dominant feature as a 'blot on the landscape'.[13] Rugeley represented the acme of modernity and an optimistic future of productive employment for the West Midlands during an era when Britain's economic performance was imagined in terms of modernised manufacturing and energy industries along with their workforces. The station was powered by five 120-megawatt transformer sets.[14] Ken found work at the successor station, Rugeley B, in the late 1960s, having been discharged from an Air Force mechanic position and then leaving a manufacturing job in aerospace engineering.[15] The new plant was built around a decade after the A station. Demonstrating the advance of technology in the decade between the construction of the two stations, as well as Britain's growing appetite for electricity in homes and industry, it consisted of two 500-megawatt sets.[16]

These advances were a product of government design which fused industrial and social engineering. The British Electricity Authority (BEA) shared much in common with the NCB in both its Labourist imprints and its relentless emphasis on concentrating production in new, large modern power stations.[17] Walter Citrine, an electrician originally from Merseyside who went on to become a paid official of the Electrical Trades Union (ETU), was the BEA's first chairman. As a time-served man and a keen student of political ideas, along with electrical theory and accounting, Citrine exemplified the self-educated skilled craftsmen who played a formative role in British trade unions as well as in moulding their connection to the Labour Party and the state.[18] Citrine was an exponent of careful, corporatist politics and a sworn opponent of communists and radical socialists. He was the general secretary of the Trades Union Congress (TUC) throughout the crucial period between the defeat of the General Strike in 1926 and the 1945 general election. Citrine played a central part in shaping the TUC's influence within the Labour Party. He also ensured that unions were still consulted on relevant industrial legislation even under Ramsay MacDonald's Conservative-dominated National Government. Despite MacDonald having broken away from Labour in 1931, Citrine accepted a knighthood from his pro-austerity administration in the 1935 New Year's Honours.[19]

The most lasting contribution Citrine made to the practices

of British trade unionism was perhaps his authorship of a set of rules and a code of conduct, *The ABC of Chairmanship*.[20] These achievements are revealing of both the world of strict structure and hierarchy which Citrine endorsed and shaped, and his emphasis on legitimising patterns of consultation and dialogue between government, employers and workers through official trade union channels. His anti-communism and opposition to unofficial strikes marked Citrine's response to walkouts over bonus payments at four London power stations in December 1949. Citrine and the Minister of Fuel and Power, Hugh Gaitskell, were not just concerned at the economic motivations of the strikers but also suspicious of the presence of union representatives who were members of or sympathetic to the Communist Party of Great Britain (CPGB) in the electricity industry. The Labour government responded by ordering soldiers to break the strikes and operate the power stations.[21] In a letter to Gaitskell, Citrine described union activists as 'fomenting dissension' and organising 'an attack on the community by disorganising a vital public service'. Citrine feared the strikes were only 'a rehearsal for something bigger'.[22] He was 'strongly in favour of prosecution of the ringleaders as soon as possible under the Conspiracy and Protection of Property Act 1875', archaic legislation which bound workers to the expectations of Victorian relationships between masters and servants.[23]

In other respects, Citrine was enthused by modernisation through the potential which reorganisation and concentration held in terms of economic efficiency. Electricity production was increasingly concentrated within a smaller number of larger, more efficient units, of which Rugeley was just one example. In 1948, the nationalised industry inherited around 300 power stations from a mixture of municipal and privately owned undertakings. These were primarily located in cities.[24] For instance, Pinkston power station in Glasgow powered the city's tram network. In London, there were the well-known Battersea and Bankside plants on the Thames. Electricity production expanded greatly in the decades which followed nationalisation. Annual generation grew from 43 terawatt hours to 245 over a quarter of a century from 1948 to 1973. This was a major and never since repeated achievement for British public enterprise. By the early 2020s, domestic production had only increased to 310 terawatt hours, a far smaller rate of increase.[25] It was in the immediate post-war decades that electricity shifted from being a relatively marginal energy source to becoming a dominant concern in the everyday life of the home, in industrial production and in the delivery of public services like healthcare and rail travel.

Under nationalisation, a new dramatic form of rationalisation was realised through the transmission of electricity at higher voltages over larger distances through 'supergrid' technologies. Supergrids were powered by superpits and encouraged the development of gigantic new power stations in semi-rural coalfields. The supergrid, first launched in 1953, more than doubled the voltage of the National Grid's trunk transmission lines. An even more powerful 400-kilowatt grid was developed soon after, with rollout beginning in 1965. Tellingly, the first line on the new grid ran between West Burton power station in Nottinghamshire and a substation in Bedford, connecting the Home Counties to the large new generating units placed along the Trent.[26] At Longannet in West Fife, which began electricity production in 1969, mechanical conveyors directly supplied the power station from modern, highly productive drift mines which even pioneered the introduction of computer technology into British mining. Longannet comprised a vast unit, replete with a massive cooling tower which dominated the Forth Valley. It was giant by the prior standards of the Scottish electricity system, sustaining one-third of Scottish demand.[27]

Longannet maintained men in mining jobs as the Scottish coalfield workforce contracted at an even faster rate than overall British coal employment, declining from over 85,000 colliery wage earners to less than 24,500 between 1957 and 1974.[28] The power station provided cleaner and safer jobs, and sustained a larger share of skilled trades posts than older collieries had. John Wilson began working in Fife collieries in the 1950s; he climbed the ranks to become an official, taking advantage of the opportunity the NCB gave him to improve himself by attending a night school training class. His mining career ended at Solsgirth, one of the drift mines that supplied Longannet. Solsgirth 'must have been the highest producing mine in Europe at one point', he recalled. 'This place put coal out like naebody's business.'

John sought to break the 'natural progression' which would have led his son Mark to follow him into the pits. Instead, John looked to the example of his younger brother, Mark's uncle, who worked at Longannet power station. Working above ground, even burning coal, was a social advance for men who had no wish to see their sons entering a dirty and dangerous line of work.[29]

Other miners' sons shared the same experience. Ken Rochester became an Air Force mechanic after his father discouraged him from going down the pit at Lea Hall. The West Midlands offered opportunities in a range of industries, which meant that there were more options for young men to work in better conditions than in the Northumberland pit villages the Rochesters and many of their neighbours had left behind.[30]

Atomic factory

John Harvey was also a power station worker. He left Durham to find work in engineering. He initially found this employment in the military-industrial complex at the Aldermaston Atomic Weapons Research Establishment. The site was integral to Britain's nuclear bomb programmes and targeted by the nascent Campaign for Nuclear Disarmament. John, though, spent most of his life in civilian power generation, working with coal like his father, uncles and brothers, but in far larger quantities. He installed large new boilers at Didcot A power station in Oxfordshire, supplying the energy-thirsty booming economy of southern England with coal-fired electricity. In a written testimony which he sent me in 2022, John described a meticulous system of publicly owned collieries supplying the fifty-wagon merry-go-round trains operated by nationalised British Rail. With each journey these specially designed trains transported hundreds of tons of coal, arriving at power stations as frequently as every twenty minutes. While power generation worked to the rhythm of highly capital-intensive processes, it remained reliant on manual human labour. For Didcot to function smoothly, John and his colleagues had to ensure a swift turnaround on train repairs to prevent bottlenecks and keep the station in production. 'If you were working on the tracks or equipment, you had a very small time to do the repair,' he remembered, while coal had to be swiftly weighed and sampled to ensure that it met the requirements of the boilers John was responsible for maintaining.[31]

The supergrid was also of value to coal's competitors. Nuclear power was a new technology which was purposely placed outside of cities to avoid risks to large population areas. In some older industrial areas such as West Cumbria, there was an overlap between the two sectors, with former coal miners finding work building the new nuclear reactors known as 'piles' at Windscale (later renamed Sellafield). The facility later came to serve both military and civilian atomic purposes, but its origins lay in manufacturing weapons-grade plutonium for Britain's first atomic bombs. Joe Bell was a second-generation Sellafield worker and a trade union representative at the complex. During an interview at his home in Whitehaven in 2022, Joe explained that, to his father, working at Windscale had meant opportunity. The nuclear industry offered a comparatively cleaner and safer environment than working down Cumbria's ageing and dangerous pits. Joe, like his father, had worked processing weapons-grade plutonium:

> A lot of people think that Sellafield was built for nuclear electricity, but it wasn't built for that. All the shit we've got over there. It doesn't belong to West Cumbria. It belongs to all four nations. Scotland wanted the bomb. England, Ireland, Wales wanted the

> bomb so we could sit at the big table and that's what Sellafield were built for.
>
> We used to blend what you would call plutonium, and you would blend what you call A grade plutonium. As far as I know there's only one use for A grade plutonium. We blended it and we sent it to different countries. Exported it from my little plant. As far as I remember understanding A grade is what you use for the bomb.[32]

The military purpose of the piles and the industrial prosperity they sustained conditioned defensiveness and secrecy. As early as 1958, British servicemen who had been subject to nuclear weapons tests were raising concern over the impact of exposure to hydrogen bombs made with material from Sellafield.[33] By contrast, there was no outcry locally after a serious fire at Pile No. 1 caused the dispersal of radiation across Cumbria and further afield in October 1957. Historian Lorna Arnold explained that the nuclear industry had brought 'pride as well as economic benefit' to West Cumbria, providing 'employment and considerable prosperity to a severely depressed area'.[34]

Joe Bell's perspective concurred with Arnold's assessment: he mused that, in contrast to the depression endured during the decades between the World Wars, in the late 1940s and 1950s 'people outside of it [West Cumbria] called it the Gold Coast because of the money they were making'. The area became 'a magnet, tradesmen were brought in from far and wide'.[35] These motifs were not merely nostalgic or anachronistic. As early as 1951, the *Sunday Express* covered Windscale's prosperous skilled craft workers, referring to '£40 men' working on 'a desolate wedge of bleak Cumberland coast'. The report emphasised the scale and modernity of the new enterprise: 3,000 'workmen are drawing the fattest pay packets in Britain' at the new 'atomic factory', it continued. While these men laboured in arduous conditions to build the vast reactor chimneys, there was a fundamentally egalitarian dynamic to employment with the Ministry of Supply. Commenting on

standing alongside the construction workers who were returning home to meet their families, the reporter noted that they could afford to, and chose to, present themselves in the manner of professionals: 'except for their craggy hands and weather-beaten faces they look like company directors as they wait for the London express that now stops at Sellafield'.[36]

This was modern Britain in its Labourist image: prosperous, productive and patriotic, with all that entailed in late-imperial, militarist terms. Public ownership established an important new coordinating mechanism for planning the future of electricity generation which facilitated the linking of Lea Hall and Rugeley, and the larger development of coal, electricity and nuclear in tandem. These rising sectors secured the basis for the new communities, and the material comfort and predictability which they promised, for those willing to leave their picks and shovels behind. The egalitarian dignity that the suit-wearing Windscale men carried suggested a country where old markers of class were in decline and where the legitimation of trade unions and publicly owned industries could help to sustain a more equitable social order. At Windscale it came at the price of a Cold War arms race and the radiation spewed out by nuclear accidents and atomic-weapon test explosions in Australia and the Pacific.

Affluent workers

Major changes to working-class households were made possible by workers in publicly owned enterprises. Electricity was the energy of the future, and the new national enterprise was delivering vastly increasing quantities of an essential resource to industry but also to homes and farms. The BEA undertook to reach poorer working-class households and rural areas erstwhile excluded from access to all the mod cons that electrical currents powered. Electricity emerged as a truly national utility as a result, but also one which was used and depended on much more intensively by households that had previously enjoyed more limited amenities. Consumer prosperity saw affordable television sets begin displacing radio during the 1950s, and electrically powered vacuum cleaners, cookers, fridges and washing machines were all becoming common in the households of better-paid workers by the end of the 1960s.[37] Trips to the cinema and football match attendance dwindled as more families had the opportunity to watch television at home. Women were spared the long drudgery of the wash house in favour of the washing machine in the home, though this replaced a communal activity with a more secluded one.

Manufacturing employment in Britain only peaked in the mid-1960s, although some sectors like electronics and carmaking kept expanding even after that. Historian Selina Todd has traced how national imaginaries of 'the people' became synonymous with the manufacturing workforce.[38] This was highly visible in the concerns of government and its propagandistic economic messaging around raising exports and productivity, and curbing wage growth among weekly waged (as opposed to monthly salaried) workers.[39] The success of *Coronation Street*, Britain's first regularly broadcast television soap opera which depicted the lives of a fictional community in Greater Manchester, from 1960, confirmed the dominant and sympathetic place which urban 'factory Britain' exercised in the national imaginary.

Despite its seemingly traditional setting, 'Corrie', as it has been nearly universally known, was symptomatic of the new world of labour. It was often watched on televisions made in Britain by relatively feminised workforces in modernised assembly line processes. Television ownership was itself symptomatic of rising living standards and availability of new technologies. The electricity which supplied the growing demands of weekday evening viewers was produced through burning the increasing quantities of coal dug by the NCB at publicly owned power stations. At its peak viewership in the late 1970s, *Coronation Street* could draw an audience of over 20 million, more than a third of the total British population at the time.[40] Patterns of electricity consumption underlined these connections. Evening surges structured peak output as electricity generators ensured that they could match demand when television viewers made cups of tea during advertisement breaks.

Coronation Street confirmed the extent to which mid-twentieth-century British popular culture was produced for working-class audiences, often by working-class people. Another television staple which leant on older traditions from industrial communities was provided by two former music hall performers, the Lancashire-born Eric Morecambe and Ernie Wise, son of a Leeds railwayman, who became a celebrated duo. Their slapstick comedy drew on the style of variety entertainment which had dominated working men's clubs. As these older forms of community life themselves entered abeyance, they were given a new lease of life and recognition by the ultimate signifier of national culture, the British Broadcasting Corporation. The Morecambe and Wise 1977 Christmas special surpassed the highs of *Coronation Street*, reaching 28 million viewers, or around half of the UK population.[41]

Even when presented in the form of light entertainment, the powerful cultural working-class presence on British screens and airwaves could also spill over into more overtly politicised and philosophical discussions. One notable example was the debate between Clydeside shipbuilding trade unionist Jimmy Reid and actor Kenneth Williams on Michael Parkinson's talk show in 1973. Parkinson, who was the son of a Yorkshire miner, found himself moderating a passionate discussion between Williams, who had grown up as a barber's son in London, and Reid, concerning the meaning of freedom. Williams championed economic individualism. Reid rebuked Williams by counterpoising appeals to 'abstract freedom' with the realities of a Merseyside pensioner who had recently been found dead after eating cardboard due to being unable to afford food. In place of vague notions of liberty, Reid argued for freedoms he viewed as substantive: freedom from war and poverty and the freedom to realise human potential.[42] Reid's presence on the nation's leading Saturday night talk show is demonstrative of a cultural context moulded by a strong recognised working class whose leaders shaped the tenor of public discourse. The clash between Reid and Williams took place after Reid had emerged as the nationally prominent leader of the occupation of the Upper Clyde Shipbuilders yard in the previous two years. Reid was still serving as a workplace trade union representative at Fairfields shipyard in Govan and was a prominent CPGB activist.

Factory life was the stuff of sociological research and commanded the attention of government as well as soap opera storylines. Television and home-owning car plant employees became the emblematic 'affluent workers' of the 1960s thanks to a landmark study of Vauxhall Luton workers by John Goldthorpe and his collaborators. The authors concluded that affluent workers increasingly displayed minimal enthusiasm for labour itself and were in fact willing to exchange more intrinsically enjoyable artisanal work for the higher wages on offer in duller repetitive assembly line jobs. Affluent workers nevertheless remained class conscious, primarily through the crudely materialist understanding that 'union membership pays'.[43] Historian Jon Lawrence reassessed Goldthorpe's papers in 2019 as he examined the changing meanings of class and community in England. Lawrence underlines that the affluent workers tended to clock up hours of overtime and that their wives' earnings were also important to sustaining higher levels of material comfort. Affluent workers valued collective as well as individual achievements, and they were overwhelmingly Labour voters. In essence, their worldviews accorded with the values of Labourism as they were articulated by trade union and Labour Party leaders in the middle of the twentieth century: they wanted to earn more, work less and spend more time on holiday.[44]

Outside the factory, working-class life was being transformed by slum clearances, the demolition of dilapidated miners' rows, and the building of new terraced public and private housing estates along with city high-rises. Scottish playwright Tony Roper's 1987 drama, *The Steamie*, tells the story of a Glasgow wash house on a 1950s Hogmanay (New Year's Eve) thirty years earlier through the entertaining intergenerational solidarity a group of Glaswegian women show one another as they contend with a hapless drunken male attendant. It was adapted for a Hogmanay broadcast by Scottish Television in 1988, marking a lament for a world of tenement living and neighbourliness.[45] Yet generally families very willingly vacated these social worlds. They were the people who had to bear its high costs in cramped and damp housing along with intensely patriarchal family lives built around often precarious and relatively poorly paid jobs in Clydeside's shipyards and locomotive works.

The sociologist Richard Hoggart polemically bemoaned the death of communities structured around the street, the pub and the mill in his home city of Leeds during the late 1950s. Communal bonds were being eroded, he argued, by the corrupting influence of US-style commercial culture and the increased anonymity afforded by extended commutes as a result of rising car ownership.[46] Eric Hobsbawm, the historian and influential CPGB intellectual, characteristically retained a more orthodox perspective in the early 1960s. He insisted that 'proletarian reflexes and habits live on intensely', pointing to the strong retained Labour vote among the manual working class in new environments. These old alignments were given expression through the *Andy Capp* cartoon series in the *Daily Mirror* which depicted the life of an everyman industrial worker from the shipbuilding town of Hartlepool in the North East of England. For Hobsbawm, Capp epitomised 'the British worker dear to tradition, at home with his cloth cap, a fag in the corner of his mouth, in short-sleeves and braces, lording it over his wife as his grandfather did'.[47]

Hobsbawm's certainties overlooked Andy Capp's eternal unemployment being the central running joke in the series. More importantly, it also undervalued the role which workers and their families played in reshaping their own lives and in remaking the social and economic order that they demanded more from. One Wallsend shipbuilder condemned *Andy Capp* as a dated and derogatory image of life on Tyneside when he was interviewed by social researchers in the late 1960s. These interviews also evidenced generational distinctions, with younger men eschewing the deference for employers, elders and trade union leaders shown by their fathers.[48] The growth of companionate marriages and the pursuit of more autonomous leisure lives by couples were concurrent with shrinking family sizes. This was in part an outcome of another important achievement: tumbling rates of child mortality in the age of the National Health Service and improved material living standards. Decisions which were made by millions of women and men were reinforced by the shared growth of incomes and economic security that industrial employment now underpinned.[49]

Car ownership complemented new conveniences, establishing a new form of individualised freedom and mobility. Even coal mining trade unionists celebrated the petrol-powered motor car. Joe Gormley, the Lancashire collier who served as president of the National Union of Mineworkers (NUM) from 1971 to 1982, said that his ambitions were for British miners to enjoy high-quality housing, education and living standards. For Gormley, material improvements were encapsulated by his aspiration for a future where the miner would drive a luxury Jaguar car to work, supplemented by a more practical Mini for his wife to take shopping.[50]

The sense of growing material prosperity associated with ownership of consumer durables was increasingly financed by hire purchase. Such debts more than tripled in nominal money values between 1955 and 1970. This development was legislatively encouraged by the repeal of the 1947 Finance Act under Harold Macmillan's Conservative government in the late 1950s.[51] Macmillan's famous boast that households had 'never had it so good' as they did under his Tory administration was partly made possible through the increased availability of debt financing to workers which created the appearance of a sudden expansion in living standards. As historian Peter Hennessy notes, though, Macmillan was already growing concerned about levels of inflation that were associated with Tory anxieties over wage drift caused by the empowerment of workers in tight labour markets.[52]

Increasing levels of homeownership enmeshed sections of the 'affluent' working class in a credit–debt nexus and mortgage payments. Yet unlike Margaret Thatcher's later expansion of homeownership through Right to Buy, discussed in chapter 4, these new financial obligations were not a dampener on industrial mobilisation. Instead, workers in the 1960s and 1970s who were unwilling to delay further improvements to living standards saw collective mobilisation as the way to obtain them.

Discontents

Class antagonism remained integral to British society in the 1960s and 1970s. Powerful workplace mobilisations brought workers into conflict with nationalised industries and governments which were failing to fulfil long-standing promises of incremental material advancement. The aspirations for affluence and economic security communicated by miners, electricity workers and their leaders were informed by a sense of falling behind their friends, family members and fellow union members in other sectors. Ostensibly, this marked a conservative dynamic within Labourism: time-served electricity workers looked to the earnings of craftsmen in manufacturing and other utility industries, just as miners contrasted their earnings with those of their former colleagues who now worked on car factory assembly lines. In practice, these changes, along with the impact of restrictions on wage rises imposed by successive governments, fuelled workplace conflict and politicised wage disputes in nationalised industries which were essential to the functioning of the economy and society.

The foundations of latent discontent were visible as men poured out of the coal mining industry as the 1960s went on and found jobs in newer, still-expanding areas of manufacturing. These experiences also shaped the outlook of the miners who remained employed in the coal industry. In some cases, they still lived in the same communities and in others they continued to congregate on the same football terraces. During an interview in 2014, Peter Downie, a Lanarkshire miner from the village of

Greengairs, recalled that as a young man he continued to meet former colleagues who had left mining to take jobs at the new Linwood car factory to the west of Glasgow. Initially it was Rootes, the Coventry-headquartered manufacturer, who owned the Linwood plant before it was subsequently taken over by the US firm Chrysler in 1967.[53] Peter's memories centred on the unsatisfactory wages he earned in a dangerous but essential job for the national economy compared with the pay his ex-workmates could command in the safer and cleaner conditions at Linwood:

> We were standing at Ibrox in 1966 and '68. Linwood was open. Linwood. The Imp. The making of the Imp motorcar. We were going from our village in Greengairs, in to watch the Rangers playing football, and we're standing with boys that were working in Linwood, working in the motor factory. And they were coming home with thirty-five pound, and our wages was twenty-two fifty. That was the difference for leaving the pit to go to industry.[54]

Tensions between union members and officials had spilled over into confrontation in central Scotland during the opening months of 1962. After the NUM Scottish Area (NUMSA) postponed a day of strike action against pit closures, 3,000 men walked out unofficially in Clackmannan. When union leaders attended a meeting of strikers in Fishcross, they were barracked by strikers chanting 'throw them in the pond!'[55] Around a decade later, NCB officials looked back ruefully on the impact of coalfield restructuring, concerned by the removal of links between social standing, effortful work and economic reward that had previously prospered in the 'small mining villages' which grew up around Victorian and Edwardian collieries. The 'expressive' miner of 'a generation ago . . . was involved in his work and had a sense of duty and obligation'.[56] By contrast, the younger miner, who commuted to a 'cosmopolitan' colliery, was frequently absent and had a utilitarian rather than communitarian relationship to his job:

> A man's status at home depends much more on being a conspicuous consumer. Moreover, the bureaucratisation and mechanisation of the Board has made the miner only one of a number of important inputs to a complex economic organisation. A miner's orientation to his work is therefore expected to be instrumental: he is expected to view the job as a means to an end.[57]

Two years before the confrontation at Fishcross, Karel Reisz's cinematic adaptation of Alan Sillitoe's novel *Saturday Night and Sunday Morning* profiled the life of a discontented young worker in the Midlands. Arthur Seaton, the film's anti-hero, works at the Raleigh bicycle factory in Nottinghamshire where he labours hard to meet production quotas only to spend his wages frivolously at the pub, rejecting what he sees as the staid norms of his parents and the older men at the plant. In the opening scene, Arthur begrudgingly makes the last of the spokes needed to reach his daily target of 1,000 before he can clock off and enjoy a Friday evening. The film ends with Arthur having reconciled himself to living conventionally as the reward of mind-numbing employment while glancing over a new-build suburban-style housing estate with his partner Doreen as they discuss the life they will build together.[58]

There is no simple story of consumerism and individualism unpicking Labourist industrial politics. Such extrinsic motivations also encouraged collectivist orientations and trade union mobilisation. Class consciousness and conflict adapted to conditions of increased material expectations. Labourism had provided the platform for state policies which were now helping to erode the old basis of class affinities, but new collectives formed around the demand for greater improvements.

Cohorts of workers who had grown up in relative stability and prosperity were often less patient and deferential than their parents had been when it came to either tolerating disruptions to their improving economic standing or what they increasingly came to view as the lagging pace of change. Younger men were less content to await improvements than their fathers had been.

Generational differences became a feature of shifting orientations to culture, work and trade union mobilisation. In 1974, delegate A. L. Robson from Kent addressed a conference of power-supply shop stewards. Jovially drawing attention to differences in fashion, he praised what he saw as the more educated and more demanding nature of younger workers. Robson emphasised that these qualities had shown through despite appearances: 'The apprentices I have come up against – I am talking about Transmissions and Area Boards – may have long hair and wear unisex clothes, but they certainly know what it is all about.'[59] Along with the representatives they elected, these men were less patient when it came to relations with the Labour Party.

The role of managerial authority in industry and the bureaucratised structures which dominated trade unions, along with the petty officialdom of the public housing offices or the world of mortgage lending, all contributed to rising frustrations and became the subject of discontent. Those changes had party political implications which challenged the institutional affiliations that had undergirded the making of the British working class during the first half of the twentieth century. There were indications of the weakening of the Labour Party's base of support in the 1960s as industrial constituencies rebelled against a now-established party of government which could be interpreted as the upholder of the status quo rather than as a vehicle for societal change. The pressures of City financial interests and conflicts within government between the Treasury and Harold Wilson's government's ambitions for faster growth and manufacturing expansion were resolved on the Treasury's deflationary terms during the mid-1960s. As a result, growth slowed and price increases were stoked by the devaluation of sterling against the dollar. During a 1968 conference of electricity shop stewards, T. Spellman, a London supply worker, challenged the leaders of the ETU's successor, the Electrical, Electronic, Telecommunications and Plumbing Union (EETPU), who called on workers to moderate their demands to avoid conflict with the Wilson government and its insistence on tying wage rises to demonstrable improvements in productivity: 'Why have trade union officials become sensitive about the economy and sensitive about whether the government should fall or stand, especially as it is a Labour government? What is so sacred about a Labour government?'[60]

Unofficial strike action sparked the hostility of the Wilson government on terms reminiscent of Citrine and Gaitskell's suspicions of the London power station strikers two decades before. Wilson appointed a Royal Commission headed by Lord Donovan to investigate industrial relations. Donovan's report emphasised the problems for trade union leaders, employers and government created by the devolution of power within unions to workplace representatives known as shop stewards. This encouraged workshop conflict and recalcitrance over levels of employment (bringing managerial allegations of 'overmanning'), restrictive practices exercised by skilled workers and low levels of productivity, as workers were motivated by overtime earnings.[61] Labour historian Jack Saunders underlines the patterns of inequity and authority which conditioned Donovan's perspective: it was manual and not white-collar professional workers whose pay negotiations were 'expected to be conducted with the interests of the national economy in mind'.[62] Tensions between class interests and the purported national interest played a powerful role in conflicts between the managers of nationalised industries, the governments they served and the trade unions they bargained with. These conflicts dampened faith in Labour administrations.

Important nationalist breakthroughs occurred in Wales and Scotland in 1966 and 1967 respectively, when coalfield constituencies in South Wales and Lanarkshire voted for opponents of a centralising Labour government that was then overseeing the shrinking of mining employment and championing nuclear energy as 'the white heat of technology'.[63] Within the Scottish context, nationalism became understood as a phenomenon concentrated among the 'new working class' residing in recently constructed public housing schemes, working primarily in semi-skilled factory jobs. These constituencies were unmoored from the norms of work in shipbuilding or coal and life in tenement housing or miners' rows which had fortified commitment to the Labour Party in previous decades.[64] Of course, moving workers into productive manufacturing industries, along with a drive to build new homes and new communities in place of the old single-industry settlements, was precisely the agenda of Labour governments in the 1940s and 1960s.

In England, Labourism was also strained by rising racism and far-right nationalism, most markedly following Enoch Powell's anti-immigrant 'Rivers of Blood' speech in 1968. Powell, then Shadow Secretary of State for Defence, had been anticipated in the Midlands by Peter Griffiths, the Conservative candidate for Smethwick who beat the national trend at the 1964 general election, unseating the incumbent Labour MP after campaigning on the slogan 'If you want a n***** for a neighbour, vote Labour'. Griffiths' racist campaign exploited housing shortages by appealing to the racial prejudices of white industrial workers and their families in a booming part of Britain that had attracted workers from Commonwealth countries in South Asia and the Caribbean.[65] When Powell was sacked by Heath from the Conservative shadow cabinet the day after his speech, fifty building workers walked out of the Rugeley B site, which was then two years away from completion.[66] Most notoriously, thousands of London dockers also walked out in Powell's defence.

Workplace rebellion

The operational workforce at Rugeley was part of a major but less well remembered work-to-rule late in 1970 which caused intermittent blackouts as electricity workers demanded that their wages keep pace with those of the workers in the factories their power stations supplied. This dispute revealed the potential friction between the priorities of government and the demands of organised workers. It is a reminder of the centrality of workplace order and trade union politics to both daily life and high politics in Britain in the 1960s and 1970s.

Electricians and their colleagues wanted their dues from their assistance in streamlining their sector. The general secretary of the EETPU, Frank Chapple, an ex-Communist turned leading labour movement right-winger, was broadly successful, along with the leaders of the other unions representing manual workers, in maintaining support for modernisation efforts. He was forced under pressure from his members, though, to lead demands for higher wages and industrial action which ultimately threatened electricity supply.

Electricity workers experienced a similar dissociation of their work from its older communal bonds to that experienced by coal miners. As power stations and depots closed, and workers were made more mobile under successive agreements, they became more frustrated with what they saw as the meagre financial rewards which they were compensated with for major disturbances to their lives. These changes, along with the attendant shrinking of the workforce, came with increasingly unsociable hours and weekend working for many, all with the loss of the avenue of supplementing earnings through overtime pay that had often provided a safety valve in the past.

With income controls continuing and inflation eroding the value of wages, goodwill further ebbed following the election of Heath's Conservative government in June 1970. Bad-tempered negotiations eventually led to a work-to-rule and an overtime ban by the unions representing manual electricity workers which lasted from 7 to 14 December. Reflecting on the dispute in 1978, Thomas Breakell, the EETPU's president, boasted of its impact, telling electricity-supply workers that they had the power to inflict the same economic damage in six minutes that it took miners six weeks to achieve through industrial action which ran down coal supplies.[67] The electricity unions called off their action following the offer of a Court of Inquiry chaired by Richard Wilberforce, a peer and Court of Appeal judge who was the great-great-grandson of the famed abolitionist William Wilberforce, and an embodiment of Britain's staid class hierarchies.

In the febrile atmosphere of the dispute, power workers were subject to denunciation, mistreatment and violent confrontation. During a televised address, Conservative Secretary of State for Industry John Davies encouraged viewers to confront power workers and make their views known. Anthony Barber, the Chancellor of the Exchequer, accused unions of employing 'industrial blackmail'.[68] Power workers were refused service at shops and petrol stations, while their wives and children were targeted at work, in the street and even in school playgrounds. Some participants in the work-to-rule had their car tyres slashed or were subject to physical assault. In one incident, workers were fired at with a shotgun. *Contact*, the journal of the EETPU, condemned Davies for 'a declaration to all the bully boys that it was open season for power workers. Let every crank have his day. A minister of the crown with a nod and a wink says, "have a go."'[69] Ken Rochester participated in the work-to-rule at Rugeley B, taking part as a plant operative and member of the National Union of General and Municipal Workers. He remembered the feeling of workgroup isolation and the public backlash that the industrial action provoked: 'There were people in town who if they knew you worked in the power station, they wouldn't serve you in some of the shops, filling stations, cause they knew everybody. It was only a small town. And we had a blacklist of places [where workers had been refused service].'[70]

While the weapons and boycotts were largely put to one side when the lights were switched back on without further interruption, a war of words unfolded which revealed bitter enmities. Furious letters were sent to Wilberforce by members of the public before the inquiry began. Alan Ross McWhirter, company director of McWhirter Twins, and resident of Enfield on the outskirts of London, condemned what he saw as the absence of a suitably authoritarian response from the government. McWhirter underlined that, under the Electricity Supply Act of 1919, if an electricity worker 'wilfully and maliciously breaks a contract of service' by depriving the public of electricity, 'he is breaking the law'.[71]

This intervention was revealing of the anti–trade union forces that were gathering on the political right. Ross McWhirter and his brother Norris were perhaps best known for developing *The Guinness Book of Records*. He was also a right-wing Conservative activist. Before Ross McWhirter's assassination by the Provisional Irish Republican Army in 1975, he and Norris helped found the National Association for Freedom, which played a formative role in rallying opposition to trade unions at the landmark Grunwick dispute explored in the next chapter.[72] The objections to worker mobilisation which McWhirter voiced were not confined to celebrity opponents. G.W. Searle, a Middlesex resident who worked in a solicitor's office, angrily observed that although he held two university degrees, power workers already typically earned more than he did, 'for work that is in comparison almost unskilled'. Searle angrily remonstrated on the plight of 'lowly paid [white-collar] workers', adding that 'employment in a solicitor's office entails a profound knowledge of the law and special skills not required from power workers'.[73]

Searle was articulating the lot of the anxious salaried man in an era of narrowing economic and social hierarchies. The gap between non-manual and manual employees was receding, along with the divide between skilled and unskilled workers. Professional middle-class opinion was resentful both of trade union power and of the relative decline in standing revealed by the experience of the dispute and its outcome. Following Wilberforce's inquiry, the wage offer made to the power workers and accepted by their unions stoked outrage on the Tory right and in the pages of anti-collectivist publications. The *Economist* fumed that 'those workers who operated the illegal electricity go-slow last December will be rewarded' with wage increases of about a fifth, around double the rate of inflation. Wilberforce's proposals were 'a farrago of anti-social and uneconomic rubbish'.[74]

During the inquiry, a similarly combative tone was struck from the other side by trade union representatives. John Torode reported on the antics of the 'power court jesters' in the *Guardian*, making it clear he had enjoyed a day watching 'the Treasury's knights being smacked around unmercifully' by more streetwise union officials. Torode mused that 'senior civil servants can seldom have been held up to such sustained ridicule and abuse as they suffered at the Wilberforce Inquiry into the power dispute'.[75] Questioning focused on the employers' demand that power workers prove that their labour had definitively been the cause of rising productivity, as separate from the increase in capital within the electricity system. This was deemed necessary for power workers to merit a wage rise, revealing great inequities in the expectations placed on manual workers and middle-class professionals.

Jim Mortimer was a former union official who was then a member of the National Board for Prices and Incomes. He would subsequently go on to become the general secretary of the Labour Party. Mortimer probed Sir Douglas Allen, the Permanent Secretary of the Treasury, on a recent large pay award to doctors. He asked why already well-salaried employees should be treated differently to electricians and fitters: 'If it was good enough to escalate for doctors, why not for power workers?' Frank Chapple questioned the Permanent Secretary in a more immediately personal way that 'rubbished' the 'national interest' remit of the court, which centred on the need to tie wage increases to proven advances in productivity. These limitations seemingly only applied to manual workers but not to those appointed to decide their wages. Chapple emphasised that, over 1970–71, Allen's pay had increased by over a third, from £9,800 to £15,000, following a large salary increase for senior civil servants and judges, including Wilberforce. Senior public servants in receipt of these salary increases were not subject to any of the performance 'yardsticks' which prior power worker awards had been dependent on.[76]

Wilberforce is better known for another inquiry he sat on the following year, after industrial action once again jeopardised electricity supply. On this occasion it was a famous strike by coal miners which put the lights out and led to a major pay award. Solidarity from other industrial workers was central to the miners' success, and to a similar result two years later. This included power station workers, who in the coal strikes of both 1972 and 1974 demonstrated solidarity with the miners by refusing to handle coal deliveries or to replace coal with other sources such as oil.[77]

Here was the working class at high tide. The class antagonisms of industrial society were brought to bear on the structures of the British state in a struggle fought by organised manual workers to realise a greater share of the wealth they produced. Miners and the power workers were not just in receipt of material improvements but also improving their place in the 'wages league'. In the mid-1970s, British politics came to revolve around managing industrial conflicts, centred on the coal industry. Labour won a general election in February 1974 which Heath called amid the dispute, hoping to mobilise dissatisfaction with union power and blackouts. Heath had run his campaign on the theme of who governed the country, stoking anti-union sentiment. Labour's victory was secured on the back of a promise that, unlike the Tories, it could work with organised workers constructively. The 1979 Winter of Discontent strikes across large swathes of the public and private sector demonstrated the difficulties Labour governments faced in continuing to rely on wage restraint to manage inflationary pressures and spending curbs. In the short term, Labour's new Plan for Coal was hailed as offering a secure future to coal miners and the larger energy workforce, including men like Ken Rochester and John Harvey in coal-fired power stations.[78] As part of a modernised industrial workforce, their representatives and sentiments had at least temporary success in moulding government policy.

But the 1960s and early 1970s had revealed inherent tensions between the interests of manual workers and the national interest as formulated by nationalised industries and by Labour and Conservative governments. They had also stoked the forces of the political right, which were fired by a commitment to de-organise the workforce by facing down trade union power; this became a defining feature of the two decades which followed.

2

Grunwick: 'The Shape of Things to Come'

Jayaben Desai lived a life shaped by Britain's imperial and global history. She was born in the early 1930s to a relatively privileged family in Gujarat and took up the cause of Indian independence as a young teenager. After marrying a Tanzanian Indian man and relocating to East Africa, Desai and her husband, who managed a tyre factory, were among the tens of thousands of Asians displaced under the Africanisation agendas embraced in recently decolonised countries. These policies were targeted at Indians who often occupied comparatively senior roles within industry, commerce and public administration. By the mid-1970s, Desai and her family had found themselves in reduced circumstances. She had taken a job as a mail-order worker at an obscure company, Grunwick, in Willesden, North West London. It was here that Desai entered history, leading an iconic strike and being heralded in British trade union folklore as the sub-five-foot tenacious 'Mrs Desai' who stood on the picket line for nearly two years.[1] Desai was perhaps the first woman of colour to play such a prominent role in a nationally recognised British industrial dispute. Along with the image of her fellow 'strikers in saris', this novelty has been central to how the Grunwick strike was appraised at the time as well as how it has been remembered since.[2]

In 2007, Desai recalled, during an interview recorded to commemorate the thirtieth anniversary of the strike, that she had never worked outside the family home to earn wages before she arrived in England as a refugee in the early 1970s.[3] Desai began dressmaking, before finding work at a photo-processing factory, initially in Wembley, which later moved to Willesden as Grunwick expanded. George Ward was the company's Anglo-Indian managing director. He became the other celebrated – and vilified – face of the strike. To his supporters, Ward was the voice of the small employer toughing it out against trade union bullies. Desai mused that just a few years earlier he had begged her to stay at work. Ward needed willing workers and increasingly came to rely on the Gujarati-speaking East African Asian community of West London as a supply of both male and female labour for his plants.[4]

Workloads at Grunwick ramped up during the long summer days of 1976 when demand for processing holiday snaps was highest. Management was oppressive and wages were poor, running at just over half of what women in London typically earned at the time. Even the overtime inducements were meagre.[5] In a book-length account of the strike published while the dispute was still ongoing, South African journalist Joe Rogaly reported that Malcolm Alden, the mailroom manager, had a reputation for being an unjust and intolerant disciplinarian. Rogaly detailed that Alden, who was a white Englishman, blared out Capital FM over the top of what he referred to as the workforce's 'oriental' Indian music.[6] Following a deprivation too far – being forced to work mandatory overtime on Friday, 20 August 1976 – Jayaben Desai and her son Fasil walked out. This followed on from another small group of Asian workers leaving the plant earlier the same day to protest the sacking of Devshi Bhudia after he refused to complete his mail-order work at the pace demanded by Alden.[7]

As she walked out, Desai emphasised that Alden would not dare to treat white workers in the same way he treated her and her primarily Asian colleagues. She called on the workforce of the Grunwick 'zoo' to refuse to be compliant 'monkeys' and to instead stand as striking 'lions'. Desai ended her rallying call by exclaiming that there were no 'white girls' left among the Grunwick workforce, before declaring 'I want my freedom!' in both English and Gujarati. The workers who followed Desai out of the plant formed the kernel of the strike which began the following Monday. The dispute was initially concentrated among the mail-order employees at Chapter Road but also extended to workers from Grunwick's photo-processing facilities nearby at Cobbold Road. By the end of the month, 137 strikers out of a workforce of 490 had joined the dispute. The striking workers were organised by the Association of Professional, Executive, Clerical and Computer Staff (APEX) union. Ward had reacted by sacking all of the strikers, leaving them demanding reinstatement along with union recognition.[8]

Therein began an epic British workplace battle, which Jeremy Corbyn described as 'one of the seminal strikes of the 1970s' in a film released not long after he became Labour Party leader in 2015.[9] Corbyn was far from an isolated voice in commenting on Grunwick either contemporaneously or retrospectively. The dispute ran on for almost twenty-three months. In the face of managerial intransigence, the strikers called for reinforcements from fellow trade unionists. Grunwick regularly made newspaper front pages over the summer of 1977 when the strikers and their supporters clashed with police. Television news reports broadcast footage of large crowds vying with police on West London streets while Grunwick drivers tried to force ageing buses carrying 'loyal' workers through to the plant.

In June 1977, the strikers called for a mass picket and were supported by students, feminists and socialist activists. Support grew and reached deep within and beyond the capital. Jack Dromey, the secretary of the Brent Trades Council, sat on the Grunwick strike committee as a non-voting member. Dromey retrospectively lauded 'the big battalions' of the labour movement who became crucial to the mass picketing strategy.[10] The largest pickets were bolstered by Fleet Street print workers, London dockers and miners from Yorkshire, Kent, South Wales and Scotland. In an obituary for Jayaben Desai published shortly after her death in 2010, Dromey commended Desai's courageous leadership but also underlined her pivotal role in giving these well-organised and comparatively well-rewarded workforces 'an understanding of the grim reality facing too many' women and migrant workers.[11]

Dromey's sentiments have formed an important core of how Grunwick has been remembered and heroised. Grunwick stands out as an occasion where the white-dominated structures of British trade unions extended support to striking Asian and black workers. Contemporary commentators such as Amrit Wilson, a prominent Asian socialist and anti-racist journalist, contrasted events in West London with earlier recent experiences of workplace mobilisation, such as a major strike at Imperial Typewriters in Leicester during 1974. At Imperial, the trade union branch and full-time officials had collaborated to undermine the strikers. As at Grunwick, the workers were primarily East African Asians who had relatively recently arrived in England.

Wilson quoted George Bromley, a Transport and General Workers' Union (TGWU) official, who responded to the Imperial Typewriter strikers with indignation, condemning their impatience and ignorance of labour movement procedure: 'The workers have not followed the proper dispute procedures, they have no legitimate grievances, and it is difficult to know what they want.' In Wilson's view, Grunwick was 'an important exception' to the trend, and an occasion where 'the rank-and-file of the labour movement demonstrated their support for black workers'. These dynamics were mediated by a labour movement left politics increasingly informed by anti-racism. Wilson noted that its exponents in many cases came from migrant backgrounds too.[12] Jack Dromey was born to Irish parents in London. His comrade, Tom Durkin, who was chair of Brent Trades Council, had arrived in England after fleeing poverty in Ireland in the 1930s, where he found work in the building industry and joined the Communist Party of Great Britain (CPGB). Durkin still spoke with an Irish accent when he lent support to the Grunwick workers four decades later.[13]

Grunwick is identified in Satnam Virdee's history of race and class in modern Britain as a central manifestation of working-class anti-racism. Along with mobilisations against the violent street fascism of the National Front in nearby Southall and in Lewisham, the dispute was a crucial marker for a more inclusive version of class consciousness in London. It was also a polarising moment, drawing stark divisions between opponents and supporters of a multiracial working-class politics.[14]

There were tensions as well as solidarity on display at Grunwick. Sundari Anitha and Ruth Pearson note how the dispute, which would end in defeat in the summer of 1978, left the strikers disappointed with union officialdom. They caution against overemphasising fleeting moments of support.[15] White male solidarity 'was about workers per se and not about migrant workers', epitomised by a Yorkshire miner who explained he was attending pickets to back the Grunwick 'lads'.[16] This refusal to distinguish between British and migrant or male and female workers was made by a trade unionist who was travelling a long distance to risk arrest or physical harm on the picket line. It demonstrates part of what was at stake in Grunwick as the labour movement attempted to expand its presence into new sections of the workforce that had traditionally been excluded from and on occasion actively demobilised and belittled by trade unions.

Within less radical sections of the trade union movement, APEX's support for the strikers encompassed new strategies for managing the forms of workplace conflicts that attracted George Bromley's ire at Imperial Typewriters. Ambalavaner Sivanandan, the London-based Sri Lankan Marxist who edited the journal *Race and Class*, wrote in 1977 that APEX aimed 'to bring the dispute within the Social Contract framework' then being pursued by Jim Callaghan's Labour government. The Social Contract centred on exchanging wage restraint for enhanced workplace rights and other legislative gains. Sivanandan interpreted APEX and the Labour Party as domesticating the militancy on show at Grunwick by imposing orderly mechanisms on Asian workers who had been at the forefront of a series of recent disputes.[17] Assimilation was employed as part of a two-pronged strategy along with tightened restrictions on immigration. On the one hand, as Sivanandan underlined, the Callaghan government believed 'fewer blacks make for better race relations'. On the other, it sought to manage remaining tensions through integrating black and Asian workers within systems of legal equality as set out in the 1976 Race Relations Act and incorporating them within unions.[18]

The Grunwick dispute powerfully anticipated the deep challenges facing Callaghan's Labour government as it pursued the Social Contract through to its politically disastrous culmination in the 1978–79 Winter of Discontent. The Labour government pursued wage restraint, concerned by the value of sterling along with worries about Britain's trade balance and public sector borrowing levels as the capitalist world experienced its most serious economic crisis since the end of the Second World War. Labour's own social base, unionised private and public sector workers, were asked to pay the price for the inflationary impact of spiralling oil prices amid conflict and revolutions in the Middle East and a global downturn. British workers faced the worst of both worlds – 'stagflation'. This ugly term referred to the unpleasant experience of economic growth stagnating while inflation continued to erode the value of earnings that were subject to tight controls. The Social Contract bargain which exchanged wage restraint for favourable industrial relations reforms and welfare inducements broke down towards the end of 1978 as living standards stagnated and unemployment grew.

Two years earlier, on 28 September 1976, just a few weeks into the Grunwick strike, Chancellor Denis Healey was at Heathrow airport, not far from Willesden. The chancellor did an about-turn and abandoned his international travel plans and dashed for Whitehall as sterling entered a new crisis amid market worries over whether the government would make debt repayments. Healey announced soon afterwards that Britain was applying for a record loan from the International Monetary Fund (IMF).[19] This 'heavily mythologised' moment of fiscal theatre played a crucial role in helping Callaghan and Healey justify their decision to implement spending cuts to party members rather than the capital controls advocated by the Labour left. Only half the loan was used, and it was repaid in full by 1979. Nevertheless, the symbolism of a British government appealing to the IMF for emergency credit buttressed right-wing narratives of national 'decline' and the failure of Labour's attempts to govern in dialogue with trade unions.[20]

Callaghan, who was on the right of the party and deferential towards the Treasury, saw wage restraint as necessary medicine for resuscitating the British economy, specifically through manufacturing exports. The prime minister addressed the Labour Party conference on the same day that Healey left Heathrow. His leader's speech abandoned Keynesian reflation of the economy, counselling members and union affiliates to prepare themselves for tough times ahead. Not even a Labour government could guarantee a return to full employment, averred Callaghan. The new premier warned in recriminatory terms that 'for too long, perhaps ever since the war, we postponed facing up to fundamental choices and fundamental changes in our society and in our economy'. Callaghan added that Britain had been feckless and 'ready to settle for borrowing money abroad to maintain our standards of life, instead of grappling with the fundamental problems of British industry'.[21] Wage costs were rising, making British factories uncompetitive, which led to plant closures and growing dole queues. Only a disciplinarian and austere response agreed in conjunction with organised labour could save British industry.

At Grunwick, the Labour government policed the trade unionists who were meant to be its social base far more harshly than it did a recalcitrant employer opposed to extending basic rights to workers. Not long after the dispute ended, Callaghan and his cabinet colleagues were plunged into a conflict with trade unionists across the country. After four years of restraint, by autumn 1978, union members were unwilling to carry the can of Britain's economic challenges any longer. Just a couple of months after the last picket lines gathered in Willesden, an unofficial walkout by Ford car factory workers marked the beginning of a series of major disputes across the public and private sectors over late 1978 and early 1979.[22]

Wage strikes were instantly historicised within sensationalist narratives of national decline and social disorder which already incorporated the motif of the disgrace brought by a Labour government going 'cap in hand' to the IMF. Key features of 'crisis' accounts of the Winter of Discontent include the extent and duration of rubbish piling high and graves going undug thanks to uncaring striking municipal workers, and hospital staff walkouts. A small number of chickens that perished due to the impact of a national strike by lorry drivers became a centrepiece of media coverage. The 'tyranny' of pickets who were a threat to their colleagues, employers and 'the public' (which did not include unionised workers themselves) dominated hostile interpretations of industrial action. Political scientist Colin Hay has examined the power of this episode of powerful narrative-making in paving the way for a Tory election victory. Projections of a society under 'siege' by trade union militancy convincingly helped Thatcher's Tories to triumph at the 1979 general election.[23] Anti-union sentiments built on narratives that emerged from Grunwick. The siege metaphor became a dominant right-wing framing of the threats to the British economy and society posed by labour militancy, along with the oppressive nature of draconian union mobilisation and the threat to public order posed by mass pickets. Conversely, the Labour Party failed to demonstrate that it could deliver sustained improvements in pay and conditions or support trade unionists mobilising for the most basic of workplace rights.

From picket lines to Parliament

It was the huge picket lines outside the plant which brought Grunwick to the nation's attention. Addressing the House of Commons on 14 July 1977, three days after the largest mass picket had seen tens of thousands of supporters assemble in Willesden, Robert Adley, the Conservative MP for Christchurch and Lymington in the South West of England, stated that 'the violence shown on television has been profoundly disturbing to many people'.[24] William Molloy, the Labour member for Ealing, a constituency which borders Willesden, responded. He pointed to the prior forty-four weeks of 'exemplary' picket-line behaviour which preceded the adoption of mass picketing. Molloy blamed management hubris for the dispute's continuation and violent clashes.[25] These details were by and large lost in reporting which emphasised the drama and danger of the mass picket instead of the workplace grievances behind the dispute.

Molloy's argument demonstrates the central dynamic at Grunwick, and its place in the unmaking of the British working class. The mass picket lines of 1977 were a response to the inability of a supposedly powerful trade union movement to enforce recognition on a relatively small employer.[26] Their opponents succeeded in presenting unions as a malignant bullying presence. Yet their repeated failure to either physically close the plant, starve it of supplies or deter strike-breakers only demonstrated the limitations of 1970s British trade unions when it came to organising poorer marginalised workers, especially migrant workforces. Employers like Ward and workplaces like Grunwick which thrived on offering jobs to workers excluded from better employment opportunities were an anticipation of Britain's future of increasingly precarious and non-union employment. The incremental de-organisation of the British working class across the five decades which followed the Grunwick dispute was not an accident or a straightforward outcome of economic changes. It was achieved through the agency of employers and their political allies. Robert Adley articulated a widely shared stance when it came to Grunwick and its place in the organisation of anti–trade union public opinion by the Conservative right. When journalist and historian Andy Beckett knocked on doors near the Willesden plant in the mid-2000s, he spoke to the wife of a local trade unionist. Her husband had been supportive of the strikers, but she herself simply felt frustrated by the dispute engulfing her doorstep and its long endurance.[27]

Violence on the street and the menace organised labour posed to employers like George Ward in pursuing their right to manage became the prevailing explanations of the strike and the need to end it. The dominant labour movement strategy of using newly legislated mechanisms for obtaining union recognition through the Advisory, Conciliation and Arbitration Service (ACAS) failed, but so did the more militant response embraced by the picketers. Grunwick was a victory for Ward and his supporters in the libertarian capitalist pressure group, the National Association for Freedom (NAFF). They assisted his firm and moulded the anti-union agenda pursued by the Thatcher government following the 1979 general election. As we saw in the last chapter, the NAFF had been formed in response to trade union strength within industrial sectors often characterised by largely white male workforces such as coal mining and electricity supply, but at Grunwick it intervened in a very different kind of workplace and sector.

Grunwick matters because it was an important event in and of itself, but it was also crucial to the halting of organised labour's 'forward march'. The dispute was a moment where emergent sections of the working class attempted to organise at a firm offering the forms of consumer-facing services which were growing in the British economy. It was also anticipatory and an inflection point in the history of workplace power in Britain. In the words of David Miller, a Scottish miner who worked at Kellingley colliery in North Yorkshire in the 1970s, the dispute exemplified 'the shape of things to come'.[28] Along with several other protagonists referred to in this chapter, Miller was interviewed in 2007 by Chris Thomas for a commemorative film which marked the dispute's thirtieth anniversary. Miller had played a leading role in organising for the Yorkshire Area of the National Union of Mineworkers (NUM) to attend picket lines by the busload, motivated by 'righteous indignation' at the exploitation of the Grunwick workers and the treatment of pickets by the police. He viewed Ward as a nineteenth-century throwback to employer despotism worthy of Victorian Britain's satanic mills but not a late-twentieth-century workplace. The militant picketers on the one hand, and the constitutionally minded union leaders who advocated using ACAS and recourse to legislation as the primary methods to achieve recognition at Grunwick on the other, were united in the view that draconian anti-union bosses were an anachronism. It was Ward, however, who represented the future.

Grunwick exposed the failings of Labourism in both guises. These outcomes were in part rooted in sociological factors, and by the retained association of the British labour movement with a core constituency of white male industrial workers. But they were primarily conditioned by the failure of unions or the Labour Party to effectively respond to challenges from employers and their allies in the Conservative Party in a shifting sectoral landscape. It was the nature of production at Grunwick and the logic of profit-making which shaped the walkout. The key flashpoint which triggered the strike took place in a mail-order room, which bears closer resemblance to contemporary logistics employment than a factory production line. Moreover, while it had industrial qualities, Grunwick was a service provider. Its primarily migrant workforce was episodically swelled by students over the summer months of high demand. Competitive advantages were secured by low wages and 'flexible' conditions, which were imposed by an employer keen to provide the greatest and cheapest convenience to a mass of consumers. In this sense, Grunwick was an important anticipation of the forms of work which characterise twenty-first-century Britain. It parallels employment in similarly draconian conditions at warehouses which often rely on migrant workforces and temporary workers.

The result of the dispute was a victory for the class struggle from above waged by Ward, the NAFF and their allies in the Tory Party. Grunwick succeeded in defying government urges to recognise APEX while relying on the Metropolitan Police to maintain production and beat back pickets on the ground. Its national significance lay in the political implications of associating even moderate demands for union recognition with industrial chaos and economic disruption. Grunwick had lasting political effects even before a potent anti-union narrative was further popularised during the Winter of Discontent, when public sector workers across areas like refuse collection and the National Health Service walked out against the Callaghan Labour government's pay restraint. Political forces committed to the de-organisation of the labour movement were emboldened by Grunwick. Their new-found confidence shaped the unmaking of the British working class, by preventing union expansion into growing sectors of the economy, but also by encouraging an offensive against remaining strongholds of workplace organisation.

Back to the future

Employment at Grunwick was presented by the strikers and their supporters as a dangerous throwback. The regular bulletin produced by the strike committee condemned the conditions endured by 'sweatshop employees' at the photo-processing company. Going further still, the bulletin accused management of abusing 'slave labour'. Perhaps more revealingly, the appeal to fellow trade unionists underlined enlightened self-interest through the potential of using the dispute to reach the ranks of Britain's non-union workforces: 'the eyes of the millions of unorganised workers and their employers are on this dispute. So too are the eyes of the immigrant communities.'[29] The strike at Grunwick from this perspective was a litmus test. It was a trial of the labour movement's commitment and ability to organise in a sector and form of enterprise it had not prioritised in the past, as well as to unionise a group of workers it had previously not enjoyed traction with.

Similar sentiments were relayed in Parliament by Laurence Pavitt, the Labour MP for Brent South, who was a consistent supporter of the strikers. On 4 November 1976, Pavitt lambasted the conditions at Grunwick, which he negatively contrasted with other local unionised workplaces such as the Heinz and

United Biscuits factories as well as the Guinness brewery at Park Royal. By comparison:

> Grunwick is a sweat shop with a management which could have been lifted straight out of the Dickens era. Conditions and management attitudes such as these have never been seen in Willesden since the First World War. They are a blot on an extremely good area.[30]

Working life at Guinness strongly reflected the trajectory of British industry at large, or at least its predominantly white and male components. By the middle of the twentieth century, unionised workers could often count on a job for life. Tim Strangleman's history of Guinness records the strong sense of affinity and belonging this created. At the peak of trade union strength, Guinness workers were industrial citizens who expected to be afforded rights, dignity and security in return for the responsibilities they undertook for their employer.[31] After the defeat at Grunwick, these gains were reversed as the workforce contracted. Work became more precarious and less rewarding, ahead of the brewery's eventual closure in 2005.

Grunwick was also representative of a side of British working life which had never fully disappeared through the transformations to politics, the economy and workers' rights between the 1940s and 1970s. Guinness employees enjoyed some similar experiences to the coal miners, power station operators and nuclear workers considered in the previous chapter, including unionised employment and enhanced status in the workplace. Such improvements, however, were not universal. The extension of mid-twentieth-century industrial citizenship was never complete, and in some sectors and localities the Victorian expectations of master and servant relations remained. These trends were particularly marked in smaller firms, lighter areas of manufacturing, construction and private service-sector employment, especially where members of the workforce were more likely to be women or come from a racialised minority background.[32]

Yet the advances which had been made by the growing portion of unionised workers shaped attitudes in the remainder of unorganised workplaces. Grunwick and the solidaristic responses the strikers received demonstrated the cultural reach of trade unionism in 1970s Britain and its appeal to even the most seemingly marginalised workforces. Female trade unionists in a small London firm had even inspired a contemporaneous television series. As the Grunwick strike rumbled on in 1977 and 1978, the BBC broadcast *The Rag Trade*, a sitcom set in an East London factory. It starred Miriam Karlin in the role of 'Paddy', the shop steward who leads a group of women machinists in perpetual conflict with the factory owner, Harold Fenner, played by Peter Jones. *The Rag Trade* is best remembered for Paddy's strike-happy catch phrase – 'Everybody Out!' – but the portrayal of the personalised battle between her and Fenner also paralleled reporting on the workplace battle taking place on the other side of the city between Desai and Ward.[33]

While they took the form of a lampooning caricature, Paddy and her colleagues were intelligible to a society where trade unionism was a dominant feature of public life. By the mid-1970s, most British workers were covered by collective bargaining agreements negotiated between employers and unions. At the peak of union strength in the late 1970s, more than seven in ten British workers were employed under collective bargaining conditions.[34] More than 13 million British workers were then members of trade unions, accounting for a majority of the workforce. They were concentrated in large firms within manufacturing, but increasingly within the public sector too.[35]

Events on Grunwick's doorstep encapsulated some of these changes. Another high-profile industrial dispute that overlapped with the strike at Grunwick took place at the Trico factory in Brentford, where women workers engaged in Britain's longest equal-pay strike. The strikers walked out after male workers, who had previously been employed on the nightshift, retained higher rates of pay for doing the same jobs as the women on the dayshift.[36] There were important parallels with Grunwick in the form of a supportive coalition of feminists and allied trade unionists from the left of the engineering union. A twenty-four-hour picket was maintained across twenty-one intense weeks, which led to confrontations between strikers and strike-breakers. As at Grunwick, management used convoys of vehicles to break through picket lines. Unlike at Grunwick, the Trico workers won a famous victory.[37]

It was easy to view Trico as part of a forward march of women's union activism in the 1970s, but the plant closed down just six years afterwards. It followed a general trend of American multinationals shutting down or downsizing in Britain. Multinationals undertook international restructuring in the face of global recession, but they were also motivated by subsidies available to them in other parts of the UK or globally.[38] In their 1978 account of the Grunwick strike, Jack Dromey and Graham Taylor of Brent Trades Council cited Trico as another significant strike which they had been involved in supporting. Dromey and Taylor also described Brent as a 'declining' industrial area, referring to local factory closures and job losses. Even North West London, one of the capital's last major manufacturing areas, was following the city's larger trend.[39]

In important respects Grunwick was significantly different from Trico and the more celebrated heroes of equal pay from the other side of Britain's capital, the Ford Dagenham strikers of 1968.[40] Grunwick was not owned by an American multinational, nor was it a publicly listed company. It did not have an existing union recognition agreement and it was not part of an already well-unionised sector like automotive manufacturing. In sharp contrast to Trico, which sold components to large car companies, Grunwick sold its services directly to consumers. It was also in the mid-1970s a firm that had decades of London-based activity ahead of it. Andy Beckett wrote in 2009 that George Ward remained in charge of Grunwick, which had been renamed after its Bonuspool brand but continued trading.[41] Circumstances then changed. The *Independent* reported in George Ward's 2012 obituary that his firm had wound up the previous year, citing the impact of changing technological and consumer wants following the popularisation of cheap digital cameras.[42]

George Ward's company's lifespan was integrated with the rise and fall of the colour photo–processing technologies, which improvements in workers' living standards (examined in the previous chapter) had created a mass market for. The labour regime at Grunwick was based on gaining a competitive edge by ensuring customers enjoyed a cheap and speedy service. Such was the combination of high-technology and consumer demand that industrial sociologist Les Levidow found in 1981 that 70 per cent of Grunwick's custom was processing 'amateur snapshots from working-class holiday makers'. The remainder were institutional customers, including, with no shortage of irony given events on the picket lines, the Metropolitan Police. Grunwick secured its markets, including international custom transported via nearby Heathrow airport, through a quick turnaround of typically around four days on mail order, which was less than half as long as its rivals.[43]

Grunwick sold a service that was a product of the affluence which the industrial citizens of Guinness's Park Royal brewery and other unionised workplaces enjoyed. The leisure lives of affluent workers were both increasingly mobile and documented. These trends were further encouraged by the growth of package holidays and more affordable air travel by the 1970s. Pictures were no longer the preserve of professional photographers, nor were they confined to formal occasions. Instead, they captured moments of intimacy and fun for couples and families. Demand for workers surged during the summer months at Grunwick as eager customers submitted their film rolls to bask in the memory of their days at the beach, whether it was in Blackpool or Benidorm. The Mancunian punk poet John Cooper Clarke bitterly satirised the Spanish package holiday in 'Majorca' (pronounced with a *j*) in the late 1970s. His tale of unpleasant flights, boozed-up tourists and shabby hotel rooms ended on a sardonic political note which drew attention to the more heroic history of the anti-fascist British volunteers who had travelled to Spain four decades earlier.[44] Grunwick revealed the complexities of the divisions of labour within Britain which made the lives of affluent workers possible. The dispute also unveiled the relations of exploitation and solidarities they could inspire.

While the extent of support that they received afforded Grunwick strikers a public platform, George Ward was also given a prominent stage to make his case. When the dispute was still ongoing, Ward published a memoir titled *Fort Grunwick*. It tells the story of a self-made man who defied the odds. Ward profiled himself as an enigmatic entrepreneur. The England of the 1960s 'was associated in my mind with hardship, discomforts and racial discrimination'.[45] Ward's firm, of which he was one of three partners, had expanded considerably through the offer of mail-order colour photo processing. By his reckoning, the company's growth was fraught with tension and personal risk, borrowed money and many hours of toil in 'sweatshop' conditions. A steep £20,000 loan was necessary to finance the switch to colour printing, and the move towards mail order also came with a credit innovation: the 'pay later' scheme. Customer loyalty was further secured by the convenience of awarding free vouchers for future pictures where an image was not worth developing. Eventually this paid off, and Grunwick began 'to make some real money'. The firm merged with a competitor and expanded, later relocating from Wembley and St John's Wood to its two sites in Willesden. Ward was contemptuous of the allegation that he ran an exploitative business, insisting on the quality of the bathroom facilities and the canteen. They were starkly better than the facilities had been in Grunwick's ramshackle earlier days. Ward mockingly referred to the 'air-conditioned sweatshop' his company had spent £70,000 upgrading at Chapter Road, where the trouble brewed in 1976. He also conceded, though, that in fact the air-conditioning system was not up and running over that long hot summer![46]

Ward's defence of his plant was largely predicated on chasing phantoms, at least when it came to his account of working conditions. Worker complaints primarily rested on the relatively low wages, poor treatment by superiors and the unwillingness of management to negotiate their terms and conditions. Wages as low as £28 were reported for a forty-hour week, which was fully £12 below the average for a woman in London in 1976 and less than half of the average male wage of £66. It was Ward's uncompromising stance that shone through most of all. Joe Rogaly incisively characterised the Grunwick management's insistence on 'unquestioned obedience' in his 1977 book on the strike. Ward imposed these conditions on largely immigrant workers from former colonies because native-born white workers would not have tolerated them. Rogaly saw employment at Grunwick as below the standards of contemporary expectations in British workplaces: 'We live in a world in which the power employers have traditionally wielded over employees is no longer accepted by most people.'[47]

Ward's most ardent supporters were galvanised by the prospects of downgrading the working conditions which most people would accept. One of his closest allies was John Gorst, the Conservative MP for Hendon North, not far from Willesden in North West London. As perhaps his most vociferous backer, Gorst was keen to rubbish allegations 'that Mr Ward, who is himself an Anglo-Indian, is a racist employing slave labour'. Instead, Ward's opposition to unionisation at Grunwick was conceived as a stand for sovereignty and liberty: 'His defeat would be a serious blow to the freedom of the individual, to the rights of small businessmen and to the future of democratic government in this country.'[48]

Yet the supporters of Grunwick management also told another story of eagerness to defeat organised labour and worker expectation in altogether less idealistic terms. These ends were nakedly displayed in the pages of the *Spectator*. An article in the right-wing periodical from late June 1977 spoke in racialised, 'othering' terms about Grunwick's primarily migrant workforce, essentialising the 'Asian women, dressed in saris who can lunch at the canteen off biriyani, chapati and mango juice' but who would not make excessive demands on their employer. The article was enthused by the prospect that employers such as Ward could exploit immigrant labour for lower wages than they would pay unionised white British workers. It emphasised that 'foreigners work harder for less'. Grunwick was orientalised in these descriptions as an outpost of a post-colonial economy in the metropole: 'The sight of an Asian factory actually here in London might make clear to the British trade unions the competition they face from abroad.'[49] By the autumn, the blunt purpose of Grunwick as a symbol of the future again occupied the pages of the *Spectator*, when Peter Peterson praised George Ward as 'a hero' who had taken a stand on behalf of 'small employers all over the country'.[50]

A more materialist understanding of the political economy Ward defended was summarised by Robert Taylor in the *Observer*. Ward's firm stood at the apex of markets, technologies and labour organisation, which created demands for low pay and subordination. Grunwick 'processes family snapshots at competitive prices and mostly employs immigrant and part-time student labour. The film-processing industry operates on tight margins with low profits, poor wages and a large labour turnover.'[51]

Employment at Grunwick anticipated a host of other high-tech customer service jobs that developed in Britain in the decades to come based on exploiting female and immigrant workers on low wages under draconian conditions. The mail-order room at Grunwick perhaps most strongly anticipated the contemporary Amazon 'fulfilment' centre in its form of labour process, intensity and cost minimisation. It also had in common authoritarian management and a derisory view of efforts to unionise large numbers of racialised and migrant workers.[52] In this sense, Grunwick is a crucial instance of the remaking of the British workforce but also of the unmaking of the British working class through its de-organisation at the behest of aggressively anti–trade union employers.

As a proprietary self-made man, Ward encapsulated the petty bourgeois perspective which animated the Thatcherite radical right of the Tory Party.[53] Grunwick stood against the bureaucratic 'establishment' embellished by Labour's Social Contract and union leaders regularly visiting Downing Street. Ward was opposed to both ACAS and a Court of Inquiry which Callaghan's government called in the summer of 1977 as a way out of the dispute. He was not going to be told what to do in running *his* business. Keith Joseph, a key lieutenant of the leader of the opposition, Margaret Thatcher, was second only to Gorst when it came to fighting the firm's corner, describing the dispute as 'a make-or-break point for British democracy, the freedoms of ordinary men and women'.[54]

Many more Grunwicks mushroomed after Ward won. Twenty years after the dispute finished, small firms in the booming South East of England were among the least likely to recognise trade unions. They were also disproportionately likely to rely on predominantly female workforces and to employ among kin networks from racialised minorities.[55] North West London was the epicentre of the redrawing of authority and legitimate expectation in British workplaces in the late 1970s. Grunwick's business model was intimately linked to Heathrow airport and dependent on high technology as well as employing from among the area's growing migrant populace. At the airport itself, a racial division of labour confined immigrant workers to menial and often contracted-out roles such as cleaning, while an ever more vicious and restrictive migration regime was implemented by the British state.[56] The two years of picketing at Grunwick demonstrated the political and repressive force that was needed to institute Ward's labour regime as the norm across large parts of Britain's economy.

The limits of Labourism

A few months after the strike at Grunwick ended in bitter defeat, Britain's best-known Marxist intellectual, Eric

Hobsbawm, published his thesis that labour's forward march had halted. Hobsbawm did not reference the dispute in Willesden. His comments instead underlined what he saw as the contradictions that had grown within the labour movement and the decomposition of an industrial working class formerly centred on miners, factory hands and especially male craft workers. The Winter of Discontent narrative of uncollected rubbish, unburied bodies and unattended patients strongly chimed with Hobsbawm's emphasis on the tendency of industrial action to be directed against the public rather than capital. Britain was not marked by increasing class consciousness but instead mired by 'a growing division of workers into sectional groups, each pursuing its own economic interest irrespective of the rest'.[57]

The following summer, just weeks after Margaret Thatcher had come to power, Hobsbawm debated his thesis at the 1979 Communist University of London educational event hosted by the CPGB. Hobsbawm was up against another party talisman, Michael 'Mick' McGahey, who was also vice president of the NUM and president of the NUM's Scottish Area (NUMSA).[58] McGahey had been instrumental in organising miners' support for Grunwick. Just a few years earlier he had emerged as a well-known figure in British public life after he played a leading role in organising the coal strikes of 1972 and 1974. During the Grunwick dispute, McGahey referred to George Ward as a menacing 'industrial hooligan' who needed to be stopped by a show of labour movement strength. To help achieve this, McGahey brought the NUMSA executive and a representative from each colliery in Scotland to the picket lines in 1977.[59] The next year, he reminded the Scottish Area's annual conference that 'picket force', and not the Court of Inquiry led by Lord Wilberforce, had delivered victory to the NUM during the coal wages strike in 1972.[60] McGahey was a product of a period of growing working-class confidence and expanding trade union organisation. His stance in the debate with Hobsbawm rested on these foundations. An assertive British labour movement was improving its position in the 1970s through working-class unity. From McGahey's vantage point, Grunwick was an important occasion to demonstrate that race, nationality and gender were no barrier to organising workers around demands for basic standards of dignity.

Archive news footage from the largest day of picketing at Grunwick, 11 July 1977, includes a Yorkshire miner explaining to a television news journalist that having been made aware of the treatment of the Grunwick struggle, 'the working class are responding the only way they know how. With a display of solidarity.'[61] Around two weeks earlier, the *Guardian* had recognised that it was no longer just 'young students with far-left views' who were supporting the strike: 'Now Grunwick is attracting manual workers from all over British industry.'[62]

When Mahmood Ahmed, who was a young Grunwick worker in his early twenties at the time of the strike, reflected on the ramifications of the dispute thirty years later, it was the extent of solidarity from other trade unionists that stood out for him. Ahmed recalled 'there was thousands and thousands of people turned up, and we didn't believe it would be like that'. As 'plain labourers' and 'just some, you know, about a hundred or so Asian people', the strikers had not anticipated receiving this groundswell of support. Grunwick became a *cause célèbre*. As the strike committee's secretary, Ahmed found himself giving speeches and taking in large donations on a tour of workplaces including shipyards in Glasgow, collieries in Kent, and factories in Edinburgh, Paisley and Kilmarnock.[63] Vipin Magdani, a Cobbold Road worker who led a walkout of strikers who joined the Chapter Road strikers, recalled the dispute as a similarly powerful but more localised experience. Soon after the dispute started, a trembling Magdani gave a speech to a large public meeting in Euston. After this, he found himself touring factories closer to Willesden: 'It was an all-white type of environment, and we were getting support.'[64]

Dockers, miners and building workers helped bring mass picket lines to a sleepy London suburb, and at least in isolated incidents they were able to win momentarily. David Miller chortled thirty years later when he remembered that when he travelled to Grunwick from the Yorkshire coalfields, he saw some London dockers successfully using a banner to topple the mounted police who were deployed to disperse the pickets.[65] On 11 July 1977, the bus driving workers into Grunwick was stopped and turned around. Subsequently, the plant was closed for several hours during the period of peak customer demand for the company, at the height of summer. Dromey and Taylor triumphantly recalled that 'a phalanx of dockers and building workers who stood their ground against the horses until they turned around and trotted back to demeaning chants of "Workers united – will never be – defeated!"'[66] Yet this was the biggest halt in production achieved by pickets at Grunwick, despite the tens of thousands who attended to support them. They paid a heavy price. The Metropolitan Police reported that over 500 arrests were made at Grunwick during 1977 and that 37,000 police officers were estimated to have been deployed to the picket lines during the busiest period of mass picketing between June and November.[67] Around 550 arrests were made over the course of the dispute. This is approximately double the number of arrests made in the national coal strike of 1972, which involved around 300,000 miners, more than 2,000 times the number of workers on strike at Grunwick.[68]

Policing at Grunwick was distressing and violent. Its political function was to undermine the legitimacy of the strike by closely associating picketing with criminality.[69] Here, then, were the limits of Labourism. The unmaking of the British working class flowed through the contradictions between the objectives of wielding government power to legitimate organised labour and the role of police authority in suppressing trade unionists in the name of upholding social order. While workers attempted to win the basic rights of union recognition, supported by large constituencies of the Labour Party, the Metropolitan Police's Special Patrol Group were deployed to defend George Ward's right to resist unionisation under a Labour government. Union recognition was far from an obscure or divisive aim within the labour movement. Shirley Williams, who was the Paymaster General from 1976 to 1979, and positioned on the right of the Labour Party, visited the pickets with two other ministers who were also APEX members on 18 May 1977. Williams encouraged the strikers to maintain their resolve: 'You've shown a remarkable degree of courage and solidarity and we're here to recognise that fact.'[70] She also articulated her confidence that the union would succeed.

Just a few weeks later, one of Williams' colleagues, Audrey Wise, the Labour MP for Coventry South West, was arrested and charged with obstructing a police officer. Wise would testify in court that she was detained after objecting to a police officer dragging a woman by her hair. She was found guilty and fined.[71] The day she was arrested, Stephen Kelly, who was reporting on the picket line for the Labour left publication *Tribune*, was punched in the face by a police officer. He wrote that Wise had attempted to pass a message to her comrades following her arrest but was prevented from doing so by police, who slammed the door of their van shut. Kelly also documented the targeting of the strike leaders. Mahmood Ahmed described having become a 'marked man' the previous week, while Jayaben Desai had been charged with assaulting a police officer.[72] Ahmed and another arrested picketer were subjected to punitive measures. He was left languishing in Brixton prison after refusing to accept bail conditions which debarred him from going within a half-mile radius of the Grunwick plants. These stipulations were only lifted after a challenge in the High Court.[73] In 2007, Ahmed reflected on the political conditions which lay behind his arrest while he was picketing his own workplace and striking for union recognition under a Labour government. The problem was that Grunwick had become a 'national issue' where the animating subject was public order and not the demands of the strike: 'We were just basically asking for a decent wage, you know, decent working conditions, and, you know, those of us who were outside should be taken back to work.'[74]

These tensions were summarised thirty years later by Albert Booth, who was the Secretary of State for Employment throughout the strike. In 2007, Booth remembered that Grunwick was episodically discussed at cabinet meetings, through the lens of managing and ending the dispute and minimising further bad press coverage: 'The discussion then was around the issue on how we could terminate the dispute. The concern of cabinet ministers was over the nature of the demonstrations that were taking place.'[75] Before becoming an MP, Booth had worked as an engineering draughtsman and been a trade union activist. He was seen as on the left of the Labour Party. Booth was naturally on APEX's side against Ward, but his commitment to the Social Contract as a means to achieve an orderly system of industrial relations became a form of paralysis at Grunwick.[76] Even three decades later, Booth bemoaned the Grunwick strike, saying it 'was a classic case of how not to obtain recognition', and that the workers and their union had effectively placed themselves outside 'procedure' which had been tilted in their favour under new legislation which had enhanced workers' rights since 1974 through agonising efforts in parliamentary committee rooms: 'The legislation which had taken so long to obtain . . . had not been used in any way to obtain trade union recognition in this particular case where I thought it was highly necessary.'[77]

Booth's dilemmas reveal the limitations in his strategy. His comments from 2007 were reminiscent of those made by union officials about the unruly character of Asian strikers at Imperial Typewriters in 1974. Ultimately, the pressure of mass picketing, along with the 'blacking' of Grunwick mail by the postal workers at Cricklewood sorting office, created the impetus for a Court of Inquiry that was held over the summer of 1977 under Lord Justice Scarman. By refusing to sort Grunwick's post, the Cricklewood workers created a pivotal threat to the mail-order business model, but they were also in breach of their own legal responsibilities and attracted the ire of their union. Scarman's findings presented a paternalistic perspective on the Grunwick dispute: 'the strikers had no knowledge of trade union procedures and organisation' but they were responding to the pressures of a 'long hot summer', mused the patrician judge.[78] Jack Dromey had encouraged this view when he appeared before Scarman on 19 June 1977. Dromey described himself as being contacted by 'chickens without a coop' following the walkout in August 1976.[79] Scarman largely endorsed the strikers' aims but was also condemnatory of mass picketing and supportive action taken by the postal workers. These mobilisations had forced his inquiry in the first place but fell outside of 'the spirit of the law', as did Grunwick's intransigence. The inquiry findings included appeals to Ward to reinstate the workers and recognise a union 'no matter what the legalities are', and to make an ex-gratia payment to workers where demand for labour was not sufficient to warrant reinstatement.[80]

Scarman's appeals to the spirit of fair play got nowhere with Ward, but in the meantime the firm's stonewalling, the impact of hundreds of arrests and Labour Party pressure on trade union hierarchies all contributed to isolating the strikers. The Metropolitan Police's operation had much more consistency and force behind it than Scarman's requests for humane employment practices. Days of clashes led Grunwick to make front page news. On 23 June 1977, the *Guardian* reported that the previous day two young feminist activists, Mary Davis and Maria Duggan, had been hospitalised and were left reliant on a wheelchair and crutches respectively.[81] On 16 August, Energy Secretary Tony Benn found himself in the unusual situation of appearing in court as a cabinet minister, to appear as a character witness at the trial of his Parliamentary Labour Party colleague Audrey Wise. Despite Benn insisting on Wise's kindness and commitment to non-violence, she was found guilty of obstructing a police officer.[82]

Benn titled his diary of the period *Conflicts of Interest*, which could also summarise the position of the Labour government at Grunwick. He bemoaned the fact that Callaghan's main priority, over and above the legitimate concerns behind the strike, was insisting all parties involved 'cool it'.[83] The president of the Yorkshire Area of the NUM, Arthur Scargill, became a subject of paranoia for Callaghan. The prime minister requested that MI5 personally inform him of Scargill's movements with regard to Grunwick.[84] Historian Matt Myers records that both Callaghan and the Metropolitan Police were primarily concerned about the picketing miners 'displaying military-style discipline, self-confidence, and physical power'.[85] Booth unhappily recalled that Scargill was among the 'rogue elements' who were responsible for stoking Trades Union Congress (TUC) support for mass picketing, which only contributed to his government's problems.[86] The hysteria which Scargill inspired was demonstrated following the last mass picket on 7 November 1977. A Commons debate on crime was dominated by Grunwick. William Rees-Davies, the Tory MP for Thanet West, claimed that as many as 18,000 miners had attended picket lines at Grunwick, when the number had in fact been only in the hundreds.[87]

Ministers made a virtue of acquiescing to public order demands. On the same day, the home secretary, Merlyn Rees, commended the thousands of police who had kept Grunwick open, condemning the 'considerable disorder' brought to the plant by pickets from around the country.[88] Rees had earlier responded to the largest day of picketing on 11 July 1977 by reiterating his full backing for the Metropolitan Police, referring to his previous experience as Secretary of State for Northern Ireland from 1974 to 1976: 'When I am asked to support the police, I support the Commissioner in taking his decisions. This is something which we all learned in Northern Ireland when politicians were taking these decisions.'[89] These comments were perverse and hyperbolic. More than 850 people lost their lives in violence related to the armed conflict in Northern Ireland across the three full calendar years.[90]

A crescendo of pressure built on Rees and the government after Special Patrol Group officer Trevor Wilson was hit by a glass milk bottle during the intense day of picketing on 23 June 1977. The incident added to perceptions of disorder and thuggery. Wilson was described as 'badly cut about the head' in a press report which profiled him as a young husband. It was accompanied by images of Wilson lying in a pool of his own blood.[91] Following Wilson's injury, a young black worker, Richard Maull, was arrested and charged. Maull was described by Dromey and Taylor as having a Caribbean background and being a computer programmer at a local factory where he was a member of the white-collar union, the Association of Scientific, Technical and Managerial Staffs.[92]

Maull's union branch raised money for his legal case and appealed for witnesses. The Trotskyist newspaper *Workers' Action* celebrated these developments, emphasising that, unlike at Imperial Typewriters just three years earlier, 'white scabs' were not dominating the union response to Grunwick.[93] Workplace solidarity beyond the episodic blacking at Cricklewood came from Fleet Street printers. Bill Freeman, who was a union activist at the *Observer*, led objections to an NAFF advert which attacked the Grunwick strikers on the grounds that the printers 'had a responsibility to the rest of the movement' to demand a right to reply.[94] In 2007, Ann Field, Freeman's wife, who was also a print worker active in organising solidarity with Grunwick, recalled that union activism had succeeded in insisting on a right to reply for the union perspective on Grunwick at the *Observer* and the *Telegraph* as well as pressurising positions at other leading newspapers.[95] These important displays of print worker power did not change the larger narrative of the dispute.

Maull was convicted and sentenced to two years in prison following a trial at the Old Bailey in March 1979. Two contrary accounts had been given by witnesses. Ronald Hollis, a free-lance photographer who was present at the picket line on 23 June 1977, insisted that the bottle was thrown at Officer Wilson by a tall man with a pale complexion. The *Guardian* reported that Hollis was contradicted by a Canadian television journalist – Ann MacMillan – who claimed to have seen a man with an Afro hairstyle, fitting Maull's description, throw the bottle.[96]

Jurors were divided but convicted Maull on a majority decision, presumably swayed by police evidence: 'Fragments of a bottle bearing Mr Maull's fingerprints were subsequently found under the officer's coat.'[97]

By the time of Maull's trial, the defeated Grunwick strike was being linked with protests against the National Front in Lewisham and Southall in influential accounts of London disorder involving black and Asian people clashing with police. The strike's aims for workplace trade union recognition, which were enshrined in the Social Contract, were buried under the depictions of a public order emergency. Racialised strikers, and their supporters, were presented as a problem to be managed, not deserving workers exercising their rights. Senior police officials referred to Grunwick, Lewisham and Southall as major episodes of disorder when they gave evidence to a parliamentary committee on public order legislation in 1979.[98]

The month after Maull's conviction, Blair Peach, a local teacher and anti-fascist protester, was killed by a Special Patrol Group officer in Southall.[99] While it was the 'strikers in saris' who dominated coverage and retrospective accounts of Grunwick, Maull's story and the links with Lewisham and Southall point to a larger context of political blackness in the period too.[100] As concern with 'law and order' increased, black men became key figures of public anxiety and fear closely associated with disorder. Lord Scarman would go on to chair another inquiry following riots in Brixton during the early 1980s. The violence meted out by Commissioner David McNee's Metropolitan Police had been a defining feature of the events in question.[101]

The image of police under attack by picket lines made up of Asian and black workers, militant trade unionists, and feminist and socialist activists was used to encourage sympathy for police in the line of fire. McNee's annual report for 1977 emphasised the extent of support for officers of the Metropolitan Police institutionally and individually:

> The fortitude and restraint with which my officers met the demand of duty outside the Grunwick plant evoked a wave of sympathy and admiration from members of the public. At times, the telephone switchboard of New Scotland Yard was inundated with calls from well-wishers and over 600 letters of appreciation were received, many containing donations to police charities.[102]

McNee's ascendency was illustrative of the rise of increasingly authoritarian policing which was used to delegitimise labour movement activism on picket lines and in opposition to fascists in the 1970s. Liam Turbett's history of racist violence and anti-fascism in Glasgow records that in 1975, while he was chief constable of Strathclyde Police, McNee oversaw a huge policing operation which led to violent confrontations and the arrest of scores of senior Scottish trade unionists picketing a meeting of the National Front at Kingston Halls.[103] McNee's 1977 report uses militaristic motifs. It discusses police 'casualties' but primarily dwells on their successes in the face of the picket-line threat. New stronger helmets with 'special protective lining and a more effective quick-release strap' allowed the police to retain 'control', all the way through to the 'final trial of strength' when the last mass pickets were mounted in November.[104] As McNee's comments demonstrate, the significance of Grunwick lay in physical control and state violence, but it was also an ideological struggle over designating the boundaries of legitimate workplace authority and constraining trade union tactics.

Class struggle from above

George Ward's full-throated anti-union stance came to embody what Ralph Miliband later termed the spirit of 'class struggle from above' which animated the assault on trade union rights in the 1980s by Thatcherite Conservatism.[105] The key conditioning here was the New Right's preparedness to get its hands dirty and be seen to openly support a reactionary employer in a struggle against their workforce. Self-presentation was crucial to the popularity and political successes of this positioning. The liberal and broadly left-leaning journalist Joe Rogaly was far from sympathetic to Ward. In his 1977 book on the strike, Rogaly judged Ward to be a recalcitrant employer who refused dialogue with his workforce. Nonetheless, he presented Ward and his allies in the NAFF and on the right wing of the Tory Party as rebels who had defied Britain's 'new establishment' which was defined by the corporatism that reached its apogee in the Social Contract.[106]

Ward's own memoir of the dispute, which was published around the same time, profiles him as standing up to unwarranted official expectations and interference in his business. The defiance shown against the trade union 'siege' of Fort Grunwick was fuelled by determined opposition to the demands of pushy union officials and the government bureaucrats who refused to stand up to them. In language that clearly crossed over with the perspective of the NAFF, Ward described demands for union recognition as 'an affront to liberty'. He accused unions of attempting to impose membership on his workers through a closed shop system.[107] This was a repeated inaccuracy raised by Ward and his supporters throughout the strike. It incensed Robert Taylor, the *Observer*'s labour correspondent, to the extent that he wrote a letter to the *Guardian*, correcting the claims made in a quotation from John Gouriet, the NAFF activist seconded to assist Grunwick management throughout the dispute.[108]

Gouriet was a Conservative outrider with influence over shadow ministers and the leader of the opposition. Following the publication of the Scarman report in September 1977, Keith Joseph rushed to the defence of Ward and his obstinate refusal to recognise a trade union, which he hailed as crucial to maintaining British freedoms. The front page of the *Guardian* showed a ventriloquist Margaret Thatcher speaking through a Joseph dummy.[109] The Margaret Thatcher Foundation has retrospectively described the Scarman report as having had 'major' importance in shaping the future prime minister's approach towards trade unionism and strike action.[110] Grunwick is discussed as a formative episode in Thatcher's memoirs. She referred to the dispute as 'a clear case of the outrageous abuse of trade union power'. Thatcher went on to explain that she 'gave NAFF as much support as I could', emphasising the threat that Labour's legislative changes in favour of union recognition posed to employers. An additional crucial dynamic was the public reaction when 'thousands of demonstrators crowded the narrow suburban streets'.[111]

Thatcher and her confidants spotted a favourable opportunity to create a spectacle. With her encouragement and even orders, Conservative MPs made themselves present at Grunwick on Ward's side. John Gorst had long championed anti-union activism, having previously founded an anti-union pressure group tellingly called the Middle-Class Association. On 24 June 1977, Gorst rode the bus with the Grunwick workers through the crowd of strikers and their supporters.[112] Afterwards, the member for Hendon North indulged in extremely unparliamentary language:

> No one who stands on his rights and is then faced with rioting on the streets can accept responsibility for what has happened outside these gates. Most of the people out there are bloody-minded thugs. I will tell you they are shits. People are being trained to bring policemen down.[113]

Gorst became a close friend of Ward during the dispute, creating a crucial link between the plant management and the parliamentary Tory Party. Thatcher insisted that Adam Butler, her Parliamentary Private Secretary, and Barney Hayhoe, a junior shadow employment minister, follow Gorst in taking a Grunwick bus journey. They attracted further media attention and in Thatcher's recollections shone a light on not only the 'fear' but also the 'courage' demonstrated by the majority of Grunwick workers.[114]

It was the strike-breakers who became the face of respectability in this presentation of Grunwick. Women and men who wanted to get on with their lives and support their families rather than risk politicising their workplace or allow themselves to be coerced into withdrawing their labour. Rogaly described strike-breaking at Grunwick in terms which anticipated the mass sale of council housing to come in the 1980s, explored in chapter 4, stating that many of those workers who crossed the picket lines each day between the summers of 1976 and 1978 were helping to meet mortgage payments in low-income households. Homeownership was an important resource and marker of respectability to migrant families who had only recently arrived in England, particularly those who had previously enjoyed comparatively middle-class positions in East Africa.[115] Those reference points would later become powerfully assimilated in Thatcher's embrace of the strike-breaking miners during the great strike of 1984–85. On that occasion she also championed the willingness of men and their families to defy union, workplace and community expectations by continuing to work.[116]

George Ward presented his 'willing' workers in glowing terms. They were a highly diverse multicultural workforce with origins in the Caribbean, Africa and the Indian subcontinent, and even included a dissident from Communist-ruled East Germany who knew a thing or two about coercive collectivism. Grunwick's loyal labourers were united in opposing union recognition. Ward proved this when he convinced APEX President Roy Grantham to endure a very hostile meeting with some Grunwick workers who made clear their objections to joining a union. Furthermore, he organised a poll of his workforce using the reputable public opinion firm MORI, which recorded overwhelming objections to union membership and recognition, or to reinstating the sacked workforce after a year of bitter picket-line confrontations. The reliability of such a study, in the face of Ward's well-known attitudes, is obviously dubious, especially given his boasts of successfully opposing attempts by ACAS to legally enforce union recognition through a successful High Court appeal.[117]

A potent class consciousness buttressed Ward's anti–trade unionism. He characterised the Scarman Inquiry, which was led by a High Court judge, a senior union official and Pat Lowry, the personnel manager at nationalised car firm British Leyland, as an insult to 'private business'. Ward went on to insist that he was 'just a small businessman' who had been fortunate to be assisted by his political 'friends'. Ward's language, comparing union recognition to having to share his wife with another lover, underlined his own sense of patriarchal proprietorship.[118] Yet he also clearly enjoyed the intrigue that lay behind Grunwick's ability to defy the pickets and distribute mail orders when the Cricklewood postal workers blacked his firm. As much as courtroom drama or political speechmaking, it was do-it-yourself anti-union activism that defined Ward and the support he received from the NAFF.

The buses which drove Grunwick workers through the mass pickets were archaic, barely roadworthy vehicles that the firm had improvised as a measure to beat the pickets, initially borrowing them from a school and later purchasing them. Managers Malcolm Alden and Ken Pearson drove the vehicles, protecting 'frail Asian girls' from 'the bully boys' outside. Ward also hailed his workers' defiance. He claimed that an Asian supervisor, Jessie Khan, had hobbled through picket lines with a bad leg, determined not to be beaten back. Additionally, Ward underlined the commitment of the police to keeping his plant open, singling out a Special Patrol Group officer who was willing to burn his hands on the bus radiator to ensure that the workers got through the picket lines.[119] In these comments, Ward summarised the Grunwick strike not simply as a defence of managerial prerogative and the right to sack workers, but also as a stand for the right not to join a union. Grunwick was willing to offer significant inducements to its remaining workforce to ensure the company won the dispute. The firm awarded two large wage rises, cumulatively totalling around a 25 per cent increase during the dispute in 1976 and 1977. These were in breach of another component of the Social Contract –

its wage restrictions! – but clearly demonstrate that Ward's overriding concern was workplace power, which he was willing to secure even at the expense of Grunwick's financial margins.[120]

The most audacious action undertaken by Grunwick was 'Operation Pony Express'. NAFF volunteers assisted Ward and the management to move around 100,000 items of undelivered mail from the plant to the Home Counties countryside over the weekend ahead of the largest mass picket on Monday, 11 July 1977. A convoy of vehicles removed the bags and £12,000 worth of stamps were applied to the mail orders which were then distributed to post boxes across London and the surrounding area. As historian Jack McGowan notes in his analysis of this episode, members of the NAFF were content to behave as collectively minded industrial activists when it suited them![121]

While Ward had the backing of Thatcher, the sorting office workers at Cricklewood were disciplined by the Union of Post Office Workers for embarking on the illegal blacking and eventually forced into delivering Grunwick's mail after their action had already been significantly undermined by the NAFF. Local union officials were fined considerable sums ranging from £50 to £500 by the union for their actions and insubordination.[122] Jayaben Desai still fondly remembered the 'beautiful' sight of 'the pile of bags' of unsorted mail left by the Cricklewood workers when she was interviewed in 2007. She looked back with anguish, though, on the absence of sustained support from the Labour Party and the TUC. Towards the end of 1977, Desai and a small group of strikers launched a hunger strike outside the TUC headquarters. Len Murray, the general secretary of the TUC, incensed Desai by insisting that she had been put up to it by Dromey and other outside agitators. Desai employed the same sharp rebuke that she did to a Grunwick manager who mocked her for wearing a sari on a picket line. On that occasion she pointed out that Indira Gandhi, India's then prime minister, wore a sari and exercised far greater power than anyone at Grunwick. She dressed Murray down by affirming that the hunger strike was an established method of struggle in India. Desai explained she was appealing to her own national tradition when she felt abandoned by Britain's trade unions.[123]

Mahmood Ahmed, reflecting on the support Ward was able to count on and the treatment he and other strikers had received at the hands of the police, underlined his own exasperation with Labour Party and TUC expectations that a legal route would hand victory to the Grunwick strikers: 'We were just plain labourers . . . unless we break some laws we're not going to get anywhere,' said Ahmed thirty years later.[124] In her testimony, Lakshmi Patel, who was a young striker in the late 1970s, insisted that despite the grim costs of defeat, she experienced a moral and political awakening from the strike through the rest of her life: 'I'm not scared. I can fight for myself.'[125]

Despite these sentiments and the lifelong influences that the dispute had on men and women like Desai, Ahmed and Patel, Grunwick was a formative episode in the unmaking of the British working class, specifically through the de-organisation of its industrial and political presence. It was during the two-year-long strike in suburban West London that the limitations of trade union expansion were confronted in the late 1970s. Workers in low-waged and increasingly insecure roles in the private service sector became the core of Britain's working class when factories closed down and the public sector shrank in the 1980s and 1990s. Anti-union bosses were able to follow George Ward's lead in either resisting or ripping up recognition agreements, but with much less difficulty than he had, especially after the Thatcher government's legislative offensive against secondary picketing made a repeat of Grunwick even less likely.[126] The extent of solidarity evidenced at Grunwick rested firmly on the conviction that all workers ought to enjoy rights akin to the industrial citizenship which had developed in heavy industry and public sector employment.

The strikers and their supporters were animated by a decisive rejection of the master and servant traditions of British employers. Solidarity mobilisations demonstrated that important sections of British organised labour were, at least on these terms, supportive of a broadened multicultural understanding of the contemporary working class, even where these efforts also transmitted gendered and racialised worldviews. There was clearly a marked contrast with union support for the 'colour bar' policies of racial discrimination which were a feature of workplace struggles in Britain. These dynamics had been central to major disputes such as the Bristol bus boycott in 1963, when the Bristol Omnibus Company branch of the TGWU was exposed as complicit in ensuring black workers did not find jobs at the firm. Since then, the boycott, along with Grunwick, has become a formative moment in labour movement interpretations of anti-racist struggles and important transformations in trade unionism.[127]

The defeat which unions and striking workers suffered at Grunwick demonstrated that the most politicised and mobilised trade unionists who had exercised industrial power to considerable public effect earlier in the decade were unable to meaningfully effect change in growing sectors where workers were employed on vulnerable and precarious terms. These were the parts of the economy where women and racialised minorities were more likely to work. Labourism's fragilities were exposed through Ward's determination to keep his workplace open and his ability to rely on police support to do so, and by the fact that Labour government ministers were far more moved by public order concerns than a strategic setback for union organisation. The result was that the language through which the Grunwick strike was described focused on alleged problems of metropolitan public disorder through violence instigated by Asian and black people either in their capacity as picketing workers clashing with the forces of law and order or in facing down the National Front. By comparison, the workers who stood on the picket lines did underline a shared working-class interest in expanding union organisation to achieve dignity at work and improved economic rewards.

During the Grunwick dispute, one lesser-known message of solidarity was sent to the strikers by Jessie Stephen. While she was now an ageing socialist stalwart, as a young Glaswegian woman Stephen had been one of the leaders of the Domestic Workers' Union of Great Britain, a fledgeling union for Britain's domestic servants formed in 1912.[128] At that time, domestic service had been the largest sectoral employer of women in Britain. Stephen moved to London to help run the union, organising the women employed under the same intensely patriarchal master and servant relationships which the Grunwick workforce was trying to break the mould of decades later. She was a bold reminder of the past struggles of British workers against deprivation and paternalism. The strikers were battling for what were considered in the 1970s to be basic workplace rights and conditions. Terms and conditions at Grunwick were the shape of workplace relations which growing portions of the British workforce would be employed under in the decades which followed, across the powerful divisive markers of race and gender. Grunwick can be viewed as an important indication of the potential of workers to fight against oppressive conditions like those experienced by the growing numbers of British warehouse workers in the 2020s. The defeat of the strike in 1978 was a sign of things to come, along with the emboldened politics of class struggle from above.

3

Closing Cardowan Colliery: 'The Price of Coal'

Margaret Wegg never forgot the morning of 27 January 1982. She vividly recalled the day thirty-two years later when I interviewed her at her home in 2014. By then, Margaret was a retired woman in her early seventies. She lived where she had grown up, in a housing scheme in Stepps outside the mining village of Cardowan to the north-east of Glasgow. When she was young, Margaret's family were offered a house purpose-built by the Scottish Special Housing Association for miners at the colliery where her father was employed. It was a cold day with winter in the air, but Margaret's living room was being kept warm by a coal fire. Coal and Cardowan were a continuous thread that ran through her life. While her neighbours had moved over to gas, Margaret insistently stuck by coal: 'It's a better heat, you get more hot water.' Three decades earlier, coal had been a source of risk and fear as well as security and familiarity. Margaret was meant to be resting after finishing on the night-shift at the Cardowan colliery canteen, but instead she immediately rushed down to the pit to help her colleagues after hearing news of an explosion underground.[1]

Thankfully, the explosion left no fatalities, but scores of men were badly burned and hospitalised. Before she worked at the canteen, Margaret, like many other wives and daughters of Cardowan miners, had taken a job at the Black & White whisky bond, which was powered by the gas from the colliery. Although it was beneficial for Black & White, the gas also made Cardowan a particularly inhospitable environment, and a dangerous one. Miners were warned sternly about the hazard of contraband, with matches and cigarettes strictly forbidden. Just a year after the explosion, Margaret and the Cardowan miners were left facing a new threat: the closure of the pit. Not only did Margaret work at the colliery, but her husband Jerry was a miner too, just as her father had been.

Coking coal mined at Cardowan had supplied the Lanarkshire steel industry for over fifty years, but the colliery had been deemed uneconomic by the National Coal Board (NCB) which ran Britain's publicly owned mining industry. Cardowan had faced similar threats before, overcoming moves towards closure in the 1960s and 1970s through a combination of determined mobilisation, improved industrial performance and favourable coal market fluctuations. Nothing could save Cardowan in 1983, however, as the NCB discarded its traditional approach of negotiating closures with unions and pursuing workforce dialogue to achieve consensual aims, preferring instead to use financial inducements to divide the workforce. This forceful imposition of managerial authority was a taste of things to come in Britain's coal industry but also across the wider economy. The working class was being unmade where it had formerly been strongest, assertive and recognised. Its key strongholds were targeted for closure and de-organisation.

This chapter examines the closure of Cardowan as a defining episode which exemplifies the pivotal dynamics of coercion and delegitimisation in the Thatcher government's offensive against trade unions in publicly owned industry. Coal was at the centre of these changes given the strength of union organisation and the economic power miners could wield. The closure of Cardowan was a formative experience in the lead-up to the 1984–85 miners' strike, the definitive conflict which ended in a decisive historical defeat for collectivism and organised labour. It was also an exemplary instance of the disempowerment of workers and the redistribution of agency and authority towards management in late-twentieth-century British workplaces. These were the outcomes of the de-organisation which the anti–trade union agenda promoted. Lasting consequences subsequently mounted across four decades marked by plummeting levels of union recognition, membership and confidence.

The conflict over Cardowan's future juxtaposed two perspectives on the 'price of coal'. On the one hand, it was understood in narrow financial terms by the Thatcher government and its allies within Coal Board management. On the other, however, Cardowan miners knew the true price of coal through their endurance of danger, injury and deaths at the colliery along with the maintenance of community and the supply of a vital resource for powering local industry.

The price of coal

The gas explosion on the fateful morning of 27 January 1982 realised the long-standing fears of the Cardowan miners and their families. Their colliery had been the site of fatal accidents in the past. In a previous explosion on 25 July 1960, four men had died and others suffered serious burns. During a discussion with members of the Cardowan Community Meadow organisation recorded in 2023, local women, all of whom were daughters of miners, talked about the scarring long-term impact of the 1960 explosion on the miners who survived as well as the families who lost loved ones. Joan explained that her father had been a young miner tasked with helping to carry dead bodies from the scene and felt it had contributed to later difficulties he experienced in self-medicating with alcohol to cope with the mental impact: 'They were just young men and they were asked tae, they said, you'll need tae come and help tae get some o these bodies out, and that's what they done. And ma dad never came tae terms wi that and he said, ah think no wonder people drink, and he said when he went down it was the state o the bodies wi the gas, you know. It was horrendous.'[2]

These were the collective memories that were flowing through Margaret's mind as she rushed out of her house to the pithead on 27 January 1982. Thankfully for her, Jerry had also been working on the nightshift so was not at risk. Then forty years old, Margaret was joined by older retired miners the same age as her father. The explosion left a legacy of mental and physical injury in the community. Some men were simply unable to face returning to the colliery again. Another was left mentally impaired, while many more suffered serious burns. For Margaret, it was a particularly severe event, and markedly worse than the earlier mining accidents she had lived through as an adult. In 2014, she remembered 'that was a bad one'. Jerry explained that in Cardowan, coal and community were synonymous, and sadly reflected on what happened in the village after the colliery closed down: 'The pit was a community anyway, underground and in the actual [housing] scheme . . . so it disappeared.'[3]

Willie Doolan, who was a miner in his mid-twenties in 1982, was the workmen's safety inspector at the pit. This was both a considerable burden of responsibility and an important mark of trust invested in him by his workmates. The election of safety inspectors was an important victory in an industry which had recorded annual death rates in the thousands during the early decades of the twentieth century, with even higher levels still of serious injuries.[4] Along with the election of a checkweighman (who was responsible for weighing coal which determined pay), the safety inspection system was part of the unique structures and working cultures of British coal mining. Under nationalisation from 1947, these systems were extended still further, through consultative committees that also comprised elected workforce representatives. They met regularly, discussing production, the future of collieries, and health and safety. Another distinctive feature of colliery life was the Mines Rescue Service, which originated in the privately owned industry but was reinforced under public ownership.[5] Willie's father was a member of the Lanarkshire branch. He had responded to the worst pit disaster in Scotland during the twentieth century on 18 September 1959 at Auchengeich colliery, which sat at the northern fringes of the village of Moodiesburn where Willie grew up and still lives. Forty-seven miners were killed and local families were left bereft after the loss of sons, brothers and fathers.[6] Afterwards, Willie's father was silent about his experiences of responding to the horrific accident. He lost workmates, neighbours and friends to the underground fire. In 2019, during an interview recorded close to the sixtieth anniversary of the Auchengeich disaster, Willie remembered: 'And I think it was a pretty common occurrence with the likes of a lot of miners at that particular time. Mining was a dangerous game, a dangerous industry to work in. Deaths were pretty commonplace within the industry. Fatalities were a common thing. But I think you could say it was a trait of the miners nationally that they never spoke about these things.'[7]

It was difficult to face these harrowing memories when they resonated with the dangers of work faced each day in the here and now. Miners were at risk on every shift, which was well known by the rest of their families too. Alice, another member of the Cardowan reminiscence discussion, recalled that she was in her primary school playground when she heard the alarms going off on 27 January 1982: 'But that's what you saw was all the women running towards the pit wi the kids and all that. Ah was aware ma dad was in the pit at work.'[8]

Unlike his father, Willie did discuss his own experiences of facing danger in the mining industry, including the Cardowan gas explosion, during the interview I recorded with him. He still vividly recalled his day on 27 January 1982. After seeing several of his workmates rushed to hospital, some having to be carried on stretchers, unsure as to whether they would all survive, Willie had to carry out his duty as an inspector. This meant travelling to the scene of the explosion with a representative from Her Majesty's Inspectorate of Mines: 'There was a case o somebody had been burnt. We had a report. This is the underground phone system. At that particular time, we were told that one person had been burnt. So right away you're not for a moment thinking it was gonna be the magnitude of forty men suffering severe burns and life-threatening injuries. We then got requested as things developed, we got requested to come back up the pit.

'We came up in the cage from number one pit and within minutes they were starting to bring some of them men up. Now this was men that you'd spoken to in the canteen maybe that morning. You'd spoke to them maybe before they went down. An automatic reaction when you seen them, it was your colleagues and you knew that they were suffering. Some of them were walking, some of them were in stretchers, coming off the cage. The immediate reaction when you see them is to embrace them, try and help them. But the skin was peeling off with the effects and clothes, like some of the jumpers that they maybe had on had melted into their skin and everything like that.

'That particular day, once all the men had been cleared out the area, we went down in the afternoon with the government inspector. And Ewan, the minute you walked in you could smell burning flesh. It was horrible. Horrible. We done the inspection down there that day. I mean it was horrible. Horrible. It was a thing that will stay with me for the rest of ma life.'[9]

The next year, Willie and his workmates embarked on a different struggle for survival. Closure was a threat to the jobs and welfare of over 1,000 miners and their families during a time of growing unemployment, but it meant even more than that: Cardowan was Lanarkshire's last pit. During the nineteenth century, Lanarkshire coal had fuelled the development of Neilson's hot blast technique, which transformed iron smelting.[10] The county had been decisively important to Scotland's industrial revolution, powering the steel works and factories that sustained Clydeside as one of Europe's major conurbations when Glasgow was home to over a million people. At its peak, the Lanarkshire coalfield had employed around 60,000 men in the early 1920s, when British coal mining sustained a workforce of over a million.[11]

Lanarkshire miners were centre stage in the development of British working-class politics. James Keir Hardie first worked in Lanarkshire collieries and cut his teeth unionising local miners. He also famously stood for Parliament for the first time as an Independent Labour candidate at the

Mid-Lanarkshire by-election in 1888, anticipating the eventual formation of the Labour Party and affiliation by the miners' union.[12] Cardowan itself was a storied pit. It had a radical reputation stemming from a significant presence of members of the Communist Party of Great Britain who played a dominant role in its union branch. Willie was among them. He succeeded an earlier generation which included his own father as well as Michael 'Mick' McGahey, who was president of the National Union of Mineworkers Scottish Area (NUMSA) from 1967 and became the NUM's vice president in 1973. In the previous chapter, McGahey was present as a senior union leader supporting the picket line at Grunwick. As a younger man, McGahey had worked at Cardowan, which was formative to his life as a trade unionist. Cardowan remained foundational to McGahey's trade union worldview all the way through to the bitterly contested closure of 1983. His late brother John had also worked alongside Willie at the pit when Michael was a full-time union official.[13]

A colliery's life

Willie was not meant to be a miner. He was actively discouraged by his father from following him down the pit and upset his Catholic mother by becoming both a miner and an active Communist. Willie explained that obtaining employment at Cardowan in 1971, and abandoning his job as an apprentice motor mechanic, took some deception. It was worthwhile, though, to pursue the working life he wanted, standing in family tradition and, in Willie's view, affirming community identity and camaraderie: 'Unbeknown to my mother and father who had sworn that I would never ever go underground, ah had went along tae Cardowan pit. Seen at that time we call them the personnel manager, human resources now, and asked him for a job. And he knew that ma father worked in the pit, and he asked me if my father was aware I was seeking employment in the coal mining industry. I told a lie. I said yes, he knew all about it. So, they gave me a start. Ma father and ma brother, both of them went off their head.

'But I wanted to work with the people ah knew, Ewan. People ah knew. People I'd grown up with. Families that I'd grown up with. And ah knew the hardship and the struggle that was attached to the mining industry throughout Britain at that particular time. The hardship that was involved. But that was a route that I wanted to go down.'[14]

Willie's recollections underline the strong bonds of family and localism which still structured the mining industry even after it had markedly shrunk in the 1960s. By the early 1970s, Lanarkshire had a diversified industrial economy in which coal was increasingly marginal. These changes were demonstrated at Tannochside, a former mining village which was made derelict as older miners' rows and pits made way for modernised industry along with newer and improved housing schemes. Caterpillar, the American earth-moving-equipment manufacturer, opened a large new factory atop the remains of the colliery settlement. The plant and the new homes built around it represented a hopeful and safer future. Its workforce was swelled by former miners and their sons, along with incomers who arrived from Glasgow as part of the population 'overspill' associated with urban slum clearances.[15] John Slaven's family moved to nearby Birkenshaw from Glasgow so that his father could work at Caterpillar, with his mother later joining the factory's payroll team: 'You werenae down an old decrepit pit that's seam was running out. You were in this big modern factory that had computer design pay systems. That were making big yella tractors that everybody knew aboot. You know, they could pay high wages.'[16]

As the coal industry shrank and concentrated into larger modern units, the overspill incomers were complemented by an accompanying exodus. Thousands of miners and their families left Lanarkshire for the more promising coalfields of Clackmannan in Central Scotland and the Lothians and Fife in Eastern Scotland. Smaller numbers later found jobs in the English Central Coalfields of Yorkshire and Nottinghamshire during transfer schemes. This restructuring was termed by the Coal Board as a model of rationalisation and efficiency, concentrating production in new or redeveloped collieries which served large new coal-fired power stations such as Longannet in Fife and Cockenzie in East Lothian. Despite labour market competition from engineering factories and other workplaces demanding male labour, the Board's officials were confident it had sufficiently appealing conditions of employment whereby 'greater amenity, safety and security offered by modern pits' would even attract former Scottish miners back to the sector if necessary.[17] Under the terms of mid-twentieth-century Labourism addressed in chapter 1, work would be easier, the conditions would be better and the rewards would be higher.

Cardowan appeared something of a survivor and outlier in this industrial scene. It was older than the pits the NCB had pioneered for the electricity industry. Scottish coal masters Nimmo & Dunlop had dug Cardowan during the 1920s.[18] Its purpose was distinctive from the Board's newer collieries. Cardowan produced coking coal by the hundreds of thousands of tonnes each year. It was an important supplier to the Lanarkshire steel industry which had prospered in the previous century. Lanarkshire remained a crucial steel producer during the second half of the twentieth century, and, in turn, Cardowan coking coal remained important to the fate of Scotland's new economic structure. The Caterpillar factory and other plants, such as the car factory at Linwood in Renfrewshire and the new commercial vehicle plant at Bathgate in West Lothian, absorbed labour released from mining. Yet they were also dependent on the work of the remaining miners to produce the coking coal for making the steel they relied on.[19]

Cardowan underwent significant investment during the NCB era, including electrification, the digging of a new shaft and improvements to the ventilation system along with an upgraded preparation plant.[20] These changes accompanied the development of the vast Ravenscraig strip steel plant nearby on the outskirts of Motherwell. Ravenscraig was initially pioneered by Scottish steel firm Colvilles in the late 1950s, under pressure from Harold Macmillan's Conservative government, which was seeking to improve productivity and employment levels on Clydeside while retaining private ownership of the sector.[21] In 1967, the steel works was nationalised as Harold Wilson's Labour government embraced public ownership as an answer to the sector's perceived need for efficiency and rationalisation in the face of international competition.

Cardowan was locked into a fight as job losses in the Lanarkshire coalfields accelerated. Mining employment fell from around 13,500 to below 4,000 over the decade from 1961 to 1971. At the beginning of the 1960s, around one in ten of Lanarkshire's employed men still worked in coal mining, but by the early 1970s this had fallen to fewer than three in every hundred.[22] These job losses were felt particularly severely in the North Lanarkshire mining heartlands, which became a focus of pit closures. By the early 1970s, only Cardowan and neighbouring Bedlay, also near the eastern edges of Glasgow at Glenboig, remained open.

Closures disrupted the expectations of the men made jobless along with their families. Working lives were cut short and futures were threatened. Anthony Rooney, who grew up as a miner's son in Bellshill in North Lanarkshire, remembered that just like Willie Doolan's father, 'ma father wouldnae let any of us go anywhere near the pits'.[23] His father's last job was at Bardykes colliery in the vicinity of Cambuslang to the south east of Glasgow. After it closed in 1962, around a quarter of the workforce were men under sixty who were not offered transfers, in some cases due to illness. Some of these men found new employment for the first time only two years later.[24] Ruefully, Anthony remembered that his father had lost his job aged fifty-six, and in the process, he also lost entitlements to retirement benefits such as concessionary coal allowances before dying not long after. Even half a century later, Anthony looked back in anger, decrying coal mining as a 'dangerous and dirty job', and remonstrating that 'all ma father got out of it was I carried him down the stair in a box, sixty years old'.[25]

While the NCB was a highly bureaucratised national enterprise, mining was still strongly localised. Collieries differed in their seams, conditions and culture, while transferred miners could lose access to the best-paid roles in tunnelling and work mining at the coal face. This precarity fuelled the discontent vocalised by Lanarkshire miners and their representatives. Pit closures and slum clearances, as well as workers being required to travel further to retain industrial jobs, demonstrate the unmaking of the working class through geographical dislocation. The working class had emerged in the nineteenth century through the displacement of the rural poor who settled in fast-forming mining and manufacturing districts. Migration and movement, both within Britain and further afield, had long been a part of industrial life, particularly in extractive sectors like mining.

There was a distinctive permanency to the communally experienced changes brought by mounting closures as they gained traction between the 1950s and 1980s. The Reid twins, Charlie and Craig, who are better known as Scottish folk act the Proclaimers, ruminated on the mounting cost of economic change in their 1987 hit single 'Letter from America'. In the music video, the Reids walk by the remains of Henry Robb's shipyard in Leith, their father's old workplace, which had closed four years earlier. The lyrics drew parallels between the displaced Highlanders of the nineteenth-century clearances, who swelled the ranks of Scotland's working class, and the contemporary fate of towns suffering factory, foundry and colliery closures. 'Letter from America' was covered with a record sleeve featuring pictures from inside the recently closed Gartcosh steel works which had been subject to an intensive campaign of opposition by steel industry trade unions and the Labour Party, but which was also backed by Scottish nationalists.[26]

Gartshore 9/11 colliery lies just six miles to the north of Gartcosh, in North Lanarkshire. It had closed nearly two decades before the album was released, in 1968. At Gartshore 9/11 it was the highly localised basis of industrial employment which shone through in opposition to the closures. A representative of the Colliery Officials and Staff Association, the NUM's white-collar affiliate, expressed the resentment he felt towards the increasingly centralised nationalised industry during the pit-closure proceedings:

> It used to be that the colliery manager had to plan out his own pit. Then Area officials took control of this and now we find that the planning for the pit is done 500 miles away. Handouts were all right, if unavoidable, *but men wanted to work.*[27]

Peter Downie recalled the hostility that miners faced when they transferred to Bedlay from Grayshill, an extension of Gartshore 9/11 which also shut in 1968. These were highly personalised and hurtful experiences:

> When we went tae Bedlay, up fae Grayshill tae Bedlay. Jimmy Clelland, a man that I stayed up brought up beside his mother and faither all of ma days, and he says 'Yous are fucking up here to steal oor jobs. Get away back tae wherever you come from and get a job ae your own!' We'd no other pit we could go tae.[28]

Peter's memories of the bitter reception at Bedlay demonstrate the intense localism which underlay Labourism, and that it was magnified by difficult economic conditions. While the solidarities which underlay the politics of the British working class could extend nationally, across industries, occupations and powerful social divisions such as gender and race, they could also be highly restricted through geographical boundaries.

Miners losing their jobs at Gartshore 9/11 also objected to transfers. Sixty men refused their offers, attempting to insist instead on receipt of redundancy pay, with one of them telling a Coal Board researcher that 'the pits are finished'. Another Gartshore miner communicated his exhaustion, saying he had 'been through too many closures'. Others underscored the cumulative impact of ongoing pit closures and the running down of other sections of mining infrastructure such as the

NCB's local workshops.[29] The refusers were discussed internally by Coal Board managers as a 'resistance group' of middle-aged workers who were primarily motivated by the likely loss of piecework rates as they transferred into less lucrative day wage positions. This was a 'mass protest', concluded the board. It was aimed at management but also 'the national policy of the NUM'. The grievance was given a collective form through a legal challenge taken on by a sympathetic local lawyer of 'mining stock', rather than the union directly, but several of the men were in fact Gartshore 9/11 colliery branch office bearers.[30]

These hostile responses were perplexing to Coal Board manpower branch officials in Glasgow, close geographically but distant socially and culturally from Lanarkshire's mining villages. One commented bitterly that both the Board and the NUM felt Gartshore 9/11 had been 'the best organised closure ever carried out in their experience'.[31] The sense of collective suspicion put forward by the Gartshore 9/11 men was voiced institutionally by Kilsyth Town Council, which comprised a historic mining settlement. Writing to the NCB's Chairman, Alf Robens, following the closure, the council supported the grievances of the sixty transferees related to grading and earnings, but also argued that they 'were not gainfully employed' upon transfer to Bedlay, alleging that the NCB was 'deliberately redeploying large numbers of men into Bedlay to force a closure on economic grounds within three years'.[32]

Keeping Cardowan open became a focus of trade union mobilisation when the pit was threatened twice with closure – first during the late 1960s and again in the early 1970s. Nicky Wilson began his electrician apprenticeship at Cardowan in 1967. Unlike most Cardowan miners, Nicky did not come from a mining family background but lived in the Glasgow peripheral housing scheme of Easterhouse, not far from the colliery. He was attracted by the prospect of a career in a dynamic sector. Just two years into his apprenticeship, Cardowan was put in jeopardy status by the Coal Board, marking the beginning of procedures which could have led to the pit's closure: 'Actually in 1968, '69, Cardowan was put under threat o closure. I was only two years into ma apprenticeship. And the guys were saying, "Oh, you'll need to try and get another job."'[33]

Cardowan came under threat during the first half of 1969 in the face of growing coking coal competition between British coalfields. The link between Cardowan and the local steel industry had been weakened by the reorganisation of the new British Steel public enterprise. Coking coal could be imported more cheaply from Yorkshire or Durham, but this would come at the cost of more than 1,500 Lanarkshire jobs, with only 100 men expected to be temporarily retained for salvage and just 100 able to transfer to other pits.[34]

The prospects of closure raised considerable disquiet. The Coal Board was described by the UK government's Scottish Office as 'anxious to proceed with the closure at the earliest possible date bearing in mind their own concern with minimising the serious consequences in terms of redundancy which seem inevitable as a result'.[35] These concerns were magnified by the local context, whereby 'the situation in these areas is likely to be further aggravated by the continuing rundown of manufacturing employment in the heavy engineering sector'.[36] Other industrial closures nearby included steel works which had previously provided markets for Cardowan and other coking coal pits. By late summer, the NCB Scottish North Area conceded that, whatever economic case there was for closing the pit, it may be retained for 'political reasons'.[37] In December, David Murray, an industrial correspondent, reported in the *Glasgow Herald* that the closure of Cardowan had been abandoned after improvements in productivity at the colliery strengthened the economic case for retention. He also underlined a larger Scottish industrial interest at work: steel industry representatives were 'doubtless relieved at the reprieve' of one of just a handful of remaining Scottish coking coal collieries.[38]

McGahey took a personal interest in the welfare of his old pit and was joined in doing so by Lawrence Daly, the Fife miner and fellow left-winger who had been elected general secretary of the NUM in 1968. The future of Cardowan remained in contention despite the pit's stay of execution. Notably, Daly sought to move meetings discussing the colliery to Scotland rather than hold them in London, indicating the importance he placed on Cardowan at a national level in Scotland, but also the need to ensure the fullest understanding of the closure in localised community terms.[39] Coal Board officials subsequently unhappily took Cardowan out of jeopardy status, citing 'grounds other than financial' as having dictated their decision.[40] During 1972, question marks still hung over the long-term future of Cardowan and Bedlay. McGahey vocalised his opposition to what he saw as a determined effort by Scottish Coal Board officials 'to prove that Cardowan was finished in 1969', only for investment in the pit to have improved performance.[41]

Cardowan's colliery manager, John Frame, came to play a more sympathetic role in the eyes of the workforce and the union. Frame epitomised the commitment towards his colliery and positive relations with workers which the miners expected from managers in the nationalised era. He was another prominent exponent of localism in championing Cardowan within the Board's larger bureaucratic structures. Frame therefore occupied an intermediate position, standing on the one hand as a figure of authority over the workforce but on the other as a defender of his colliery and its miners against the more aloof Coal Board hierarchy.[42] The commitment Frame demonstrated both to his pit and to dialogue with trade unions brought him into conflict with the restructured industrial and political priorities which came to dominate the Coal Board in the early 1980s. Neither he nor the NUM nor the Cardowan miners could save their pit a decade after their 1970s successes.

A new order

British coal lost its status as a privileged fuel source subject to an extent to national protection during the 1980s and 1990s. There was a clash of economic understanding between the miners and the ethos of integrated public enterprises in mining, rail, electricity and steel on the one hand, and the privatising agenda embraced by the Thatcher government on the other. Coal had been central to the industrial strategy embraced by the Labour government elected in 1974, confirmed, as discussed in chapter 1, by the Plan for Coal, which sought to expand production and strongly link the future of coal and electricity. After 1979, however, coal was viewed by government ministers as simply another energy source among many alternatives.

These conflicting perspectives, with their attendant moral underpinnings, were apparent in an exchange between Lawrence Daly and David Howell, the Secretary of State for Energy, at a meeting in February 1981. The backdrop was a declining coal market in the face of recession, mounting unemployment and intensifying deindustrialisation, including severe cutbacks in the steel industry, along with weak demand for electricity. Daly stated that the NCB ought to produce concessionary house coal for pensioners, which he saw as 'a humanitarian gesture'. Howell objected, noting the derisory status of 'benefits in kind'. He argued from an individualistic perspective that 'allowing pensioners to arrange their affairs themselves was also the more dignified way to proceed'.[43] Coal was central to the organisation of communities in the Fife coalfields of Eastern Scotland where Daly grew up and was an essential household and industrial fuel.[44] Howell's perspective was not invested in the materiality of coal or in the social order constructed around mining; he visualised coal in terms of balance sheets and saw mining as a rightfully declining industry.

The future of Cardowan colliery was entangled in these clashing perspectives and enmeshed with the industrial politics of steel. Between the mid-1970s and the mid-1980s, the number of workers employed by the nationalised British Steel Corporation fell from 228,000 to just 54,000. Output halved and demand for coking coal slumped. A large national strike in 1980 had ended inconclusively. Although steel-workers won a significant wage rise, they did so at the cost of job losses and were unable to change the direction of their industry, which pointed only towards further retrenchment, ahead of eventual privatisation in 1988.[45] Industrial rationalisation was no longer associated with community cohesion and rising living standards as it had been in the coalfields during the 1960s. The new manufacturing sectors and power generation which had partially replaced heavy industry were themselves shedding jobs and closing in the 1980s. Steel settlements were poster children of the misery of joblessness and a lost sense of purpose in towns which lost their main employers. In the early 1980s, Consett in County Durham, along with Corby in the East Midlands, both became shorthand for economic redundancy and social misery.[46]

Corby was tied to Lanarkshire's longer history of industrial crisis. Its steel works was greatly expanded by Clydeside firm Stewarts & Lloyds in the 1930s. Lanarkshire workers and their families moved to the Midlands to escape depression and take up the opportunity of prosperity. Half a century later, following the Corby closure in 1981, Fife punk band Big Country commemorated the story in the title track of their album *Steeltown*. It was released in October 1984, when Fife, Lanarkshire and the Midlands were in the midst of the miners' strike.[47]

Steel industry managers, desperately seeking to make their plants competitive against rivals elsewhere in Britain, were permitted to seek advantages by importing cheaper foreign coal. This further encouraged ire, dislocation and a sense of betrayal among miners. Steel works in the North East of England, South Wales and Clydeside had originally prospered due to the advantages provided by the vicinity of coking coal. By abandoning British coal for imports, plant managers in effect jettisoned the economic rationale behind their establishment in the first place. British coking coal imports crept up, with Poland and Australia among the suppliers. The 1980 Coal Industry Act further incentivised imports by compelling the NCB to pursue closures and introducing pricing structures dictated by the prospective end of subsidies for domestic coal production by 1984.[48] To Nicky Wilson and his colleagues, these moves were nothing short of a scandalous misuse of national resources. Over thirty years after Cardowan closed, he lamented the sterilisation of his colliery's 'high grade coking coal'. Nicky further ruefully complained that after Cardowan had lost its steel markets, the NCB would take Cardowan-mined coal and 'mix it wi a lotta rubbish' to make it suitable for burning in power stations which were configured for lower-quality coals.[49]

Prior to this, Cardowan miners had reacted to mounting threats to their livelihoods by joining a large unofficial strike in February 1981. The walkout came after the Board announced twenty-three colliery closures. Miners in Kent and South Wales, as well as Scotland, were among the men on strike, with comrades in Yorkshire making plans to join them.[50] A Coal Board memorandum from early 1981 confirmed that Albert Wheeler, who had been appointed as the NCB's Scottish Director the year before, had been given 'his instructions to close Cardowan' during the next financial year.[51] The government withdrew its closure notice, perturbed by the lack of preparation for a dispute as well as by the support the NUM was attracting from its Triple Alliance allies in the Iron and Steel Trades Confederation and the National Union of Railwaymen.[52] Signifying the gravity of the situation, a broadcast of *Coronation Street* was interrupted with a message urging miners to return to work on union instruction to attempt to prevent further disruption.[53]

NUM leaders knew that the government's u-turn was a tactical rather than a strategic retreat. Michael McGahey was born in 1925, the year before the General Strike and miners' lockout of 1926, in which his father, also a Communist Party cadre and miner, was a highly determined participant. McGahey's reaction to the events of February 1981 was shaped by the memories his father and his comrades passed on to him. On 'Red Friday' in July 1925, the government had granted subsidies to the coal industry which protected miners' wages and conditions, but only for one year. It paved the way for the decisive battle and defeat suffered by the miners the next year. McGahey pointed to this example over half a century later in 1981, quite aware that the Board would provoke renewed conflict with the miners over pit closures. Just as the removal of subsidies in the 1920s had made conflict inevitable, so the restructuring of coal industry financial obligations in the 1980s did the same.[54]

These policies were never purely financial or economic in motivation. They were also keenly attached to ambitions around redistributing power and workplace relations in the nationalised coal industry, with significant implications for British society at large. The reconstruction of Britain's economy under the Conservative Thatcher and Major governments was grounded on ending centuries of reliance on British deep-mined coal, which had been pivotal in bolstering the power exercised by organised labour. Achieving these totemic changes began with reversing the agenda of the 1974 Plan for Coal and dispensing with policies oriented towards a future of coal-fired electricity and investment in modernised mining capacity, epitomised by the Selby complex in North Yorkshire.[55] As discussed above, incentivising steel industry coal imports created the trigger for the closure of Cardowan. Undermining the coal industry was integral to a larger agenda centred on replacing an energy sector centred on well-organised British workforces in public employment with increasing reliance on international energy markets. Government was motivated by its opposition to sustaining the true costs of British coal production – a relatively safe, jointly regulated environment characterised by unionised employment.

The NUMSA attempted to build resistance in the context of mounting fears over mass unemployment and concern for the future of the industrial economy. At the Area's 1983 annual conference, held in Ayr Town Hall, speakers articulated the cause of the Scottish miners as central to the economic and political survival of the working class. Alec Hogg, the NUM Cardowan colliery delegate, declared that there were three and a half centuries' worth of coal reserves in Britain, but these were being wilfully wasted.[56] An emergency resolution from the NUM's Scottish executive committee responded to the Cardowan closure. It made the case for 'united activity to defend our people against further deindustrialisation, closures and redundancies'.[57] Use of the term deindustrialisation communicated a strong sense of the looming threat of workplace closures and growing worklessness amid job losses across mining and manufacturing sectors. The resolution specified steel and shipbuilding as among important allied industries also under attack by Thatcher's government. McGahey's presidential address underlined the imperatives of building a large anti-closure campaign. Implicitly referencing the fate of the miners who were ultimately starved back to work having been industrially and politically isolated in 1926, he insisted that 'no industry should stand alone'. Instead, McGahey argued that 'the defence of jobs in the mining industry is directly linked with other industries in Scotland', particularly through mutual reliance with steel and the railways.[58]

Building opposition, though, had to begin by convincing the miners themselves. McGahey referenced with disappointment the recent 'No' vote result of an NUM national ballot on industrial action against pit closures. It followed the beginning of a strike in the South Wales coalfields after the announcement of the closure of Lewis Merthyr colliery in February 1983. The ballot result came months after Arthur Scargill, the NUM's new president who had been elected as the left-wing candidate in a 1982 internal union election, alleged that the NCB had plans to close a 'hit list' of seventy-five pits which would lead to 60,000 job losses, around one-third of the total mining workforce, which numbered approximately 200,000 at the time. In the autumn of 1983, Scargill's claims were dismissed as 'pure invention' by Ian MacGregor, the NCB's new combative anti-union Chairman who was head-hunted by Thatcher after leading British Steel during the national steel strike of 1980.[59] Archival records do reveal, however, that in February 1983 the NCB was planning to phase out 60,000 jobs in collieries viewed as uneconomic prospects. These were concentrated in the so-called 'peripheral coalfields' of Scotland, South Wales, Kent and the North East of England. Coal Board plans would accelerate existing downward trends in coal mining employment and further weaken already fragile regional economies.[60]

Demonstrating the political significance of these decisions, and evidencing government interference in Coal Board operations, Department of Energy officials advised the Board that it should move towards a strategy for 'rapid' closure after the 1983 general election.[61] The election produced a large parliamentary majority for Thatcher's emboldened Tory Party, which was now more able to pursue confrontation with the NUM. In February 1983, Coal Board member Harry Spanton had informed the government that in around a year's time industry management would be organised for a major dispute, foretelling with eerie accuracy the beginning of the national strike for jobs in March 1984: 'The Board would expect by Spring 1984 to have done everything possible by way of preparation, and education of the public and industry.'[62]

On 7 June 1983, two days before the general election, Coal Board officials met to plan 'strike strategy'. James Cowan, the Board's deputy director, who was himself a Scottish mining engineer, advocated a careful methodical approach to closure, worrying that 'the Board would run out of people willing to be made redundant on the present terms. The chances of precipitating a national strike would be greatly increased when the Board found it necessary to make compulsory redundancies.' Spanton supported Cowan in underlining the need to follow a 'step by step' approach, isolating individual collieries to avert a national confrontation. Robert Priddle of the Department of Energy urged a more confrontational approach, embracing the possibility of a strike as a potentially positive outcome: 'if the strategy were adopted and if the Board and government were successful in the outcome of a national strike, it might well be possible to do more' by closing more pits than the 25-million-tonne capacity cut the NCB envisioned. Cowan anticipated the events of the next year by requesting political support and financial resources in such an eventuality. The Board would need 'a guarantee of imports and, of course, of cash support, as well as determination to see the strike through'.[63]

The NCB's Scottish Area had been in the vanguard of coalfield restructuring and aggressive anti–trade union management in advance of the Cardowan closure. Kinneil colliery in West Lothian was closed in 1982. Like Cardowan, Kinneil was a coking coal producer which had undergone extensive modernisation investment under nationalisation.[64] Kinneil miners mounted a stay-down strike to protest the closure in December 1982. Twelve stay-down strikers surfaced on Christmas Day, hoping that their efforts would help to build support across Scottish collieries. They were left disappointed. Learning from the closure list setback of the previous year, in 1982 managers were able to isolate Kinneil from the national workforce. Three days later, McGahey was audibly discouraged when he addressed an emergency conference of delegates from Scottish pits. He lauded the 'heroic' stay-down strikers but condemned the 'lack of response from the Scottish coalfield'. David Hamilton, who was the NUM colliery delegate at Monktonhall in Midlothian, bleakly stated his surprise at how his colleagues had responded to pickets despatched from Kinneil to build support for a Scottish coalfield strike: 'Never at any time had he envisaged a situation developing where a large number of men at Monktonhall would pass a picket line.'[65]

Monktonhall was to emerge at the centre of the new regime of robust management instituted under Albert Wheeler. These techniques anticipated a remaking of workplace relations which only took place in the English and Welsh coalfields once the strike had commenced. Conflict was driven by the excessive application of discipline, with workers being sent home without pay for arriving to shifts a few minutes late. Union presence in collieries was curtailed too. Managers were rotated by Wheeler, discouraging the form of trusting relationships built by Frame and the Cardowan workforce. A seven-week strike at Monktonhall took place over the autumn of 1983 shortly after William Kennedy took over as colliery manager. Kennedy got rid of the previously successful system of regular consultative committee meetings between managers and workplace representatives. Instead, he threatened sixty-seven face workers with the sack if their performance did not improve. The strike began after a union meeting to discuss the offer of redundancy for up to 300 miners led to several men being slightly late for work and consequently being refused entry to the shaft. One-day token stoppages were organised across the Scottish coalfield, but the pit delegate at Frances colliery in Fife was sacked for organising a collection for the Monktonhall men. Management stoking division among miners and the isolation and delegitimisation of the NUM were dominant themes in the closure of Cardowan.[66]

Closing Cardowan

Over the spring and summer of 1983, the Coal Board, led by Wheeler, vigorously pursued the closure of Cardowan, dispensing with the structures and culture which had achieved a more consensual attitude towards previous pit closures in prior decades. Wheeler rejected the system of joint administration of closure procedures and negotiating with trade unions. Instead, he told a colliery consultative committee meeting held at the nearby Stepps Parochial Hall that he 'wanted the opinion of the 1,090 men employed at the colliery and not just the few who attended branch meetings'.[67] In place of a negotiated approach, Wheeler instead proposed an 'offer' which financially incentivised miners to break with collective solidarity and the instructions of their trade union. Redundancy payments in excess of £20,000 (over £66,000 in 2025 values) were offered to men over fifty who had more than thirty years of service with the Board along with pensions of £100 per week (over £330 in 2025 values). Furthermore, transfers were available for younger men, with payments available for travel and earnings and positions protected for tradesmen.

Wheeler voiced his 'surprise that, to date, elderly men at Cardowan had not expressed a desire for redundancy', underlining his view that the union branch officials did not represent the wishes of the miners they were elected by. His long introductory speech to the meeting also carried two threats. The first was making clear that he was not intimidated by talk of a strike at a loss-making colliery. A strike would, Wheeler claimed, in fact save the Coal Board money. Second, referring to the gaseous environment and the accident of the previous year, Wheeler sought 'to make it clear that it would be totally irresponsible for men to have a "sit-in" underground in the conditions existing at this colliery'.[68]

These pronouncements were a microcosm of the transformations to the exercise of power and authority in British workplaces during the 1980s. The culture of Labourism was being undermined, and the legitimacy of trade unions was denied, pending the de-organisation of workers. Collectivist structures and dialogue between workforce representatives and managers were swept aside in favour of increasingly individualised relationships between employers and employees. Trade unions were reclassified, from representatives of workers' interests to illegitimate actors exercising power on behalf of politicised activist minorities who were out of touch with the wishes of their membership. Both public and private employers clamped down on union activity, which was subject to increased managerial antagonism along with an incremental programme of legal restrictions on the right to strike and trade union organisation.[69] These were the mechanisms by which the closure of industrial sectors accelerated and through which their remaining workforces were disciplined for privatisation. The path was being cleared to a future of workplace relations without trade unions, characterised by growing individualism in the workforce.

Wheeler's visit in May 1983 was met by worker and community resistance. Nicky Wilson recalled that 'you had men in fae various groups ae workforce, and aw the families from Cardowan and roond aboot came. And he couldnae get oot.' Wheeler had to be protected by the police and union officials as a physical altercation began. Nicky recalled these events in light-hearted terms. An ice cream cone was smashed onto Wheeler, blemishing his suit and his pride rather than posing a physical threat.[70] Conversely, Tommy Canavan, an NUM representative who, like Nicky, had attended the consultative committee meeting, remembered a more violent confrontation unfolding that day. Tommy explained when I interviewed him in 2014 that the opposition Wheeler provoked was a response to his domineering and imperious attitude towards the miners and the community. Wheeler had conducted himself in a bullying and dismissive manner while threatening the future economic stability of the area and disparaging its trade union customs: 'Wheeler came to Cardowan. Previous to that, Kinneil went on strike [against closure]. They had a sit-in doon the pit. Cardowan was a gas tank. It wis full aw methane gas. He was aw, "This is a gas tank. We will no be responsible if anything happens in this pit or anything."

'And he went on and on. And it finished up, which wasnae a nice thing tae see. One of the guys went up and knocked him up. He just went up and banjoed him. I'm no sayin that was right, but he brought it upon himself cause he was nothin but a bully. He was sayin, "Yous are wearin ma uniforms," a boiler suit! As if we were some – he was the commander of some big army or something. It's ma, his uniform! It was his pit! It wisnae oor pit. It was his!'[71]

There was an irony to Wheeler's alertness to the dangers at Cardowan compared with other Scottish pits. Cardowan had been made relatively safe by 1983 through the reorganisation of the industry under nationalisation and the practices which led to the election of Willie Doolan as the workmen's safety inspector. Wheeler now defined himself in opposition to the industry culture which sustained these practices, but he was nonetheless attempting to use the remaining dangers to stymie resistance to closure. In the commotion that followed his pronouncement, Wheeler accidentally struck Alice, the primary-school-age daughter of a local miner who was at the scene. Wheeler subsequently wrote an apologetic letter to Alice's father, expressing his profound regret over the incident.[72]

Yet the conflict between Wheeler and the Cardowan workforce extended to the colliery manager too. John Frame was isolated and unwelcome in the new environment Wheeler had fostered within the Scottish coal industry, with its antipathy to local allegiances and working alongside trade unions. Frame remained firmly committed to his own pit. In the past, he had been permitted to join trade unionists in making the case for retaining his colliery, but this was now viewed as insubordination. Less than a fortnight after the consultative committee meeting, it was reported by Abe Moffat, the president of the Scottish Colliery Enginemen, Boilermen and Tradesmen's Association (SCEBTA), that Frame 'was leaving the industry because he disagreed with the closure and knew that the miners had a good case'. Like many miners would be in the years that followed, Frame had been 'virtually forced to accept "early retirement"' in his mid-fifties.[73]

The committed view that Cardowan had a viable industrial future was central to the trade union case for the pit's retention in the 1980s, just as it had been when the NUM had fought for its survival in the previous two decades. Levels of suspicion towards the Board and its motivations were far higher, however – to the point of active distrust. Opposition grew as the Coal Board began winding down production before the pit closure had even been legitimated through the colliery review apparatus. In June 1983, Albert Wheeler ordered the closure of a face after a section of roofing collapsed, pointing to the danger it posed to continued work. A three-day protest strike then followed, but some of the workforce, around 250 men, had returned to work before it ended.[74] Michael McGahey was once again left concerned about his union's ability to mobilise the Cardowan miners and the Scottish coalfields against closures. A minority of Cardowan men committed other transgressions against union instructions by accepting transfers before they had been legitimated. By the time the appeal against the closure was heard by the NCB in September, around 300 workers had already transferred to collieries in West Lothian, Stirlingshire, Clackmannanshire and Fife. As well as creating facts on the ground in terms of diluting resistance at Cardowan by dispersing its workforce, this policy also provoked industrial disputes at receiving collieries where transferees were seen to be undermining union practices and localist workplace norms. Transfers contributed to economic insecurity, especially at Polmaise in Stirlingshire, which was then undergoing colliery development. Local miners had been promised first refusal on new jobs at the pit while they temporarily worked elsewhere before it reopened.[75]

NUM representatives saw these steps as amounting to an irresponsible and reckless use of public funds to undermine their industry and ensure the disposal of a productive asset. For veterans of the 1984–85 strike, the experience at Cardowan also offered an important anticipation of the large bonus payments that the Coal Board offered miners in attempts to entice them back to work during the year-long dispute.[76] Willie Doolan remembered events at Cardowan as a prelude to the landmark national dispute which followed soon after: 'The Coal Board were offering, and I'm going back to 1983. They were offering fifteen-hundred pounds to an individual to transfer tae another pit. And it wis the same kindae tactic the Coal Board used during the miners' strike, '84–85. They were offering vast amounts of money to people who'd been out on strike for the best part of a year. All taxpayers' money by the way!'[77]

Nicky Wilson remembered Wheeler as a figure who epitomised the values of the Thatcher government in his pursuit of self-advancement at a high collective cost. Speaking in 2014, thirty-one years after Cardowan closed in 1983, Nicky explained that Wheeler: 'Probably suited the government at that time.

He'd no social conscience or that. He didnae care what happened tae mining communities despite coming fae that originally. Just a ruthless, ruthless, person who had ambition.'[78]

These sentiments had also radiated contemporaneously. At the appeal meeting over Cardowan's closure in September 1983, J. Varley, a Colliery Officials and Staff Association official, starkly commented that it was 'ludicrous that such large reserves should be sterilised for purely political reasons'.[79] Both McGahey and NUM President Arthur Scargill were present, with the former insisting that his old workplace was 'not a clapped out pit'. Cardowan had around a decade's worth of immediate reserves, and decades' more work could be secured by investment. In McGahey's view, the pursuit of conflict and division within the workforce through the offer of transfers and provoking the three-day stoppage were unprecedented in his working life in the nationalised coal industry: 'Never in his forty years in the industry had he experienced such irresponsible conduct by the Board.'[80] McGahey and several other union officials emphasised the harassment miners were subjected to by the NCB when it came to accepting redundancy terms, underlining that these were breaches of what were meant to be collectively negotiated procedures. Alec Hogg, the NUM colliery delegate, had told journalists earlier in the summer that management had passed notifications of transfer inside miners' lamps during the early hours of the morning, after union officials had left the pit.[81] Scargill bluntly summarised that 'the death sentence was being carried out before the Court of Appeal sat'.[82]

Closure was inevitable after a strike ballot only gained support for action from a minority of NUM and SCEBTA members in August 1983. Almost 40 per cent of ballots cast were in favour of a strike, but a majority of Cardowan miners voted to accept closure.[83] Over thirty years later, Willie Doolan still remembered the experience in bitter and demoralised terms: 'It was difficult. We were battlin against the elements and some people decided that they wanted this money. And when other people saw some people leaving trickles and trickles and trickles and eventually, we had tae say, "We accept, we accept." We had tae reluctantly accept.'[84]

The closure of Cardowan was part of the build-up to the national strike that engulfed the coalfields in 1984, and an important exemplar of the tactics deployed by the Board and the government in that dispute. Over 1984–85, the possibilities of a British economy without British deep-mined coal were demonstrated through the expansion of imports. Nuclear and oil power-generating capacity helped to keep the lights on, avoiding the power cuts which had been so pivotal to the miners' victories in the strikes of 1972 and 1974, but so did coal imports.[85] Steel works also continued to be supplied with imports. In each case, workforces who had in the past demonstrated solidarity with miners refused to do so, in the context of mass unemployment, political pressure, anti–trade union legislation and mounting worries over the industrial future. Ravenscraig steel-workers broke their agreements with the miners, the rail unions and the Scottish TUC to maximise production.[86] The plant nevertheless closed eight years later, just four years after British Steel was privatised.

In 1984, miners organised their strike based on the localism which was so strongly visible in the lifetime of Cardowan colliery and the opposition to attempts to close it in earlier decades. The slogan 'Close a Pit, Kill a Community' was second only to 'Coal Not Dole' in shaping the NUM's case to save jobs and retain the legitimated role of trade unions in the industry. These dynamics were fundamentally visible in the daily life of organising coal production efficiently and safely as well as in negotiating responses to more extraordinary moments of change and crisis such as accidents and threats of closures. The year-long strike was a pivotal industrial conflict which engulfed 180,000 miners and their families across the coalfields of Scotland, England and Wales. More than 140,000 miners were on strike at the peak of mobilisation.[87] Striking miners garnered support from across the UK, primarily in the form of large donations, sometimes organised on a trans-local basis through systems of 'twinning'. These connected localities and union branches in towns, and especially large cities such as London, to collieries and mining villages. Relationships which had grown up around Grunwick, as explored in the previous chapter, were reciprocated when black and Asian activists organised to support the strike. Public servants in sectors such as local government and the National Health Service played an important role in these mobilisations, alongside more traditional groups of unionised workers such as printers.[88] These shifts reflected the changing composition of Britain's labour movement as deindustrialisation progressed and the public services membership grew, but also the disappointment which miners often experienced when it came to obtaining backing from other industrial workers or from the Labour Party hierarchy under Neil Kinnock.

Cardowan exemplified the exercise of political and industrial coercion, of class warfare as practised from above, that brought an end to the world which produced Labourism and British workers' power. Both physical and economic force, along with the delegitimisation of trade unions, were crucial to this episode in the unmaking of the British working class, and so was the exercise of state power on the picket lines and communities at the centre of the 1984–85 strike. Willie Doolan was among thousands of British miners arrested while organising to defend their jobs in the course of the strike.[89] Division was also fostered through the offering of economic incentives which were used to create consent for a new economic order. Gone was the collective negotiation of industrial change and workplace discipline. It was replaced by the imposition of managerial dictate, bought at the price of redundancy payments, pensions and transfers to new jobs. Those who accepted them hoped that they would at least sustain a modicum of security for themselves and their families. Often, these hopes proved fruitless. Colliery closures accelerated after the strike, leading to many more 'Cardowans'. Deep coal mining came to an end in Scotland in 2002, and across Britain in 2015, but this belies the brutal swiftness of the decade of closures that followed the strike. There were just

7,000 miners remaining in 1994, when the industry was privatised.[90] Britain's new workplace order bore the imprints of the violent ending of the old one. Industrial affairs were no longer the stuff of high politics in the 1990s as they had been for around a century beforehand.

The erosion of trade union strength and links between collieries and communities were a crucial phase in the unmaking of the British working class. Moral as well as material losses were incurred at Cardowan and other collieries across Britain which closed in the 1980s and 1990s. It was not just the jobs of miners or even the NUM itself which were under attack. The very standing of organised labour and the role of trade unions as the collective representatives of workers were eroding. To accomplish this, huge state resources had to be mobilised during the 1984–85 strike, and the structures which had underpinned energy production and the national-industrial economy which it supported since the 1940s were rapidly and wilfully dismantled. Achieving this entailed erasing the strong connections between coal mining and villages like Cardowan, dissociating housing schemes and settlements from their reason for existing. Nigel Lawson, who had recently been promoted from his role as Secretary of State for Energy to become Chancellor of the Exchequer in 1983, later estimated that the expenditure on fuel imports, policing and other costs represented £2.75 billion in additional state borrowing.[91] This was approximately the cost of the Falklands War, which the Thatcher government had fought against Argentina just two years earlier. On 31 July 1984, Lawson defended the vast spending on the strike in the House of Commons, arguing that it was an insurance against future losses but also justified due to the alternative being compromise with the NUM: 'Even in narrow financial terms, it represents a worthwhile investment for the nation. That is before taking into account the wider issues at stake in the dispute.'[92]

For Lawson and his most committed cabinet colleagues, the strike was an essential struggle for liberty and breaking with the tyrannies of collectivism. As the tenth anniversary of the strike was marked, the former chancellor went so far as to compare the Thatcher government's preparations for the strike with rearming before the war against Nazism.[93] The very idea of a British working class with valid forms of distinctive organisation or interests or traditions was severely dented, if not erased, as a political and cultural orientation and increasingly denied as a sociological reality. A contrasting literary vantage of the true price of coal, and of the miners' defeat, was offered by William McIlvanney's 1985 novel, *The Big Man*.[94] The story unfolds in a mining village in McIlvanney's native Ayrshire, to the south west of Lanarkshire, revolving around the fate of Dan Scoular, an unemployed former miner who was victimised while picketing in the 1984–85 dispute. In the 1990 Hollywood film adaptation, Scoular, who is played by Liam Neeson, is depicted as having been arrested at a steel works, which resembles the draconian policing of picket lines at Ravenscraig.[95] *The Big Man* storyline sees Scoular having to fight for his own survival and his family as his wife Beth courts more economically successful men. He winds up as a participant in a brutal prize fight organised by Glasgow gangsters but, despite emerging victorious, he is repulsed by the aftermath and the fate of his blinded opponent.

McIlvanney's portrayal evokes desperation and dislocated masculinity in the dissolution of a world centred on physical prowess exhibited through work underground along with the relatively high wages it sustained. It mourns the end of a communally mediated order centred on face-to-face interactions and deliberation. Instead, the market had won, triumphing over the rules which previously policed social life. These were both highly patriarchal and far from universally pleasant in McIlvanney's telling. Scoular is portrayed as having had a difficult relationship with his father, which included an induction into a life of fighting. Yet this was a way of living based on morality and standing by a code that centred on restraint and not picking on weaker people. It stood in stark contrast with the immorality of the big-money prize fight Scoular is lured into as an unemployed and criminalised former striking miner.

Robert Gildea's extensive oral history of the miners' strike illuminated the views of some of the 206 Scottish miners who were sacked for their activities during the strike but also women who were involved in the dispute as family members, trade unionists and feminists. He recorded stories of increasing levels of divorce in deindustrialising coal mining communities after the dispute but underlined that these were often remembered positively as affirmations of women taking control of their own lives.[96] Similarly, Florence Sutcliffe-Braithwaite and Natalie Thomlinson underline that some of the Scottish miners' wives they interviewed in 2018 also remembered divorce as a positive outcome induced partly by their involvement in activism but perhaps also formed by the longer trajectory of increased employment opportunities and expectations within dual-income families.[97] Yet rising male unemployment and the precarity and lower wages often on offer to working-class men and women in regions afflicted by mine and factory closures also conditioned the shifting economic and cultural landscape which materially disadvantaged women.

Margaret and Jerry Wegg shared another experience, that of a married couple who weathered the storm of closures, the strike and its long aftermath together. It was Margaret who lost her colliery canteen job in 1983 when Cardowan shut, but she became a leading local activist in 1984–85, motivated by saving her husband's job given the threat to the future of deep coal mining across Scotland. Following the closure of Cardowan colliery and the strikers' defeat, the local miners' social club was demolished to make way for a car park, and the former pit site was repurposed to build new privately owned houses. These losses were symptomatic of an evolving landscape marked by starker inequities and the retreat of collective organisation and socialised provision of either employment or housing. In a 2023 reminiscence I recorded with three daughters of Cardowan miners, these changes were remembered together. The de-organisation of working-class power and collective presence in the workplace unfolded hand in hand with the end of

Saturday evenings spent at a busy social club and annual excursions organised for miners' children every summer, as well as the demise of the deliveries of concessionary coal which miners' households had enjoyed. Alice described having been 'left behind', now inhabiting, along with her family and their neighbour, 'a forgotten land'.[98] Notably, Alice's emphasis stood in contrast to predominant depictions of the left-behind working class, which were often dominated by politics of nationalist or racial resentment. She instead emphasised the experience of lacking the means to engage in the suburban commuter lifestyle brought by increasing home and car ownership. Alice and many others faced the cataclysmic end of lives founded on the pit, the whisky bond, the union, public housing and the club.

4

Right to Buy: 'We Are Proud of Our Homes'

Less than a week after Margaret Thatcher resigned as prime minister on 22 November 1990, an unlikely High Court judgement seemingly put one of the political triumphs of her premiership into question. Making an unexpected legal ruling on a historical and sociological debate, Mr Justice Harman declared that the working class continued to exist. The context for the ruling was a dispute between the Duke of Westminster and Westminster City Council concerning the attempted sale of seven blocks of flats in Central London, which the local authority had been gifted decades earlier by the duke's family for housing the area's working class. Lady Porter, the Conservative leader of Westminster Council, spoke in terms that resonated with the ethos of the recently departed prime minister: the local authority was 'extremely disappointed' that the duke was using his aristocratic privileges to block 'opportunities for homeownership on this estate'. Justice Harman dismissed the case made by the municipal lawyers, who argued that, as parliamentary housing legislation had removed reference to the working class, this should also apply to the dwellings held by the council on a 999-year lease. Harman disagreed, underlining that 'the phrase "working class" was still relevant in contemporary society'.[1]

The relevance of the working class, and its right to state-provided housing, won out in this battle over what the judge himself described as a 'dry, bare legal issue'.[2] Yet it had been severely dented by the selling-off of millions of council homes under Right to Buy over the prior decade. Council housing was valued at around half of the public realm, amounting to 46 per cent of fixed state assets at its peak in the late 1970s. Municipal homes also accounted for around 40 per cent of the entire British housing stock by value and around a third of households by tenure.[3]

Those statistics underline the extent of Labourist achievements in public housing, which were a powerful factor in shaping British working-class politics. Understanding access to good-quality housing as a right, and one that should be met by the local state, had important implications for political affiliations as well as government policymaking. The Labour Party claimed to speak for and represent the interests of public tenants. These advances secured important changes from the cramped inner-city slums or the poorly maintained miners' rows from which the labour movement had powerfully emerged in the late nineteenth and early twentieth centuries. The marked decline in public housing tenure levels and the diminishing prospect of them recovering fundamentally challenged these outlooks, contributing towards the marginalisation of the sensibilities which had conditioned class consciousness in Britain. Labour became a party run by and for homeowners, and this trend continued into the 2020s. Less than a year before he became prime minister, in his 2023 Labour Party conference leader's speech, Keir Starmer promised that a Labour government would deliver the 'security of homeownership'. Starmer's argument rested on his own family's experience of owning a 'pebbled-dashed semi' outside of London which paved the way for his university education followed by a highly successful legal and political career.[4] Private ownership here figures as a realisation of more individualised and familial aspirations, of social mobility over shared social improvement.

Right to Buy was the most significant privatisation of all during the 1980s. The sale of the publicly owned gas, electricity and telecommunications industries was, like Right to Buy, closely associated with 'popular capitalism' and relied upon popular participation as immortalised by the 1986 'Tell Sid' television adverts for British Gas share subscriptions. It was the transformations wrought by turning council house tenants into owner-occupiers which were the most monumental change in economic relationships, and one which had profound political implications. Between 1980 and 2002, more than 2 million homes were sold under Right to Buy, and another 700,000 were voluntarily transferred, primarily from local authorities to housing associations.[5] Accompanying sharp increases in rates of indebtedness became rationalised based on growing property prices and the rising common sense which equated owning bricks and mortar with wealth and stability. These shifts were concentrated in places closely associated with the labour movement and especially with Labour Party local authorities. Public tenants in cities, industrial conurbations and factory and mining towns where Labour councils had housed large portions of their population were eager homebuyers.

Councils were compelled to sell properties under the scheme, which offered huge discounts on market valuations following the passing of the Housing Act in 1980. These began at 33 per cent for tenants of three years or more, rising on an annual increment to a maximum of 50 per cent for tenants of twenty years. In 1984, further legislation lowered the minimum tenancy to two years and increased the maximum discount to 60 per cent for tenants of thirty years. It also extended rights to some housing association tenants. Right to Buy incentives contributed decisively to British rates of owner-occupation rising from beneath 55 per cent to around 70 per cent in the last quarter of the twentieth century.[6]

Justice Harman's judgement continues to resonate in the UK during the 2020s. The links between class and status and housing tenure run deep in a country where homeownership has become a strongly engrained marker of personal success. Enthusiasm for homeownership reached a mania in the explosion of property programmes which punctuated television listings in the 2000s, epitomised by Channel Four's highly successful *Location, Location, Location*. It even spawned a spinoff series, *Relocation, Relocation*, which typically profiled affluent couples buying a second home.[7] Subsequently, passions have cooled into a more subdued response to persistently falling rates of owner-occupation and the rise of the private rental market.

Growing numbers of working-class people have now lost the chance to own their own home given increasingly insecure jobs, low wages and rising house prices. Poorer people never enjoyed the opportunities in the first place. Housing scholar Chris Allen found that 'the struggle for survival' continues to dominate daily life in inner-city Liverpool. A pragmatic material version of the bricks and mortar view of housing, not an asset-based one, preoccupied households even at the peak of owner-occupation in the early 2000s.[8] Private renting grew in the first two decades of the twenty-first century and the owner-occupation rate shrank as the effect of council house sales since the 1980s reached its full expression. The British private rented sector nearly tripled in size from around 2 million to comfortably more than 5.5 million households between the early 1990s and the early 2020s, or from fewer than one in ten to around a fifth of households by tenure.[9] Yet homeownership levels have been consolidated as a measurement through which the success and failure of not just people and their families but even governments are judged.[10]

Political discussion continues to demonstrate the strong connections between class and housing. Bridget Phillipson, who was appointed Secretary of State for Education upon the formation of Starmer's Labour government in July 2024, elaborated on her upbringing and her understanding of 'working-class aspiration' on *The Rest Is Politics* podcast a few weeks before the 2024 general election. Phillipson emphasised housing, explaining that she 'grew up in a council street in Washington in the North East' of England in a context of mass unemployment and regional economic depression over the 1980s and 1990s. In contrast to Starmer's story of optimism in owner-occupation, Phillipson's story of spending the early years of her childhood living with a single parent in a council house underlined their relative impoverishment. Phillipson's comments reinforced the negatively residual nature of council housing after Right to Buy, which relegated public housing to accommodation only for those who could not afford to own or rent privately. Furthermore, homeownership and residency shaped Phillipson's view of her working-class constituents. Phillipson defined the voters who backed her as 'people who want to put an extension on their house. They want to go on holiday. They want to live in a safe community. They don't want to be blighted by anti-social behaviour.'[11]

Starmer and Phillipson's comments both underline the strongly felt connections between housing and class in Britain and betray a refusal to clearly analyse those links. Dan Evans, a Welsh sociologist and writer, has developed a thoughtful assessment of growing British homeownership since the late twentieth century which led him to conclude that 'nowhere is class more complicated than in housing'.[12] Mass homeownership among manual workers and working-class pensioners is compounded by the 'generation rent' effect and intergenerational wealth transfers through inheritance. Another important factor is the growth of landlordism to encompass around one in every twenty-one adults. As an economic group, landlords outnumbered schoolteachers by four to one in the mid-2020s.[13]

Right to Buy is centrally important to understanding the tenure changes which have reshaped class relationships since the 1980s. It could also be read in deceptively simple terms, but these overlook the longer history of housing and its formative role in working-class politics. Owner-occupation – at least in England and Wales, less so in Scotland where public housing predominated – was already a dominant working-class tenure form before 1980. However, before the 1980s, homeownership evolved under a model of public policy which historian Guy Ortolano has termed 'property-owning social democracy'. Governments, especially the Labour governments of the 1940s, 1960s and 1970s, prioritised 'managing the housing system to place renters alongside owners in a balanced whole'. Both public renting and owner-occupation tenures were championed as an alternative to the slums which had predominated under despised private landlordism. This system had roots in the inter-war period, when both owner-occupation and council housing began to chip away at the dominance of private renting, with the active support of central and local government policy.[14]

Conservative politicians consciously understood Right to Buy as a 'social revolution' shifting not just the politics of housing but social classes as a whole through increasing rates of homeownership. Those hopes were moulded by the longer history of housing and its overlap with class and party politics in the twentieth century, which had oriented Labour towards support for both public housing and increasing homeownership. Initially, the Labour Party sought to maintain this position in the early 1980s, but it failed due to the popularity of Right to Buy with Labour voters. There was widespread tenant enthusiasm for subsidised house purchases, while the council housing stock was eroded by the cumulative impact of sales. Homeownership grew in the context of rising house prices. The value of workers' homes rose much more than their wages in a period marked by rising income inequality and weakening trade unions. Right to Buy and a shift in economic identity from earning wages to owning assets powerfully shaped the unmaking of the British working class. Labourism was undermined through the workplace setbacks suffered by trade unions in the 1980s and 1990s, but its decline was further compounded by the diminishing importance of relationships between tenants and Labour councils.

Social revolution

'Another council tenancy', sang John Lydon in the penultimate verse of the Sex Pistols' 1977 single, 'Anarchy in the UK'.[15] Lyden, who is better known by his alias, Johnny Rotten, grew up in a council flat on the Six Acre estate in Finsbury Park, North London.[16] The Pistols' punk rock lyrics rested on the irony of contrasting something as mundane and everyday as the drab municipal homes of late 1970s Britain with Northern Irish paramilitaries, the Ulster Defence Association and the Irish Republican Army, and a contemporary armed group vying for national liberation in Angola, the Movimento Popular de Libertação de Angola. Yet it was council housing that was set to be at the forefront of a very different set of revolutionary transformations.

In the early 1980s, contemporary commentators recognised the breadth and severity of the changes brought by Right to Buy. James Foreman-Peck, a housing economist, published an early analysis in 1982, when annual council house sales exceeded 200,000 units. He emphasised the scale of the impact of these changes, and their effect on the public estate: Right to Buy was a policy 'to dispose of public assets in a fashion arguably not in the best interests of the taxpayer who originally financed them: or alternatively to redistribute wealth from the state to the council house-buyer'.[17]

As Foreman-Peck highlighted, the political impact of the policy was pointed and cumulative: 'Wealth is being redistributed from the state to the council house buyer in a form which they particularly value and which would be politically difficult to revoke.'[18] The swift effect of these changes is demonstrated by the trend of growing owner-occupation being matched by declining proportions of public housing tenancies, which fell from around a third to a fifth in Britain during the 1980s.[19] Furthermore, the impact of council house sales was magnified by the Treasury enjoying a portion of revenues and restrictions on the capacity of local government to invest in new housing, which was in any case vulnerable to being subject to purchase by tenants.[20] By the early 2020s, it was estimated that the Treasury had reaped £47 billion in proceeds from Right to Buy.[21] One crucial dynamic of the policy was the disempowerment of the local state by central government through a major transfer of resources and powers, even where this appeared to be empowering tenants.

The Conservative politicians who led the calls for Right to Buy were bullish in championing aspiring homeowners against socialist bureaucracy. To them, homeownership meant extending membership of a property-owning democracy to previously excluded working-class constituents. Right to Buy was the realisation of a long-established Tory aim, with roots in the decades between the World Wars. Just a fortnight after the 1979 general election, Michael Heseltine addressed the House of Commons as the new Secretary of State for the Environment. He ardently made the case for 'a positive Right to Buy'. The new government would free families from 'the appetites for power of petty Labour bosses' who lorded it over tenants from town halls and municipal housing offices across Britain. Right to Buy would deliver a 'dramatic and immediate benefit to our people' and lay 'a framework for a social revolution'.[22]

Conservative ministers, beginning with the new prime minister herself, were anxious to be closely associated with Right to Buy. John Broughton wryly commented in his history of council housing that 'it must have seemed that you couldn't open your daily paper in the early 1980s without seeing a picture of Margaret Thatcher handing over the keys to a suitably delighted if somewhat self-conscious family of new homeowners'.[23] Perhaps the strongest and most persistent example of Right to Buy *cause célèbre*, and notoriety, is the Pattersons of Harold Hill in Havering, a suburb of East London which has been repeatedly covered in follow-up press coverage. Their story both illustrates the hope and expectations associated with Right to Buy and serves as a cautionary tale when it comes to understanding the impact of homeownership, house price rises and indebtedness that followed in its wake. Right to Buy brought life-changing but far from universally positive developments to the Pattersons.

Harold Hill is a symbolic location, given that it was the estate Margaret Thatcher visited to celebrate the early success of a flagship policy in 1980, just a year into the first term of her premiership and only a few months after Right to Buy was launched. The Pattersons' house on 39 Amersham Road had been the 12,000th council house sale achieved by the Greater London Council.[24] Even before the 1980 Act, the Conservative-led metropolitan authority was a keen proponent of sales to eager tenant buyers who were especially keen to snap up properties on the fringes of the city.[25] Yet jeering locals greeted Margaret Thatcher as she made her way to Amersham Road. Right to Buy was not yet universally popular, even in Harold Hill, nor was the prime minister, during a period marked by high levels of unemployment and factory closures.[26]

Thatcher received a more positive reception from the Pattersons. The family of five was headed by husband James and his wife Maureen. They had unexpectedly found themselves able to become homeowners thanks to Right to Buy. Celebration later turned to despair, however, with high interest rates forcing up the cost of mortgage payments which contributed to the breakdown of their marriage. After James left, Maureen, who worked in a care home, was forced to sell the house. Homeownership led to homelessness. Maureen eventually ended up living in her son's flat and then in a mobile home, which was all she could afford with the money she had left over from the sale of her house on Amersham Road.[27]

Despite her misfortune, Maureen Patterson remained an unrepentant Thatcherite, even imposing the logic of personal responsibility onto her own misfortune. Nostalgically looking back on having been a Right to Buy homeowner and the social advancement it represented, Maureen spoke to the local newspaper, the *Romford Recorder*, in the month Margaret Thatcher passed away, April 2013. As she described the recently deceased prime minister in glowing terms, Patterson perhaps perversely stigmatised her own period as a secure council tenant in the property which she was later a disastrously debt-ridden owner of: 'I don't blame anyone. It was my decision to make that investment. She was an icon to me. She was a lovely guest. I gave her a guided tour, and she said, "This is not just a house – it's a home"'.[28]

In 2013, Mr Richards, the then owner-occupier of 39 Amersham Road, also sang the praises of Margaret Thatcher. Richards told a reporter from the *Recorder*, 'I don't know where we would be if Mrs Thatcher hadn't given people the opportunity to buy council houses back then.'[29] Romford was closely associated in the national imagination with working-class Conservativism and the embrace of Thatcher's free market worldview. Steve Davis won the Snooker World Championship six times between 1981 and 1988. Davis was from Romford and had grown up on an Essex council housing estate. He was a vocal supporter of Thatcher when his snooker triumphs coincided with her election victories and as he rose to become a millionaire and businessman.[30]

Davis's commitment to taking advantage of the new opportunities created by Thatcher's policies resonated with the residents of Harold Hill. Maureen Patterson's perspective was, unsurprisingly, one that was shared by some of her former neighbours who had benefited considerably from Right to Buy. Jackie Rowland also bought her Harold Hill council house in the 1980s, when she was in her mid-thirties. By 2009, the now middle-aged Rowland still lived there when she was interviewed by *Observer* journalist Tracy McVeigh. Jackie Rowland readily acknowledged that she had been a reluctant council homebuyer, as it went against her political allegiances. If she'd known Margaret Thatcher was visiting her estate, Rowland said she would 'have gone to throw eggs at her!', only to add, 'But I'm glad I bought my house, even if I didn't stick to my principles.'[31]

For Jackie Rowland, and millions of other council tenants, the compromises entailed in Right to Buy meant trading their beliefs in the values of public housing for immediate material improvements. Rowland no longer had to wait at the back of the queue of council tenants for maintenance and upgrading. Now she could pay for it herself through access to a mortgage which both Right to Buy and the loosening of financial regulations had made possible. Moreover, Rowland was now the owner of an asset that would shoot up in value over the decades to come, vastly outstripping stagnating wages. The value of her suburban home had risen by around 450 per cent in real terms over the previous twenty-five years when she was interviewed in 2009.[32] Homeownership was a far safer bet than relying on mobilisations by workers (or tenants) for improving the lot of individuals and families. However, taking on a large mortgage was individualising and risky. It also steadily eroded the potential for more lasting and solidaristic alternatives. Yet in an era of declining unionisation, mass joblessness and rising economic inequality, homeownership became even more desirable. Collective action in the workplace and strategies based around building the welfare state at a national and municipal level were obviously in retreat.

A message of empowerment was broadcast into council tenants' homes around the country through extensive marketing by central government. In 1980, a £600,000 publicity campaign, including television advertising, accompanied the beginning of Right to Buy.[33] A further £2.25 million was spent between 1981–82 and 1983–84, while a renewed £1.4 million investment was made to attract council tenants to Right to Buy following the 1984 Housing Act.[34] A simple populist appeal centred on the benefits of homeownership, the size of discounts on offer and the support central government would give tenants in buying their homes against recalcitrant Labour councils.

An advert from 1984, produced by the government's Central Office of Information, used similar terminology to the words that Maureen Patterson had heard from Margaret Thatcher. Bearing some parallels to the Pattersons, a white nuclear family of five is depicted in the advert, which tells the assumed audience of public tenants that, thanks to government policy, 'you can decide whether to turn your house into your home'. The alternative is to forgo the 'legal right to buy your house or flat' by 'still going on paying rent every week'.[35] Additionally, the Department of the Environment produced a brief pamphlet as part of the same publicity campaign which was pointedly titled *Your Right to Buy Your Home*. The extent of the discounts on offer – for instance, the potential to buy a house worth £25,000 for just £10,000, or a house worth £10,000 for £4,000 – underlines the prospective financial benefits secured by massive discounts. Potential buyers are strongly advised that they have the Right to Buy thanks to an Act of Parliament, and that, if necessary, their local authority is obligated to find them a mortgage in case a bank or building society is not forthcoming.[36]

The leaflet shares the emphasis of the television adverts in its characterisation of the Right to Buy beneficiaries. Once again, it is a family residing in a house rather than a flat, headed by a mother and a father with children. Over the course of a colourful few pages, they are joined by the family pet, a dog, who comes with them on the revolutionary journey of making a house a home, from initial inquiries to signing mortgage papers at the building society. Ultimately, the happy new owner-occupiers are accompanied by their children and loyal pet when clutching the deed that symbolises their new-found status as property owners.[37]

Right to Buy was founded upon what journalist and historian Andy Beckett terms a 'reassuringly suburban' imaginary, extending the Conservative instincts of the property-owning middle classes to receptive new layers of the working class.[38] The results of Right to Buy consolidated the distinction between the deserving homeowner and the undeserving council-flat dweller. Increasingly, public tenants became synonymous with unemployment and poverty, and with the stigmatised poor areas within cities or estates on their peripheries which were still characterised by high levels of public tenancies. The impact has been to residualise public housing. Where it was once a legitimate housing tenure for large swathes of the working class, council housing became understood as state-subsidised support for the impoverished, who are incapable of commanding the economic resources or financial discipline to become homeowners. These trends have been particularly visible in Scotland, where rates of public housing tenure were highest in 1980, accounting for the majority of households, and where they therefore also shrank most markedly under Right to Buy.[39] Yet these changes also only exacerbated legacies of municipal housing steeped in paternalism. Seán Damer's history of Glasgow council housing underlines that patterns of allocating families to schemes which were seen as appropriately rough or respectable were practised from the expansion of publicly rented homes in the decades between the World Wars.[40]

Secretary of State for Scotland George Younger articulated the essence of the liberating 'freedom' which lay at the heart of the sell-off during a debate over Scottish Right to Buy legislation in January 1980. Younger linked this empowerment to a highly negative designation of public housing, and by implication the primarily Labour-led local authorities who predominated where council houses were most popular. He told the House of Commons that he was proudly voting in favour of laws that amounted to 'the removal of the local authorities' power to obstruct the ambitions of their tenants', conferring upon them: 'Freedom, the freedom to choose, the freedom through one's own hard work to acquire an asset which can be enjoyed and passed on to one's children, and the freedom to determine one's own way of life.'[41] Younger pointedly did not consider secure public tenancies as a form of freedom.

This appetite for freedom, or at least proprietorship, was explored in a survey conducted by the Department of the Environment. Its author, Marion Kerr, summarised the significance of the Right to Buy policy in the finding that two-thirds of the homebuyers surveyed had not expected to purchase their house otherwise. Buying their home was incentivised by the scale of the discount, but also realised aims related to social status and passing on a family inheritance:

> Almost all the purchasers surveyed were pleased they had bought, primarily because of the good investment and the sense of security they felt was provided by homeownership but also because of the freedom to improve their home and the benefit of having something to leave the family. Right to Buy offered a

> distinctive opportunity for people who had often sold their labour for a living since they were teenagers to make money through ownership. Many council house buyers felt pride in owning their own home, and some, particularly flat buyers, saw their purchase as a stepping stone to something better.[42]

Tenants who were able to buy their homes often corresponded to the projections in the publicity campaigns described above. They tended to be 'better off', meaning that 'most were in full-time work, usually manual skilled or white-collar occupation, and with more than one wage earner in the household'. The new homeowners were concentrated within suburban and rural areas, and overwhelmingly in houses rather than flats. Just 4 per cent were facing 'serious' financial problems, with Right to Buy beneficiaries enjoying considerably lower household income to mortgage value ratios than other first-time buyers. The 'typical' council house buyers were a married couple who both worked and where the husband was a skilled manual worker. Furthermore, Kerr underlined the social division between the buyers and 'economically disadvantaged' renters: in contrast to buyers, the remaining tenants were often in receipt of no income and more likely to be unemployed, single, elderly or disabled.[43] These divisions were important in fragmenting perceptions of the working class. Herein lay the foundations of the so-called 'underclass' of perpetually workshy, delinquent benefit scroungers and single mothers who came to replace the working class in media images of the 1990s. Conversely, those able to advance became absorbed into the functional plurality of socially mobile consumers.

Denis and Sylvia Abbot exemplified those who were leaving the council house–renting working class behind in the 1980s. They bought their yellow-bricked, red-tile-roofed council house in Old Coulsdon, within the borough of Croydon, South London. Just as their three-bedroom terraced house was approximate to the typical bought council house, the Abbots also fulfilled the house-buyer archetype. Sixty-year-old Denis was a lathe turner, while his wife was a filing clerk. In October 1984, Sylvia explained to *The Times* reporter David Walker that they had achieved 'a bit of freedom' by becoming homeowners: 'now [they did] not have to ask the council's permission' to make changes to the house they had lived in for decades. Like many other new homeowners, the Abbots realised this freedom by replacing their front door. The 'blue drab of Croydon council' had made way for a mock-Georgian design, which Sylvia readily recognised as a cliché, along with the name boards and new garden fences that Walker numbered among the 'signs of ownership' on the Lacey Green estate.[44]

A form of individualism which centred on personal advancement at the expense of collectively felt working-class belonging was actively encouraged and facilitated by Right to Buy. Yet the reporting on these aspirational homeowners demonstrates the difficulties the ambitious social climbers faced in achieving acceptance through the mockery meted out towards their attempts to become respectable from those who considered themselves above them. Two years earlier, *The Times* had already celebrated Margaret Thatcher's 'house proud politics' in an editorial, embracing the 'mock-Georgian doors replacing municipal drab' in council estates across Britain. Under Right to Buy, Britain was becoming 'a nation of convinced house purchasers'. The result, which the Conservative paper of record commended, was that council housing was becoming 'residual': homes only for those who could not afford to buy and therefore required some form of state support.[45]

Housing and working-class politics

On 17 May 1979, the ghosts of politics past briefly haunted the House of Commons as John Maxton, the new MP for Glasgow Cathcart, made his maiden speech. Maxton paid tribute to his predecessor, the Tory MP Teddy Taylor, but indicated that he intended to model himself on the socialist politics of his uncle, Jimmy Maxton, who had served as MP for Glasgow Bridgeton from 1922 to 1946. These nods had a powerful foundation in the politics of housing. Taylor was feted as a 'tenement Tory' who convinced respectable working-class and middle-class homeowners on Glasgow's Southside to vote Conservative.[46] By contrast, Jimmy Maxton was famed as a firebrand parliamentary orator. He is remembered for refusing to be reprimanded by the Speaker after labelling Tory MPs as murderers in 1923, following the withdrawal of food and drink provisions for mothers and their children.[47] Jimmy Maxton was also roused by the class politics of housing. He was first elected to Parliament in 1922 as a beneficiary of the Red Clydeside period of workplace and community protest in Glasgow. Perhaps above all, it was the impact of the 1915 rent strike and the Labour Party's anti-landlordism which had proven central to building a durable electoral coalition across skilled and unskilled and Protestant and Catholic divisions in the city.

Moreover, the rent strike was a formative moment too for the political economy of housing in Britain during the twentieth century. Mass non-payment of rents in a crucial centre of munitions manufacturing threatened to create such disruption that Parliament passed the Rent Restrictions Act. It founded a system of rent controls which in modified forms lasted into the 1980s.[48] The span of rent controls marks a long period when the collective interests of tenants powerfully shaped a major area of British public and private life. Housing stood along with the workplace as a formative site in the politics that rose through the making of the British working class, but it was then also pivotal in its unmaking during the late twentieth century.

In 1979, John Maxton attacked the Right to Buy proposals recently outlined in the Queen's Speech mapping out the incoming Thatcher government's priorities in its first parliamentary term. Maxton's constituency included the large Castlemilk estate to the south west of Glasgow, which he emphasised was among Europe's largest housing schemes, incorporating multistorey as well as tenement-style properties. There was a distinctly defensive tone to his address, which sought to highlight public housing achievements despite difficult conditions. Castlemilk, Maxton acknowledged, had suffered the impact of growing unemployment, vandalism and social disrepair. However, 'The problems of Castlemilk are not about the individual housing unit within the community but about the problems of a whole community.' Maxton added that 'few people will wish to buy when they examine the conditions carefully'.[49]

Debates over housing between Scottish MPs in the first term of the Thatcher government appeared to hold some of the same polarisation they had earlier in the century. On 14 January 1980, Iain Sproat, the Conservative MP for Aberdeen South, spoke in support of Right to Buy and with anger and dismay about the dominance of public tenancies in Scotland. Drawing contrasts with countries in Eastern Europe which were still ruled by Communist governments, he underlined his alarm over the fact that most Scots lived in public housing:

> I find it shocking that in Scotland still over fifty per cent of all housing – some fifty-four per cent in fact – should be under the control of the State. That is a per centage almost double that in England, almost double that in Wales, and even greater than is to be found in many countries of Eastern Europe under Communist rule, such as Czechoslovakia and Hungary. In getting rid of that shocking state of affairs, the Bill will perform a signal service.[50]

Glasgow had been at the centre of controversies three decades prior, during the early 1950s, when the future of housing had also been polarised along class and party lines. On that occasion, a municipal administration led by the Progressives and the Moderates – local Tory front parties which separately stood candidates in municipal elections – had attempted to sell newly built council homes in the suburb of Merrylee in the south of the city, within the Cathcart constituency. A strike of Corporation building workers was mounted to oppose the sale. It was soon supported by engineers and shipyard workers, along with housewives, becoming a powerful social movement across community, workplace and political spheres. The emotive opposition to council house sales helped Labour win a subsequent council election which led to the cancellation of the sales. Evocative moments from this struggle included two women who lived in dilapidated Victorian slum housing in the Gorbals attending virulent demonstrations wielding a rat and rotten plaster taken from their respective tenements.[51] These were the conditions and failures of private ownership which public ownership did so much to improve in the decades which followed.

Twenty years later, another prominent council housing struggle flared in the North Derbyshire coalfields. Clay Cross Unitary District Council made an isolated stand against council house rent increases imposed by Edward Heath's Conservative government under the 1972 Housing Finance Act. Despite initially being supported by more than forty allied local authorities, Clay Cross was quickly left fighting a solitary battle in the courts. Yorkshire Television journalist and future Labour MP, Austin Mitchell, remarked that Clay Cross was administered by 'a government of the council house tenants, for the council house tenants'. Clay Cross Labour councillors were generally miners, former miners or other manual workers. Its young leaders, future Bolsover MP Dennis Skinner and his brothers, were driven by a commitment to 'clearing the slums' and charging affordable rents. Council officials who were seen as betraying the struggle faced having their homes picketed and even physical threats or damage to their cars. Despite opposition from owner-occupiers, who organised a municipal rate-payer interest lobby against subsidised council rents, the council persisted through seventeen months of struggle marked by splits in the local Labour Party. It ended in disqualification by the courts. Mitchell was affiliated with Labour's right-wing or 'moderate' tendency. Nevertheless, he underlined the depth of commitment in Clay Cross and dismissed reporting which he felt overemphasised physical intimidation by neglecting 'the casual informality of a small town where politics are personalised, and tempers run high'.[52]

In 1976, *The Times* bemoaned the 'complete Clay Cross mentality' which the newspaper's editors claimed had absorbed the Labour government elected in 1974. The new government discouraged council house sales after they had risen under Edward Heath's Conservative government from 1970 to 1974. Yet Ernest Armstrong, the Under-Secretary of the Environment and MP for another coalfield constituency, North West Durham, put forward a quite different stance to that which *The Times* implied: 'the first consideration of all public housing authorities, whether local authorities or New Towns, must be to provide housing for those in greatest need' insisted Armstrong, but that did not amount to a policy that only prioritised public housing.[53] Armstrong was himself a former local councillor in the borough of Sunderland. He supported the property-owning social democracy which characterised Labour's approach to housing policy, especially from the 1960s to the mid-1980s. These policies sought to achieve 'balance' between owner-occupiers and public tenants, while supporting both tenures as a much-preferred alternative to private renting, which had declined from dominance to the margins across the mid-twentieth century.[54] Merlyn Rees, the Labour MP for Leeds South and a former cabinet minister, summarised this perspective in May 1979, remembering that he had grown up around archetypal proletarians – South Wales miners – who had fought hard to become homeowners. Rees clarified that Labour's position centred on improving housing standards and freedom in tenancy choices:

> In the mining village in Wales in which I was brought up, the fight went on for years to obtain leasehold reform so that the people might own their own houses. *It is the technical aspect that is important rather than the philosophical aspect.*[55]

There had been a brief phase of outright restriction on private housebuilding under Labour governments between 1945 and

1951. It was motivated by the need for an exceptional response to the extreme demand for publicly rented housing following the end of the Second World War rather than outright hostility to owner-occupation. Thereafter, owner-occupiers already enjoyed a predominance in government policymaking, as the number of private renters dropped quickly. The decline of private renting was encouraged by rent caps, and the willingness of landlords to sell properties to their tenants, marking a change which housing historian Harold Carter celebrated as a 'tenurial revolution'.[56] Comparatively local conflicts such as those over the Merrylee houses and the rent struggle at Clay Cross do not portray the dominant face of housing or national Labour Party politics. By the mid-1960s, Harold Wilson's government had already embraced owner-occupation as a standard to be expected and supported through expanding mortgage credits.[57] Labour governments continued to support expensive tax relief for mortgage holders, even after clamping down on other incidents of tax relief in the late 1960s.[58]

Between the early 1970s and the mid-1970s, the annual cost of mortgage tax-relief subsidies doubled in real terms to over £1 billion in 1976–77, or over £6.5 billion in 2025 values.[59] Additional significant subsidies included the exemptions applied to most house sales from capital gains tax as well as moneys paid to building societies to lower mortgage interest rates. By the late 1970s, around 20 million Britons were shareholders or members of building societies or held a mortgage with one. In England and Wales, owner-occupation represented 55 per cent of all tenures, whereas fewer than a third of households were council tenants. Owner-occupiers were lent mortgages based on projections of rising house prices, while local authorities also supplied mortgages as well as selectively selling existing stock to tenants and even non-tenants. In some cases, councils even built homes for the purpose of sale rather than rent.[60]

The Labour government's 1977 housing green paper emphasised the achievement of bringing a period of acute housing shortage to an end and rooting out the worst squalor. There was now a housing surplus, despite the impact of large-scale demolitions in slum clearances.[61] These changes brought major shifts to Britain's social geography, marking the movement of large sections of the working class out of city centres and into sprawling housing estates.[62] City residents actively demanded these changes and overwhelmingly took up the opportunity to relocate, even to what were later denigrated as undesirable forms of housing. Ben Jones's history of slum clearances found that 'in the 1960s many people desperately wanted to live in the modern, purpose-built tower blocks'.[63]

The housing pressure group Shelter recorded that, in the early 1970s, the main problem with clearance programmes was that they were not moving fast enough, leaving residents living in dilapidated conditions. Occupants of houses in areas of Nottingham which had been slated for demolition were still bathing in tin baths and heating water over coal fires. In Glasgow's Maryhill neighbourhood, a woman who was the final remaining resident of a tenement block that was due to be demolished lived in 'a desert of empty houses and waste'. Doors and windows in the communal close lay broken after a burglary. Children in Liverpool discovered a dead cat being eaten by maggots in an abandoned home they were playing in. A half-blind woman had also picked up a rat while looking for a duster at her terraced house on Salford's Violet Street. Her neighbours voiced their frustration in a lively protest. Demonstrators marched with homemade placards replete with slogans such as 'Get Us Out of This Hell' and 'Rehouse Us Now'.[64]

Jeff Torrington's novel *Swing Hammer Swing!* opens with the more surreal scene of a man dressed in a Victorian diving suit toiling through the streets of the Gorbals as a closing local cinema desperately tries to rouse interest for its last film showing before the residents of the condemned tenements leave for Castlemilk. It encapsulates the death of the community networks centred on neighbourhood, locality, extended family and even forms of entertainment which relocation brought about. The main character, Tam Clay, is a workshy aspiring artist struggling to navigate the process of obtaining a new home. He fails to meet even the requirements of basic decency, not visiting his pregnant wife who has been hospitalised due to high blood pressure which is aggravated by the uncertainty of where their future home will be. Clay is a suitably individualist anti-hero for a book which was published in 1992. By then, the tower blocks which had replaced the Gorbals tenements were themselves being knocked down and replaced by houses and new tenement-style flats. Torrington's novel emphasises the futility and frustration relocation could involve through the power of often seemingly arbitrary and unresponsive authorities.[65] Twenty years before it was published, Jimmy Reid, the Communist shipyard trade union leader who had recently risen to fame as the leader of the Upper Clyde Shipbuilders work-in, made his inaugural lecture as the rector of the University of Glasgow following a successful election campaign by left-wing students. Reid's address – 'Alienation' – centred on the 'frustration of ordinary people excluded from the processes of decision making'. Although Reid had made his name in leading a struggle to conserve skilled industrial jobs from the corrosive effects of market pressures and Conservative government policies, his commentary extended to municipal politics and socialised housing. Reid, who had served as a Communist councillor in the shipbuilding town of Clydebank, condemned the growing size of Scottish local authority areas as 'a blue-print for bureaucracy, not democracy'. He viewed the tower block as a visual representation and physical confirmation of the alienated tenant: 'When you think of some of the high flats around us, it can hardly be an accident that they are as near as one could get to an architectural representation of a filing cabinet.'[66]

Later analysis published by Communists reiterated Reid's condemnation of the worst excesses of impersonal bureaucracy. In their 1984 reflection on Right to Buy, written for the Communist Party of Great Britain's influential magazine,

Marxism Today, David Griffiths and Chris Holmes described the allocation of scarce housing resources before 1980 as one where 'a framework of centralised bureaucracy and a tradition of Victorian paternalism' ruled, rather than the market.[67] These were central components of the world built during the post–Second World War zenith of Labourism. Associational lives and political and residential connections linked work and employment with trade unionism on the one hand to local government, the Labour Party and council housing on the other. There were complications and particularities to these interactions. For instance, Scottish coal miners rejected the option of being housed by the National Coal Board, unlike some of their English and Welsh counterparts. Where large new schemes were needed for miners as a matter of priority, they were often constructed by the Scottish Special Housing Association (SSHA). The SSHA was a national authority which did not carry the same dangers of employer-tied housing that miners and their families had often suffered the consequences of under private ownership.[68]

In large cities and their surrounding areas, post-war housing policy, building on earlier inter-war anticipatory instances of slum clearance and council estate building, succeeded in creating lasting changes to the physical environment as well as sustained improvement in housing. Yet it did so in a context marked by enduring proliferation of hierarchies and impersonal decision making. These structures consolidated social and geographical divisions between those classified as the respectable and deserving, and the rough and residual working class. Tenants were rehoused in large numbers when over 150,000 council homes were built per annum over the 1960s and 1970s. They lived in new environments moulded by distinctive economic and social relationships. The Thamesmead estate in South East London exemplified these shifts, as a planned community of 60,000 people in a concentrated single-tenure setting. The paternalistic instincts of local councillors included opposition to the opening of local pubs as well as control and monitoring over tenant behaviour. New council homes came or were later fitted with comfortable innovations like central heating, but problems, including chronic dampness, were visible at Thamesmead in the late 1960s, not long after the first residents arrived.[69]

Glasgow's large peripheral housing schemes were also marked by councillor opposition to drinking. Municipal officials made sustained efforts to 'police, discipline and remoralise' tenants moved through slum clearance schemes.[70] By the late 1970s, the peripheral estates accounted for over 140,000 people, around a fifth of the city's population. Conflicts over facilities were a recurring feature. Tenants' movements evolved in Pollok to the south west of the city and Castlemilk to the south east, over access to schooling.[71] Activists in Castlemilk also took part in campaigns to improve housing conditions and rail against 'the dampness monster' during the 1970s. Protests were most vociferous in the Gorbals, where the tenements had been torn down and replaced by the large multistorey flats which were criticised by Jimmy Reid. Just as Gorbals tenants had been at the forefront of the campaign to stop the sale of council housing in the early 1950s, so they led from the front in the fight to improve them a quarter of a century later. A sustained rent strike over conditions in the Gorbals was supported by residents of Castlemilk and Wester Hailes, a comparable housing scheme on the western outskirts of Edinburgh.[72]

In 1983, the revisionist labour historian, Iain McLean, polemically insisted that 'Easterhouse is the last unintentional legacy of Red Clydeside'. He was rebuked for this remark by Robert Morris, a more orthodox socialist historian of the Scottish working class who underlined the centrality of workplace and community activism to the politics of Glasgow during and immediately following the First World War.[73] From a less mutually polemical standpoint, though, we can see Easterhouse was a creation of Red Clydeside. Its construction was possible thanks to the empowerment of the local state to deliver vastly improved housing conditions under Labour-led councils enjoying extensive support from central government. Easterhouse's history also evidences the trajectory of tenant mobilisations earlier in the twentieth century and their continuation in later decades. McLean meant an altogether more cutting criticism, though, in the context of the 1980s when Easterhouse was a byword for unemployment and poverty. These were the associations from which Morris sought to rescue the 1915 rent strike. In Scotland, the residual nature of council housing was consolidated in the vernacular use of 'cooncil' as an adjective to designate second best – with terrestrial television known as 'cooncil telly' as opposed to the paid subscription satellite or digital alternative which jobless council tenants have in turn been commonly rebuked for having the audacity to own.

Corruption and the illegitimate exercise of power by local government have been another recurring feature of criticisms of mass council housebuilding. These motifs have powerfully entered fictional portrayals of post-war Britain. Perhaps the best-known example is the figure of Austin Donohue who appears in *Our Friends in the North*, a 1996 television drama largely set on Tyneside. Donohue is an ex-Labour councillor turned public relations firm owner. He is depicted as being in cahoots with a housing developer to build substandard multi-storey council flats. They swiftly fall into disrepair, inflicting misery on tenants who also struggle with a descent into criminality and hooliganism.[74] Donohue is a thinly disguised T. Dan Smith, the Newcastle local government leader who was ultimately jailed for corruption in 1974.[75] Andrew O'Hagan's novel *Our Fathers*, which was published in 1999, tells a similar story through the figure of Hugh Bawn. Having been politicised at a young age by his mother's involvement in the 1915 Glasgow rent strike, Bawn became a zealous housing modernist. He entered municipal politics intent on knocking down tenement slums but became driven by putting up tower blocks as quickly as possible. Bawn loses his grip on reality and eventually dies while being latterly investigated for corruption as the high-rises he built are being torn down, written off as collectivist deviations in an age of owner-occupation.[76]

Figures like Donohue, Bawn and Smith enjoy a formative place in cultural portrayals and mass-media explanations of the distinctive role played by Labourism in shaping British housing. They potentially obscure the realities of working-class experiences of housing and the imaginations that shaped Labour Party housing policy. Under Callaghan in the late 1970s, the Labour Party remained committed to building council housing, but it also stood for expanding owner-occupation. The 1977 housing green paper acknowledged that 'more and more people would like to become homeowners', having been 'attracted to home-ownership by the opportunity for personal freedom and independence'. 'For most people', the paper continues, 'owning one's own home is a basic and natural desire, which for more and more people is becoming obtainable.'[77] Given how marginal owner-occupation had been before the 1930s, this was a recently realised natural desire! The green paper outlined that owner-occupation would be increased by further 'social emphasis in housing policy', including through local authority housing sales and mortgage provision along with continued subsidies to mortgage payers and support for building societies. These would realise 'deep-seated social aspirations' among working-class families to become homeowners. It was the very successes of Labourism in this telling which led to expanding property ownership. Stable employment and rising incomes sustained by unionised jobs, along with high-quality homes furnished by local government, were to be consolidated by a social-democratic approach to property ownership resting on state collaboration with building societies and housebuilders.[78]

A property-owning working class

'Saturday's Kids' were the council house–dwelling youths celebrated by the Jam's Paul Weller in a homage to working-class life released on the band's album *Setting Sons* in 1979. The same year, Margaret Thatcher's newly elected government began passing the legislation which led to the first council house sales under Right to Buy. Weller's portrayal of council tenancies in 'Saturday's Kids' is much more positive than the one presented in 'Anarchy in the UK'. Smoking cigarettes, enjoying seaside holidays, drinking pints of beer, listening to football results, frequenting betting shops and bingo halls as well as flirting at discos populate the song, but so do early deaths and being overlooked by 'the system'.[79] Weller grew up in a council house in a terrace on Stanley Road in Woking, Surrey, on the outskirts of London. His mother was a cleaner, while his father was a builder and sometimes taxi driver.[80]

In 'Saturday's Kids', Weller depicted a world that was ill-divided, but the song was also far from wholly pessimistic. While their lives were subject to very real constraints, there were also shared opportunities for enjoyment and individual expression along with the security of settling down and parenthood. Saturday's Kids had jobs, ambitions and expectations. They were the affectionately caricatured representation of a broad swathe of the working class who lived on British council estates in the late 1970s. When *Setting Sons* was released, the majority of Britain's unskilled and semi-skilled manual workers were council tenants.[81]

Increasingly, though, the aspirations of Saturday's Kids came to include homeownership. Builders and skilled tradesmen emerged as the archetypal council house buyers and later, especially when crossed over with running small businesses, as landlords too.[82] The white-van man came to represent the Thatcherite working class: newly propertied and determined to make 'loadsa money'. Conservative popular historian, Dominic Sandbrook, has hailed the 'revolutionary' impact of Right to Buy. It was a measure that appalled left-wing commentators and municipal officials but delighted 'hundreds of thousands of families' who 'broke free from the embrace of the state'. More than a million homes had been sold under Right to Buy by the time Thatcher resigned from office in 1990. While night clubs, courtship, fast fashion and football results still shaped the lives of young men and women, the assumption that Saturday's Kids would live in council houses was anachronistic just a decade later. Public housing was now increasingly seen as 'homes for the poor'.[83]

Weller's song lyrics evolved accordingly. Six years after *Setting Sons*, his new band – The Style Council – released *Our Favourite Shop*. Weller's new anthems took aim at the changes being wrought by six years of Tory government. 'The Lodgers' was subtitled 'she was only a shopkeeper's daughter', in reference to Margaret Thatcher having grown up as the child of a Grantham grocer. It depicted a country where old certainties were changing for the worse, underlining the insecurity suffered by the denizens who were excluded from the benefits of property ownership and growing income inequality.[84] In 'Welcome to Milton Keynes', Weller focuses his ire on the landscape of private homes and relative prosperity which was growing alongside increasing unemployment and misery. Milton Keynes was a New Town which had been built with social-democratic aspirations in the 1960s. Thatcher personally visited Milton Keynes as she built support for Right to Buy. Just four months into her premiership, she handed the keys to Peter and Patricia King when they became the new owners of their Milton Keynes Development Corporation home in September 1979.[85] Weller emphasised homeownership and the sense of purpose in property epitomised by the sight of Union Jacks waving in semi-detached homes in new private schemes.[86]

As Weller rued, Right to Buy knowingly set out to erode class consciousness as a potent political force in British society. Thatcher and her allies closely linked property ownership with full membership of the British national community and as a reward for working hard, obeying the law and achieving self-reliance. The 1979 Tory election campaign focused on 'skilled manual workers in denim overalls'. These people, who were invariably portrayed as men, are referred to as 'C2' in the wonkish but persistent Social Grades classification used by pollsters.[87] They were the group, traditionally a bedrock of Labour Party supporters, who proved most brittle during this period. In 1979, Labour began to lose the electoral majority it had enjoyed among manual working-class voters for more than three decades, winning 50 per cent of their votes at an election where Right to Buy and the tax burden were leading subjects of debate and polarisation. By 1983, Labour's support had fallen to 42 per cent.[88]

Thatcher's Downing Street memoirs, which were published in 1993, lionise her first government's 'heavy programme, designed to reverse socialism, extend choice and widen property ownership'. As early as 1982, Right to Buy was proving 'a huge success', and a major headache for the opposition: 'The wider we could extend home ownership in this way the more difficult it would be for Labour to oppose it.'[89] Fresh from her third consecutive election victory, Thatcher jubilantly chastised Neil Kinnock, the Labour leader, during her 1987 Conservative Party conference speech in Blackpool:

> Now that it's proved so popular, it must be the sort of liberating measure of which even he would approve.
>
> For years we Conservatives had talked about wanting to create a property-owning democracy. Looking back, I wonder whether we did as much as we should have done to achieve that goal. But I don't believe that anyone will be able, in the years ahead, to make a similar charge against this government, indeed, extending ownership has been one of the achievements of which I am most proud.[90]

Achieving a property-owning democracy was only possible in Thatcher's own celebratory telling through the fire sale of a public housing stock built up across prior decades. Right to Buy was long in the making. The property-owning democracy can be traced back conceptually to the writings of Noel Skelton, an inter-war Scottish Conservative. Often, a crude political arithmetic inspired Tory support for council house sales whereby homeownership could be equated with support for the Conservative Party.[91] The Right to Buy policy which was first implemented in 1980 began to take form in the second half of the 1960s. In 1968, a year associated with revolutionary change from the streets of Paris and Chicago to the Vietnamese Tet Offensive, a very different upheaval was demanded by Conservative activist and future minister, Hamish Gray. Writing for the recently established Institute of Economic Affairs, a crucial think-tank in the Thatcherite intellectual universe, Gray bemoaned council housing as inefficient, arbitrary and encouraging dependency on the state. Specifically, Gray was contemptuous of housing costs being kept down by public subsidies, insisting that 'relative rents and prices reflect the highest subjective values that could be placed on the housing stock'. Instead, council tenants lived in a crude 'quasi-barter' economy marked by rationing and families organising 'exchanges' of suitable houses when they need to upsize or downsize. Gray objected that 'local authorities therefore do not seem to have been successful in allocating their houses to the poorest families', noting that the average council tenant income at the time was around the national average. Instead, Gray championed selling homes as a matter of right, deriding objections based on the argument that this would run down the public stock: 'That seems precisely what most voters want, and many council tenants are prepared to pay for.'[92]

Gray was an influential figure who would go on to serve as a minister in both the Department of Energy and the Scottish Office. He was writing during the late 1960s as running battles over the extent of council house sales developed between Wilson's Labour government and Conservative councils. Birmingham City Council under Conservative leader Frank Griffin pursued 'a mass sale of properties' and the Greater London Council and Manchester City Council did the same following Tory gains at municipal elections in 1966.[93] Between 1966 and 1980, Birmingham City Council alone sold 21,621 homes before Right to Buy. Sales only accelerated afterwards, with around 10,000 homes sold between 1980 and 1986, when the discount regime was implemented in a blaze of publicity.[94] These earlier experiences convinced Conservatives of the potential to privatise council housing and the chance to increase the party's electoral appeal among 'increasingly affluent working-class council tenants'. By the mid-1970s, the party had adopted Right to Buy.[95]

Right to Buy did indeed influence voters, even before they had managed to become property owners. A panel of voters in the Kent town of Rochester commissioned by *The Times* ahead of the 1983 general election demonstrated that housing exercised an important role in some voters' choices. June Whyman, a twenty-year-old mother of two, bluntly told the newspaper, 'I am against Labour because they are against selling council houses.' Sandra Wildish, a twenty-eight-year-old housewife, offered a perspective which firmly situated political allegiances within housing tenures: 'Being a council tenant, the Tories are very hard, and Labour really looks after you better, but when we move out of here and buy a home of our own, I will probably swing to the Conservatives.' Notably, there was some consensus even across these divisions. For instance, Albert Sutton, a sixty-one-year-old Labour voter and council tenant, was of the view that residents ought to have the option to buy their home from local authorities: 'If you are a sitting tenant and you have got the money, good luck to you.' Others disagreed. Rosina Ramsen, another tenant in her sixties, said council homes ought to be maintained 'for people like us who could not afford to buy'.[96]

Ramsen's view, though, while seemingly favourable to public housing, also reinforced its increasingly residual nature. By the late 1970s, most supplementary benefit recipients, the majority of the unemployed and around half of the poorest 30 per cent by income lived in council housing. Rising unemployment during the sharp recession of the early 1980s exacerbated these trends along with the early impact of Right to Buy. Increasingly, council housing was oriented to the ill, single parents and the homeless. Housing academics Ray Forrest and Alan Murie concluded soon afterwards that conditions on council estates demonstrated 'economic and political powerlessness, the marginalisation of certain sections of the working class'.[97]

Contemporary press reporting confirms the role of Right to Buy in encouraging divisions within council estates, considerably augmenting existing distinctions between the employed and the unemployed. Another newspaper article from the build-up to the 1983 general election demonstrates that there were significant groups who were excluded from the benefits of Right to Buy. A report by the *Guardian* from the Hodge Hill council estate in Birmingham which was published in May 1983 underlined that the newly unemployed were unable to buy their homes. Valerie Newbold had applied to buy her house two years earlier, only to withdraw after her husband had been made redundant. Another example was Cyril Wilson, a fifty-nine-year-old ardent Labour supporter who had also lost his job. He nevertheless supported Right to Buy, just as Albert Sutton had in Rochester. Opposition to Right to Buy similarly continued to rest on the view that buyers were removing important resources from the public estate. Two elderly neighbours, Harriet Emms and Constance Jones, thought that, rather than being incentivised to purchase their council houses, prospective homeowners ought to be obliged to buy homes in private estates. The political impacts of homeownership sought by the Tories were perhaps summarised by Esther Dunford, a council house buyer who had paid off her mortgage after taking advantage of Frank Griffin's sales policies in the 1960s: 'She thinks that council sales have greatly improved the street, and she has always voted Conservative.'[98]

Even the greatest ramparts of resistance to Thatcher's vision for Britain demonstrated affinities with her housing aims. Former Labour MP for Caerphilly in the South Wales Valleys, Ron Davies, recalled during an interview with historian Richard King that he was dismayed by the 1987 general election. Constituents who had lost jobs through colliery, steel works and factory closures, and who had lived through the 1984–85 miners' strike, told him they were nonetheless planning on voting Tory at the 1987 general election due to their support for Right to Buy.[99] In his analysis of what he presents as Britain's dominant petty bourgeois worldview, Dan Evans tells the story of Rob, a self-described 'Valleys boy' and former steel-worker who is nonetheless a committed Thatcherite and a landlord thanks to Right to Buy.[100]

The transformations brought by Right to Buy were visible in other coal mining and steelmaking regions. In the Lanarkshire mining village of Cardowan, which lies on the eastern outskirts of Glasgow, council house tenants who could not or would not buy their homes nevertheless found themselves in the midst of a transformation. As discussed in the previous chapter, public housing had been built around Cardowan colliery. The pit closed contentiously in 1983 during the build-up to the miners' strike. Rising levels of owner-occupation coincided with the closure of both the colliery and a local whisky bond, as well as the withdrawal of important municipally supported bus services. During a discussion recorded forty years later, in 2023, Alice, the daughter of a local miner who still lives in the area, remembered the impact of these changes in visible social divisions which became magnified through housing. The council 'started sellin the council houses, you know, that's what happened, and the fences started gettin higher', she remarked.[101]

Ellis, who is a steel erector's daughter originally from Mount Ellen, nearby in Lanarkshire, provided a different perspective as a council house buyer, but nonetheless one that coalesced with Alice's view. In an interview I recorded with her in 2023, Ellis remembered buying her home as a major opportunity. It added to her geographical and social mobility: 'Just having that choice, we went from there, we purchased another home, just a sort of small, quite a small home. It was scary, you know. It felt good, because you had your own place to, to be able to do that, and then ultimately, you know, over the years, as you start to move into different things. And chances are it's something that's bigger as you're moving forward, maybe the area's slightly, you know, nicer to your eye at any given time than other places might be. So, it was just having those different options and then it's meant that my children growing up as well start off with something different.'[102]

Council tenancy rates in industrial villages and towns in North Lanarkshire, the local authority area which includes Cardowan and Mount Ellen, had been as high as 80 per cent in the early 1980s.[103] By the late 2010s, owner-occupation was overwhelmingly dominant, accounting for around 60 per cent of homes, with another 10 per cent in the private rented sector. Council housing tenures had fallen to just a quarter.[104] Earlier instances of public housing sales in Lanarkshire had been very popular but primarily confined to selective sales undertaken by New Town Development Corporations in East Kilbride and Cumbernauld during the 1970s. Each had attracted residents keen, in Ellis's terms, to 'move on'. Lanarkshire New Town owner-occupiers included skilled manufacturing workers, anticipating the larger numbers of homebuyers who followed in the 1980s.[105]

Notably, in Scotland, the political impact of Right to Buy did not directly increase support for the Conservative Party. The sale of council houses, along with falling levels of unionisation and the broader retreat of the public sector, did, however, erode the bonds between housing, employment and community which had formed the bonds of Labourism in the twentieth century. This frayed connection encouraged Labour's shift towards the right and abandonment of collectivist or class-based politics – including support for Right to Buy – creating the context for the later electoral advance of Scottish nationalism in the twenty-first century.

The popularity of Right to Buy created consternation within the labour movement itself. In 1980, *Marxism Today* had mused that the 1979 general election revealed that 'the perception of the housing problem itself has changed from the problem of housing conditions to the problem of housing tenure'. Right to Buy had been 'electorally crucial' and proven central to 'dividing a working class' wrought by disillusionment with a failing welfare state but attracted to the 'popular appeal to the anti-bureaucratic, individualist and self-sufficient ideology of homeownership'.[106] Reflecting on major changes in tenure over the prior decade, in 1990, sociologist Peter Saunders suggested on terms that chime with the distinctions drawn between the Lanarkshire memories of Alice and Ellis that: '"The working class" with the cars and owner-occupied houses is actually in a very different class situation from "the working class" which ends up waiting for the bus on a municipal housing estate.'[107]

Saunders' research among council house buyers in the English towns of Slough, Derby and Burnley found that housing was often significant in how they described their political choices. A female semi-skilled manual worker simply told him, 'If I hadn't voted for Margaret Thatcher, we wouldn't own this house now, would we?' A male semi-skilled worker similarly stated, 'The Conservatives [support homeownership]. Labour would stop people buying their council houses.' Even a Labour-voting skilled manual worker was among 'a number of resentful people in Slough' who were still angry that the Labour council ended a policy of council house sales in the 1970s. 'They did the dirty on us', he remembered in an interview recorded years later. Council-house buyers were more likely to vote Conservative, and more than half of those who had previously voted Labour had switched. Homeowners were also more conservative in other respects – for instance, they were less oppositional to local government cuts. Yet, overall, Saunders concluded that, at least at the level of party affiliation, the impact of changing tenures was somewhat muted between tenants and homebuyers, 'stifled by the class-based pattern of party allegiance'.[108]

Labour adapted to Right to Buy despite its early objections. In the aftermath of suffering a heavy defeat in the 1983 general election, Shadow Home Secretary Roy Hattersley insisted that 'we cannot continue to deny council tenants the right to buy their own house when the sale would do no harm to the community as a whole'.[109] The following year, Labour's annual conference voted to accept Right to Buy, albeit initially without the discount. There were 'only a handful of votes against'.[110] The same conference is primarily remembered for the controversy related to the 1984–85 miners' strike and clashes between National Union of Mineworkers President Arthur Scargill and Labour Party leader Neil Kinnock.[111] Yet housing remained a subject of bitterness and debate. At its 1986 annual conference, Labour affirmed that it supported the Right to Buy for council and housing association tenants. Jackie Rosenberg, a delegate from Westminster North constituency, struck an oppositional tone, stating: 'We are not ashamed to live in public housing. We are proud of our homes and yet we feel we have been fighting alone.'[112]

Both tenant activists and the striking miners were defending parts of the Labourist order established in the 1940s: publicly owned industries sustaining unionised jobs and greatly expanded municipal housing. Jim Phillips' analysis of the miners' strike in Scotland suggests that council housing was a positive factor in the endurance which miners displayed. Regions with higher public housing densities demonstrated greater levels of commitment. Council housing reduced the economic cost of striking. Labour councils often postponed rent payments for the duration of the dispute.[113] Furthermore, the defeat of organised labour and the diminishment of public housing are interrelated. These themes were explored by Britain's best-known trade unionist in the mid-2020s, Mick Lynch, the general secretary of the National Union of Rail, Maritime and Transport Workers, in an interview with left-wing journalist Ash Sarkar, recorded during the summer of 2024. Lynch, who is an electrician by trade, commented that in the past, skilled workers such as himself were often community as well as workplace leaders in council estates. Now they were more likely to be private homeowners.[114] Lynch grew up as the son of Irish immigrants, initially living in dilapidated slum housing conditions in 1960s West London replete with coal fires and tin baths before his family benefited from major material improvements when they moved to the Warwick Estate. He has described these experiences along with his father's union activism as having instilled 'Labour Party values' in his family.[115]

Trade union mobilisation has become more difficult as workers have fallen further and further into debt. Household indebtedness in Britain has risen enormously as a proportion of GDP since the early 1980s, doubling to a peak of over 155 per cent in 2008 before beginning to fall to around 130 per cent in the early 2020s.[116] In part, this reduction is symptomatic of the ageing population, and the fact that there are now more homes owned outright in Britain than being paid on a mortgage by an owner-occupying household.[117] A more pertinent measurement for workers is the relationship between house prices and wages. They demonstrate a striking upward trend. Since the 1980s, the average house price has increased from around four times average annual earnings to approaching nine times the average wage in 2023.[118] As a result, those working-aged people able to buy a house are highly indebted and reliant on making large monthly mortgage payments. In turn, this makes collective workplace mobilisation like drawn-out strike action even more risky, trapping workers into accepting lower pay increases than they would otherwise potentially be able to bargain for. Rents have also risen as the private rented sector has grown to a larger size than the social sector (council housing and housing association homes combined). By the early 2020s, rents in London typically made up more than a third of household income, and even in lower-priced regions, such as the North East of England, they were more than a fifth.[119]

Housing conditions have affected working conditions and the ability of workers to take collective action to defend or improve their lot, contributing formatively to the de-organisation of the working class in the community and the workplace. This trend can be explained by numerous factors, including the shrinking of traditionally well-organised industries and the breaking of union strength through privatisation and defeats suffered during the 1980s and after. Nonetheless, even where unions remained comparatively strong, such as in the public sector, another notable feature has been that all-out strikes are now rare. Such disputes were relatively common where national industrial action was organised, through to the Winter of Discontent of 1978–79 and the steel and miners' strikes of the 1980s. Since the 1990s, they have been comparatively unusual. Union leaders such as Mick Lynch led a protracted series of strikes in the 2022–23 strike wave, the first time that days lost to industrial action had surpassed the 1989 total. On this occasion, shorter days of action created battles of attrition in contexts where workers had mortgages to pay and neither the material resources nor the cohesion and organisation union leaders thought would be necessary to sustain all-out disputes was judged to be present. Nor were they demanded by strikers themselves.[120]

There is another rationality here, epitomised by Jackie Rowland owning a Harold Hill home worth several times more than it had been when she bought it during the 1980s. The less fortunate Pattersons and their property exemplify this lesson too. Thirty years after the Pattersons bought their house for £8,315, at a 40 per cent discount, it sold for £180,000.[121] Employment became a means to service mortgage debt while house prices skyrocketed, holding out a picture of wealth and prosperity for those able to maintain payments as well as for their children awaiting a hefty inheritance. Housing was a comparatively affordable asset, particularly when it was tied to Right to Buy discounts. The mass sale of council housing was a relatively short-lived feature of the 1980s and 1990s, but these were crucial decades in the unmaking of the British working class. Rising property values sustained a relatively widely shared sense of improved living standards and even enrichment.

What remained of the property-owning social democracy was further eroded in the first quarter of the twenty-first century. Both New Labour and the Conservative–Liberal coalition governments gladly continued and even extended Right to Buy, raising discount thresholds. The total number of social housing tenures fell back to 5 million, a decline of around a third and less than the total number of households in the private rented sector. Whereas council housing had accounted for around a third of homes in the early 1980s, it was in the single-digit percentages by the early 2020s.[122] Even where selling council housing proved impossible, New Labour used the aggressive implementation of stock transfer policies (from councils to housing associations) to partially privatise relationships between tenants and the state.

Stock transfer further weakened the position of the local state as a large-scale landlord and eroded the standing of the voter-tenant who had previously been a dominant factor in local politics in some areas. Perhaps most iconically, under pressure from central government, Glasgow City Council tenants voted for a stock transfer which ended the authority's standing as Western Europe's largest landlord.[123] Housing has proven to be one important area of difference under devolution. The Scottish National Party government ended Right to Buy in 2016, after around half a million homes had been sold.[124] In Wales, Right to Buy was brought to an end three years later by a Labour administration.[125] Yet substantially, the shifts in tenure that have taken place in previous decades are the same across Britain. Their impact in solidifying the imperative behind protecting the value of house prices remains a leading fact of political life.

Increased homeownership has also created a much stronger shared interest in lower borrowing rates. With house prices shooting up since the 1990s, only an era of relatively low interest rates has made high rates of borrowing comparatively affordable. This dependency has been reinforced by another dimension of the dismantling of the property-owning social democracy: mortgage subsidies. The last vestiges of mortgage subsidies, mortgage interest tax relief, came to an end in 2000. It was removed by Chancellor Gordon Brown, who made reference to the major benefits that he had secured for mortgage payers in the form of a series of cuts to interest rates. As a result, mortgages were affordable even without the subsidy.[126] Three years later, Brown appointed Mervyn King as governor of the Bank of England. In the early 1980s, King had been an advocate for removing subsidies both for the public and private sector, which he argued were inefficient and counteracted efficient housing market allocations.[127] Even in what were viewed as a comparatively benign economic context, what King termed NICE – non-inflationary consistently expanding – conditions, homeownership was still falling in proportionate terms by the mid-2000s. Loose credit and low interest rates pushed up house prices beyond affordability for growing numbers of households. From 2022, increasing interest rates contributed considerably to a cost of living crisis which encouraged the strike wave discussed above but also limited its efficacy.

Thirty years before, in 1992, the satirical television show *Spitting Image* parodied the Madness anthem 'Our House' in a comment on negative equity. Amid repossession and ruin, the revised lyrics mocked homeowners who bought their houses in the Thatcher era and were continuing to vote Conservative while being trapped in debt which even selling their property would not pay off.[128] The Pattersons appear to embody this message. Becoming a homeowner was a cherished goal for many families. Asset ownership affected class relations and consciousness by remaking dominant understandings of social hierarchy and economic and political priorities. The council home had stood alongside trade unionism and the industrial and public sector workplace in the world of twentieth-century Labourism, but it was now marginalised and subject to residualisation. Council housing was stigmatised and labelled the preserve of the down-and-outs: the poor, the sick and the unemployed.

Tenure changes were gradual. Owner-occupation had been growing for decades and was in many respects compatible with the Labourist worldview, where it was privileged alongside but not over or against council housing. Right to Buy fundamentally overhauled this housing order and made owner-occupation *the* key priority in housing policy as well as a crucial test of government economic performance. As a result, it lastingly contributed to the unmaking of the working class by drastically entrenching inequality and weakening the bonds which had secured working-class consciousness through linking mobilisations from the home and the community to the workplace and the ballot box.

However, the extent of social (counter)revolution entailed in Right to Buy was always constrained and it met its limits in the extent of house prices and rents which followed. Housing has once again emerged as an area of class conflicts in the 2010s and 2020s, particularly through the activities of tenants' unions such as ACORN and Living Rent in Scotland, which mobilise across the council housing, housing association and private rented sectors. Resistance to treating housing as a commodity to be bought and sold like any other has persisted in Britain and grew in the early twenty-first century. For younger generational cohorts, the same measures which dislocated older forms of class consciousness among their parents and grandparents may have the opposite effect. Discontent with landlordism has rekindled an antagonistic collectivist politics of housing, along with demands for state intervention and increased council housebuilding.

5

New Labour: From 'Loadsamoney' to 'Mondeo Man'

I can still remember my dad's beaming smile shining through between his moustache and beard on 2 May 1997. The Tories were gone after eighteen long years. He'd stayed up late to see the back of them, taking particular joy in watching the much-loathed Michael Portillo lose his seat. There was an optimism to our Edinburgh tenement that Friday. Not far up the street, family friends who were active in the Trotskyist Socialist Workers Party shared a sterner message: 'Vote Labour, But Don't Trust Blair', read the poster in their window. The Tories leaving government may have been welcome, but the agenda of those who replaced them was viewed with less certainty. I can recall that a few weeks earlier my dad had expressed some misgivings before he reluctantly allowed a Labour canvasser to give me a red balloon on Easter Road, a main thoroughfare in the Edinburgh North and Leith constituency.

A couple of years later, it was a sunny day in Scotland's capital, and my primary-school class was taken on a trip to watch a moment of history being made. We were given Saltire flags to wave outside Holyrood Palace as Queen Elizabeth II came past in a carriage on her way to convene the opening of the Scottish Parliament, which initially met temporarily at the General Assembly Hall of the Church of Scotland on the Mound. The opening ceremony incorporated both the royalism of the monarch's official presence and Sheena Wellington's rousing rendition of Robert Burns's egalitarian anthem, 'A Man's a Man for A' That'. Then Scotland's new political leader, First Minister Donald Dewar, gave a memorable speech which paid tribute to 'echoes from the past', beginning with 'the shout of the welder in the din of the great Clyde shipyards'. Dewar promised a forward-looking future 'for this new forum of democracy born on the cusp of a new century', centred on achieving 'social justice'.[1]

The combination of conservative tradition and constitutional reform, of supposedly integrating long-standing values with the needs of a postmodern capitalist society, reflected the genesis of the 'New' Labour Party Dewar led in Scotland. It was a new politics for 'New Times': an age no longer characterised by the shouts of shipyard workers of blessed memory. The technological and economic changes associated with the 'information superhighway', and with a global market that extended from the Clyde to Guangzhou, were hailed as an opportunity, or at any rate as an ineluctable reality.[2]

Devolution had been popularised in the Scottish labour movement as an alternative to industrial job losses and the biting effects of the Thatcherite assault on trade unions, the unemployed and local government. These commitments were symbolised in the Parliament building at Holyrood which opened in 2004. Dewar arranged for the ashes of the recently deceased president of the National Union of Mineworkers Scottish Area, Michael McGahey, to be interred in the foundations. This was a fitting tribute to McGahey's formative role in arguing for a Scottish Parliament for three decades, from the late 1960s to the late 1990s. As discussed in chapters two and three, McGahey had been an active protagonist in the struggles for expanding trade union recognition and working-class living standards in the 1960s and 1970s, before playing a key role in leading the year-long miners' strike to defend jobs and a union voice in the industry in the 1980s. McGahey hoped devolution would serve what he saw as the distinctive democratic and egalitarian ambitions of the Scottish working class. His ashes served as a memorialisation of the personalities and collectives that had been formative to imagining devolution, but which were now themselves disappearing as it took shape.[3] Devolution was formed in the shadow of the unmaking of the working-class politics which had shaped the popular demand for a Scottish Parliament within the United Kingdom in the first place.

Three and a half years later, we were into a new millennium, and Labour had won another landslide victory at the 2001 general election. Just a few minutes' walk from Easter Road, there was a decisively more bad-tempered mood in the air outside McDonald Road Fire Station in November 2002. Striking firefighters burned wood in braziers to keep warm as they braced the chilly East Coast of Scotland wind during a major national showdown between their Labour-affiliated trade union, the Fire Brigades Union (FBU), and the UK government. I can also remember seeing the archaic-looking Green Goddess fire engines manned by soldiers. The ageing vehicles looked precarious as they turned corners on Edinburgh's winding roads during the government's efforts to break the strike. The servicemen were praised by Labour ministers for stepping in and innovating tactics to deal with the impact of the dispute following eight days of strike action in November alone. Meanwhile, the firefighters were attacked by Blair's chief spin doctor, Alastair Campbell, as irresponsible and recalcitrant. Efficiency savings and job cuts – referred to as 'modernisation' – were to be the price for the significant wage rises firefighters were seeking.[4] McDonald Road was perhaps a telling location. During the 1984–85 miners' strike, the library, which is not far up the street from the fire station, had been used to store Christmas presents for the children of striking miners, illustrating the pivotal role Labour local authorities had then played in supporting workers and their families during another major national dispute.[5]

By the time the firefighters' strike was over, British soldiers had stopped crewing Green Goddesses but were instead occupying Iraq, playing second fiddle to American forces in an unpopular war which was mired in controversy and lies before it even began. I have memories of marching at a protest through the city centre of Edinburgh during the early months of 2003 along with my mum and my younger brother and sister. The four of us thought the chant 'Blair, Blair, Blair, we know you!

Your daddy was a Tory too!' was a particularly funny ode to Tony Blair's father having been chairman of the Durham Conservative Association.[6] Placards were distributed by the left-wing Scottish Socialist Party (SSP) which portrayed Thatcher morphing into Blair.

There was a more pervasive discontent expressed on the march and at the polls. In May 2003, the SSP managed to win six seats in the second Scottish Parliament.[7] Blair had cast New Labour in a binary against 'Old Labour'. In turn, Old Labour was mobilised by Blair's critics both outside and within the Labour Party to project the cohesive sense of an authentic Labour Party history which was juxtaposed with New Labour's appeasing of 'middle England', along with its close relationships to big business and the right-wing press.[8] Most of all, running through this divide like the writing in a stick of rock, were the words 'class' and 'Scotland'. Old Labour had been defined as a party by, for and with the British working class in this imagined past. New Labour, by contrast, was primarily defined by the disavowal of class as an embarrassing and regrettable feature of the twentieth century, and as an obstacle to building a modern society in the twenty-first. Under devolution, the hope remained that at least in Scotland the same transformations had not taken place, at least not as extensively, creating more space for 'Old Labour' politics. These revised constitutional and geographical ambitions affirmed how much the British working class had already been unmade during the preceding decades. Shifting views of what was achievable within the political mainstream demonstrate New Labour's crucial role in accepting, consolidating and furthering the unmaking of the British working class by arguing so directly against a collectivist or class-based politics in the 1990s and 2000s.

In October 1996, Blair made his final party-conference leader's speech before he became prime minister. He invoked a 1990s folk character who personified New Labour's reorientation towards upwardly mobile formerly working-class voters. Blair introduced conference delegates to the conundrum of a well-off tradesman who had familial ties to the Labour Party but minimal residual loyalty:

> I can vividly recall the exact moment that I knew the last election was lost. I was canvassing in the Midlands on an ordinary suburban estate. I met a man polishing his Ford Sierra, self-employed electrician, dad always voted Labour. He used to vote Labour, he said, but he bought his own home, he had set up his own business, he was doing quite nicely, so he said I've become a Tory. He was not rich, but he was doing better than he did, and as far as he was concerned, being better off meant being Tory too.[9]

While Blair referred to a Sierra driver, the electrician was anachronistically christened 'Mondeo Man' in recognition of Ford's rollout of the ubiquitous family sedan which filled suburban garages in growing numbers by the mid-1990s. Mondeo Man was both an opportunity and a challenge. Political scientist Eric Shaw later summarised that Mondeo Man was a stand-in for 'the irrevocable decay of class-configured partisan loyalties' in an era when formerly sharp, knowable social-class divisions had given way to seemingly more fungible and incremental gradients.[10]

Over the same period, divisions within the working class had grown more paramount, along with regional fragmentation. Distinctions between renters and homeowners became increasingly pronounced along with a growing gap between better-paid self-employed or securely employed skilled workers on the one hand and the unskilled, precarious and unemployed on the other. Mondeo Man was representative of these changes and challenges, as a small business owner and skilled worker earning a good income in the comparatively prosperous Midlands. New Labour assumed it could gain the votes of Mondeo Men in affluent suburbs while retaining support in working-class heartlands where, according to Blair's advisors, voters had 'nowhere else to go'.[11]

Blair would later summarise the New Labour ethos in 2004 during a speech to the centre-left think-tanks Institute for Public

Policy Research and Demos. He used uncharacteristically overt class terms: 'The purpose is however entirely traditional: social justice; to put middle-class aspirations in the hands of working-class families and their children, to open up opportunity not for a few but for all.'[12] New Labour also added a harder edge to the boundaries of the working class at the lower end, even while it encouraged the upper echelons to wave it goodbye. A workless 'underclass' was held to be a dangerous threat, closely associated with feckless habits, 'anti-social behaviour' and largesse at public expense. The only direct reference to social class in Labour's 1997 manifesto is to this 'underclass'.[13] A disciplinarian agenda focused on the lumpen 'anti-social' young people on council estates came to characterise New Labour in government. As discussed above, by 2002 the same outlook was extended to the FBU when firefighters were judged to be recalcitrant and backward in mobilising for pay increases without making sufficient concessions to modernisation. While New Labour was marked by a commitment to 'fairness' towards its traditional constituencies, it was intensely wary of attracting criticism from the right for granting clientelist 'favours' to either trade union allies or benefit claimants who received financial support from the state.

New Labour ideology, strategy and policy were inspired by the Thatcherite inheritance, including the diminished position of the working class in the balance of economic and political power. In the 1980s and 1990s, the affluent manual and white-collar sections of the workforce were seemingly increasingly difficult to categorise as straightforwardly working or middle class. The Labour Party came to view winning support from these homeowning, entrepreneurially and privately minded social layers as fundamental to achieving electoral victory. Their preferences and their perceived worries over public spending, welfare dependency and the risks of wealth redistribution or trade union power figured intimately in shaping the presentation and ambitions of the party before the 1997 election and subsequently during thirteen years of government. In answering these concerns, New Labour was in fact deeply aware of class and sensitive to forms of class consciousness, but often in a reactionary guise.

The unmaking of the British working class unfolded through the Labour Party encouraging a perception of classlessness which viewed any outward politics of antagonism or redistribution as antiquated. These changes were not merely pragmatic, even when they were presented as such. New Labour drew on core ideological tenets which emphasised Britain's changing place in a new international order. The theoretical analysis of 'New Times' was a formative perspective which had origins in the Communist Party of Great Britain's theoretical journal *Marxism Today*. Before he became Labour Party leader, Blair had even written for *Marxism Today*.[14] The New Times agenda centred on the dearth of possibilities for a national-producer-focused socialist perspective in the age of liberalising economics and microelectronics. Feminist, anti-racist and environmental activism all appeared more vibrant than traditional trade unionism. In place of old-fashioned monocultural Labourism, it argued for a broad progressive alliance.[15]

By the late 1990s, these impetuses had evolved into championing a supposed 'Third Way', which embraced globalisation and the liberalised movement of capital and goods as superseding class politics centred on industrial employment in nationally regulated economies.[16] The 'Third Way' made some noises about reordering British capitalism but proved directed much less towards capital than towards ensuring workers felt the cold winds of market forces. Martin Jacques and Stuart Hall were two of the crucial thinkers behind the New Times thesis. They had initially welcomed New Labour's intellectual curiosity and political dynamism, but even before Blair became prime minister, they warned readers of the *Observer* to be wary of Labour's limited ambitions for government.[17] Their fears were realised through an increasingly authoritarian state which set disciplining the public sector workforce and the underclass as leading priorities.

'Loadsamoney' and 'Mr Average'

Shifting landscapes of work, occupation and identity had gnawed at the Labour Party's sense of its core constituency for around four decades before Blair ascended to leadership in 1994. Writing the year before, the British historian Willie Thompson, who had been a long-standing Communist Party of Great Britain activist before the party dissolved in 1991, referred to Labourism as a political culture moulded by 'discipline, good order, submission to the rhythms of industrial life and the sober requirement of organisational bureaucracy and bookkeeping'. Putting this formulation still more drastically, Thompson stated that 'the principles of the industrial society' from which Labourism had emerged 'were irrepressible' in moulding its culture.[18] Labourism had evolved as both a political ideology and a set of organisational practices which sought to advance the socioeconomic interests of workgroups and the larger working class by respecting rather than threatening or transforming the structures of the British state. By the early 1990s, Thompson mused, the form of 'deferential Labourism' had morphed into 'pragmatic British liberalism under another name', largely maintaining the form of an industrial and political movement which remained centrally configured around the union–party relationship.[19]

Under Neil Kinnock's leadership from 1983 to 1992, Labour had already moved towards supporting European integration and accepting privatisation. Labour had also shifted away from independent foreign-policy measures such as unilateral nuclear disarmament. Yet for Thompson these pendulum swings between left and right were less important than the sense that Labour's traditional constituency was disappearing. The context of a 'two-thirds, one-third society' meant Labour was increasingly associated with the political interests of an impoverished minority against an affluent majority.[20] This was an influential but contentious framing which concluded that most British people were prospering, with only an impoverished excluded minority requiring greater assistance to reap the benefits of a liberal market economy. Following Labour's third consecutive defeat at the 1987 general election, Thompson's then party comrade and fellow historian, Eric Hobsbawm, had bemoaned the impact of rising living standards and cheap consumer goods. Workers were marred by individualism through home- and family-centred lives rather than communal orientations to either work or leisure. They were pulling away from a Labour Party still associated with staid solidaristic but bureaucratic models of public ownership and redistribution.[21]

These arguments resonated with earlier sallies by the Labour right to drop the party's formal allegiance to socialism in order to accommodate itself to post-war consumerism. In the late 1950s, Labour leader Hugh Gaitskell had caused much consternation on similar lines to those later faced by Blair when he attempted to remove Clause Four of the party's constitution. The symbolic commitment to public ownership of the means of production, distribution and exchange had been adopted in 1918, in anticipation of Labour displacing the Liberal Party as the main party of the British left.[22] While Gaitskell, unlike Blair, had failed to shift Clause Four, the revisionist creed he represented was much more successful in convincing the Labour Party towards championing a 'mixed economy', to the extent that it subsequently became a hallmark of the understanding of Old Labour which was defended by left-wingers from attack by New Labour. Formalised physical economic planning was confined to the minority nationalised sector, while managerial employees of both public and private enterprises became core to the productive economic interests which the party championed.[23]

Later proponents of 'modernisation' made even more urgent appeals during the 1980s. In autumn 1987, Neil Kinnock addressed the party's annual conference in what he described as 'the shadow of defeat' after June's general election. Kinnock discussed the 'mixed realities' workers were facing through mounting inequality, manufacturing job losses and the uneven geographical spread of prosperity and opportunity: 'We face the reality of many more people owning a few shares; and the reality alongside it of increasing poverty, of low pay and growing inequality and division.'[24]

Labour's debate on defining 'modern socialism' was driven by mounting concern over the political leanings of 'the new working class' in the South of England. Kinnock was speaking around the time that the party launched major policy reviews into regaining working-class support, particularly among higher-earning, homeowning and perhaps even shareholding workers.[25] These crucial changes were distinctive from the earlier debates over the 'affluent' workers of the 1960s. The parameters had shifted when the retained efficacy of Britain's centralised state came into question along with the obvious diminishment of the national-industrial economy which had provided the rewards of affluence for growing sections of the British working class into the 1970s. Consumption in the earlier period had remained more obviously tied to production. In turn those dynamics had shaped key parameters of the Labour worldview across conventional left and right divides.[26]

Responses to the dilemmas of the 1980s were varied and often imaginative. They included the demand for a reconstituted set of relationships between party, the local state, the national state, trade unions, tenants and social movements campaigning on peace and the environment, for feminism and against racism and fascism. A New Urban Left emerged within the Labour Party, centred on local government, orchestrating a more dynamic form of politics. Ken Livingstone's Greater London Council embodied a less hierarchical and more democratic movement. Other examples included Sheffield City Council, which was christened 'the People's Republic of South Yorkshire'. The leaders and supporters of these administrations underlined the need to fashion experimental but less deferential relationships between traditionally paternalistic local authorities and their constituencies and workforces, as well as promoting the agency of women and black and Asian communities within and beyond the boundaries of the labour movement.[27] The New Times reading was an attempt to generalise these contentions.

Yet the New Times perspectives also potentially coalesced with the revisionist view that class was no longer a galvanising feature of political mobilisation. For the 'new working class' who were so central to Labour's concerns, class itself was increasingly reserved for biography and family stories, associated with culture or heritage but also less positively linked to Britain's embarrassing continuing social hierarchies. By contrast, the office employees and skilled manual workers who lived in comfortable suburbs were less invested in class identity in their political hopes for the here and now.[28]

In 1987, Kinnock was blunt about this. He made some references to what he saw as a long-standing conservatism on the part of socialists towards workers enjoying higher wages. Kinnock remembered that growing car ownership and the rising standards of living in the South Wales Valleys were met by the moralising disapproval of local Labour Party activists when he was a young man in the 1950s and 1960s. He decried any temptation to write off 'people – not yuppies – who live in the kind of places and work in the kind of jobs that would qualify them for any certificate of working-class authenticity that any comrade wanted to award. And they did not vote Labour last time or the time before.' Exemplifying the bona fide proletarians in question, Kinnock referred to a recent speech by Ron Todd, the general secretary of Britain's largest union, the Transport and General Workers' Union (TGWU). Todd referred to his membership as now being typified by a well-paid docker who 'owns his house, a new car, a microwave and a video [player], as well as a small place near Marbella'. Todd had forcefully insisted that a union leader had no truck addressing a man who owned a Mediterranean home with the traditional mantra of 'let me lead you out of your misery, brother'![29] This was a potent rejection of the industrial politics of the past, especially given the formative role that the 1889 strike by impoverished London dockers played in shaping the TGWU.[30]

There was an irony to the choice of the docker as the key representative of the newly socially and politically mobile worker.

Just two years later, the National Dock Labour Scheme (NDLS) was dramatically abolished by Margaret Thatcher's Conservative government. This amounted to a drastic undoing of the improvements in conditions achieved in reforms implemented under Attlee's Labour government and afterwards. Casualised labour returned to Britain's ports, drastically reducing the security and earnings which had financed the foreign holidays, electronic appliances and multiple houses lauded by Todd a few years earlier. The TGWU was defeated after a strike to preserve registered employment failed. By the mid-1990s, ships were 'loaded by window cleaners and hamburger salesmen' at former NDLS ports.[31] Even the endurance of a three-year-long lockout by the Liverpool dockers between 1995 and 1998, which was supported by impressive acts of international solidarity, could not preserve their conditions locally.

Todd's and Kinnock's depictions referred to workers who had a less committed and more consumerist attitude to their politics as well as their household goods. Defeats suffered by unionised workers on the docks only reinforced perspectives on the shifting character of class consciousness. The stark conclusions drawn in these conversations were especially apparent in relation to remaining bases of Labour support, particularly within the skilled working class. Tradesmen were a prominent group within political and cultural interpretations of the new working class. They had animated the traditional labour movement through craft-based unions and mores centred around progression from apprenticeships to journeyman status. Contrastingly, by the late twentieth century, tradesmen had also come to occupy a central place in narratives of class electoral dealignment and economic change.

Harry Enfield's 'Loadsamoney' character, who fronted a 1988 hit single by the same name, cemented this narrative in a memorable pop music jingle. The music video includes a juxtaposition between the flat-cap-wearing industrial waged worker of old and Loadsamoney. The latter is by contrast an ignorant, selfish, undeserving self-employed Essex painter and decorator solely motivated by earning cash, flaunting his copious worldly possessions and being brainwashed by the soft pornography published in Rupert Murdoch's *Sun* newspaper.[32] Loadsamoney was a criticism of the Thatcherite vision of what an entrepreneurial working class ought to look like. Yet the joke was obviously on the tradesman too, as he wheels and deals and avoids tax to delude himself into thinking he's actually rich by the standards of those with serious financial clout and power who only hold him in contempt.[33]

Blair's storied encounter with a Sierra driver came to signify New Labour's bid to fasten upon and consolidate the political, economic and cultural changes which Enfield satirised. Perhaps more than any other occupational group, it was electricians, like the Sierra-owner Blair met, who were held to epitomise Loadsamoney attitudes among the employed as well as the self-employed. In the mid-1980s, the Electrical, Electronic, Telecommunications and Plumbing Union (EETPU) refused to encourage its members to support the miners during the pivotal year-long coal strike, reversing its position of not handling strike-breaking coal in the miners' strikes in 1972 and 1974. A decade earlier, power workers had helped to disable electricity production, which was formative in securing important concessions for the miners. In 1984–85, the union's general secretary, Eric Hammond, was an outspoken critic of the National Union of Mineworkers (NUM), standing out even in contrast with the leaders of other unions whose members also refused to take industrial action to support the miners. More than 80 per cent of EETPU members who voted supported Hammond's stance in a postal ballot.[34]

Soon after, Hammond and the EETPU became notorious for their involvement in the Wapping print strike. The electricians' union cooperated with Rupert Murdoch's News International in relocating the printing operation for the *Sun* and the company's other newspapers from Fleet Street to a new facility at the former docklands of Wapping in London's East End. Another major year-long dispute followed, and another symbolic defeat for trade unions eroded the strength of a formerly well-organised sector, effectively ending the power of the print unions in the media. Hammond subsequently wrote that he was glad to face down a hostile left-wing 'industrial mafia' by signing a single-union deal with News International.[35]

Cumulatively, the history of the *Sun* reveals an important story about the faltering power of the labour movement in newspaper ownership and media consumption as well as production. Murdoch bought the *Sun* in 1969 and shifted its politics to the right, to the point that Enfield could by the late 1980s closely associate it with working-class Conservatism. Yet when he bought it, Murdoch had taken over the remains of the old *Daily Herald*, a newspaper which had been part-owned by the Trades Union Congress (TUC). At its peak, the *Daily Herald* reached millions of readers each day during the 'forward march' of Britain's labour movement. Murdoch's successful takeover had been mounted following dwindling readership and advertising revenue. After the TUC's disinvestment in the early 1960s, the *Sun* had been launched as a racier newspaper pivoted towards a younger audience who were already less connected to the traditions of Labourism which the *Daily Herald* represented. Under Murdoch, it became Britain's best-read newspaper, reaching a circulation approaching 4 million in the 1980s and 1990s.[36] Union and Labour Party leaders faced a shifting strategic landscape as more hostile attitudes were conditioned among their own supporters in their workplaces, homes and communities. These conditions were markedly different from the relatively autonomous working-class political sentiment that had encouraged Labourism over the first half of the twentieth century.

The dwindling authority of Labourism and the dislocation of the institutional relationships which moulded the unmaking of the British working class were signified in 1988 when the EETPU was expelled from the TUC. Despite facing this disciplinary action, which placed the union outside of the only major union confederation in Britain, the EETPU continued to pursue single-union deals with inward investors from Japan, such as Toshiba and Hitachi, who were at the modernising apex of Britain's shrinking manufacturing sector.[37] While the electricians may have been marked by a notable divergence from the union mainstream, the EETPU also represented the logical conclusion of a broader change in direction. Union leaders were adapting to new industrial conditions and taking into account the shifting demands and expectations of their members.

After the miners' strike, and with the electricity industry facing privatisation, share ownership became a new point of contention which demonstrated changing alignments within and outside of the workplace. Internal documents from the electricity industry show that opinion polls in the late 1980s demonstrated most workers were interested in owning shares under privatisation.[38] Despite universal union opposition to privatisation (including from the EETPU), share ownership was a more divisive subject. For instance, John Daly, the general secretary of the National and Local Government Officers' Association (NALGO), which represented white-collar workers, confirmed in December 1988 that his union was seeking the maximum number of free shares and the most favourable price for purchase for NALGO members.[39]

Factsheets produced by electricity industry managers during the privatisation process emphasised the opportunities available to workers in liberating terms. One underlined that 'all who work in the industry should be offered a direct stake in the future, new career opportunities and freedom to manage their commercial affairs without interference from government', including share ownership.[40] Union leaders clashed over the efficacy of workers becoming shareholders at a TUC conference on 31 October 1988. These recriminations revealed the difficulties facing an increasingly disempowered and fractured trade union movement, derailing an event which was intended as a show of unity in defence of public ownership. Peter Heathfield, the general secretary of the NUM, warned of the dangers of inward investors from the South African coal industry, highlighting the deleterious impact such interests would have on the lives of the shrinking mining workforce who already faced difficult conditions: 'many of my members spend more time underground than a King Edward potato', remarked

Heathfield. The Derbyshire miners' leader also attacked share ownership as 'a contradiction in terms, giving workers with shares the impression that they had a stake in the industry when they had no control at all'.[41]

Heathfield was rebuked by Gavin Laird, the general secretary of the Amalgamated Engineering Union. Laird enjoyed the backing of other large unions in the power sector, like the TGWU, when he argued that unions ought to accept that 'share offers have proved to be popular with employees generally and that an unrealistic approach by them to this aspect of the privatisation plans could be divisive and damaging'.[42] Laird had been a member of the Communist Party of Great Britain in his youth. He was a former marine engineer who had also worked at the Singer factory in Clydebank to the west of Glasgow. Hammond had also been associated with the left of the electricians' union as a young workplace representative.[43]

Danny Carrigan was another former Clydeside Communist turned union official who was tasked with negotiating the difficulties of electricity privatisation. He had first worked as an electrician in the shipbuilding industry before later becoming a full-time union official, eventually rising to become the EETPU's national officer for electricity. In May 1990, Carrigan addressed his union's final conference of workplace delegates using the structures of the nationalised industry. He adopted a hard-headed approach, retelling the position he faced while conducting the last negotiations under the old system. Carrigan referred to the breakup of the nationalised industry as already in motion. Some union activists wanted to retain national bargaining in the old framework of a unitary sector despite the growing influence of the newly formed private generators:

> We were being berated by pickets outside who were saying, 'no end to the national agreement', 'it is one industry' and we looked around and saw that they were wearing PowerGen ties and carrying National Power bags and so on and so forth. So, you can see that vesting day has had an impact already because

> clearly the companies are trying to inject corporate identity into their companies, and they are indeed succeeding.[44]

During an interview which I recorded with him in 2022, Danny Carrigan said that he felt the workforce had been 'bought off' by government. The issuing of free shares, to either 'sell or keep', played a considerable role along with the availability of large redundancy packages for older workers who wanted them.[45] Electricity employment shrank after privatisation, while union membership and density levels in the utilities sector also plummeted. These trends were visible across the now enlarged private sector, even after accounting for the impact of recognition carrying over from formerly publicly owned industries.[46] Electricians were increasingly likely to be self-employed or to work to short-term contracts. Shareholding, private pensions and homeownership became alternative means of economic security and expressions of interest and identity. These acted as partial material and psychological compensation when union representation became weaker, and workers were no longer able to enjoy the levels of consultation and workplace collective interest they had exercised in sectors such as nationalised electricity generation.

The drawing on p. 170 depicts how the EETPU imagined a typical union member – 'Mr Average' – in 1992, just two years after electricity privatisation in England and Wales. The union concluded from a survey of its members that the typical unionised electrician was a skilled worker (accounting for around seven in ten members) and most likely a married middle-aged man with children. An article published in the EETPU newspaper, *Contact*, describing the survey results, informed readers they typically 'own [their] own home, a car and all the "mod cons"', depicted in the cartoon by the then-fashionable Walkman Mr Average's daughter is intently listening to. More than half of the survey respondents were paying a mortgage and a sizeable minority also owned shares. Most unionised electricians also had formal educational qualifications, and many were finding that 'the rewards are good for those in work'.[47]

'Mr Average', from 'Looks Familiar', *Contact*, August 1992, p. 1. Modern Records Centre, University of Warwick, records of the Electricians Trade Union (ETU), 1018/ETU/P/3/1.

One notable feature which differentiated Mr Average from Loadsamoney, aside from being a union member and therefore most likely in employment rather than self-employment, was that he was twice as likely to read the Labour-supporting *Mirror* than the Tory-leaning *Sun*. Unlike Loadsamoney, he was not depicted as a greedy isolated loner, but as a family man invested in friends and neighbours. Yet, as was typical of the 'well-qualified skilled worker' by 1992, his vote could not be taken for granted. Just 41 per cent of respondents reported that they voted Labour, with a fifth voting Tory.[48] Given that this was a survey of union members, it was hardly stirring reading for the Labour Party. In important respects, the profile matched the man from Blair's 'Sierra man' encounter: an electrician who was also middle-aged, owned a car and felt prosperous. Electricians were scattered across the UK, and they were employed in the newer industries and the booming construction sites of the South of England as well as the traditional centres of heavy industry. After suffering another defeat in 1992, New Labour tasked itself with fashioning a new story of a classless society for a class-afflicted country, appealing to the Mr and Mrs Averages.

'Class war is over'

On 28 September 1999, Prime Minister Tony Blair told Labour's annual conference that the 'class war is over'. Britain had finally been freed from 'the forces of conservatism', but these had been redefined to include the traditional left as much as the traditional right.[49] Blair in effect celebrated the unmaking of the British working class as a political force. Yet Blair's pronouncement of the end of class struggle did not mean the end of class itself. Britain was still, the prime minister conceded, blighted by 'a class-ridden and unequal society', adding that 'the majority of Britons are insecure and unsure of their future'.[50] This was the tension that begot New Labour's assessment of 1990s Britain: a hostility to class consciousness which was nevertheless underlain by a recognition of the continued powerful socioeconomic realities of class.

Blair was driven by developing an agenda that merged the worldview of the then still relatively solid Labour voters of his Sedgefield constituency in County Durham with the outlook of those aspirational Mondeo men and women who had left Labour behind further south. In 1997, Labour gained around 2 million voters on its 1992 total, polling above 13.5 million in total. The balance of support was skewed towards the constituencies which New Labour strategists had cited as crucial to achieving victory. Major Tory-to-Labour swings were visible in Greater London and in the South East of England as well as among readers of the *Sun*. Similarly, the Conservatives proportionately lost the most voters to Labour among professional and managerial employees but also suffered bigger reverses among clerical and skilled manual workers than they did with manual workers or the unemployed. It appeared that the appeal to the new Mr Average had succeeded.[51]

Before he became prime minister, Blair frequently referred to the heritage and experience of his coalfield constituents, arguing that their story was in fact a model for the New Labour which centred on ruling out a future based around serving narrowly defined class interests or mobilisations. In 1993, writing for the *Renewal* journal, which was closely associated with the 'revisionist' right of the Labour Party at the time, Blair hopefully interpreted Labour history in coalitional terms. In 1945, Blair judged, the Durham miners and Southern England had united by 'voting for a collectivist government because that government was going to do good by them'.[52] The problem was that by the 1990s the age of collectivism was over. Three years later, in his conference leader's speech, Blair outlined a more developed version of the gradual disillusionment of class politics, from which Labour could fashion a new progressive mission:

> In my own constituency, the miners in 1945 who voted Labour did so, so that their sons would not have to go down the pit and work in the conditions that they had. And in 1964 their children voted Labour because they saw the next generation's chance to

> go to university and do better than their parents had done. The true radical mission of the Labour Party, New and Old, is this: not to hold people back but to help them get on – all the people.[53]

During the same speech, Blair consciously sought to reach sceptical voters in similar terms. Eschewing Labour's identity as the 'political arm of the labour movement', he reassured the public both that 'the Labour Party today is not the political arm of anyone other than the British people' and that 'there will be no return to the 1970s'.[54] In contrast to the optimistic 1960s, the 1970s were present in Blair's version of Labour Party history only in the form of negative stereotypes. New Labour accepted the Thatcherite designation of the period as one ridden by industrial strife, economic failure and the political ills of class conflict.[55] These were not merely historical or intellectual motifs. Instead, they spoke to the agenda of accommodating market liberalisation, the concentration of wealth at the top and substantially higher levels of inequality which had taken form in Britain during the 1980s and 1990s. At the level of structural political economy, New Labour is best understood as a period of consolidation rather than significant innovation.[56]

Deeply ideological ramifications moulded the sense of what was possible or even desirable in the 1990s. Contemporary social science research reinforced assessments of political shifts driven by profound social and economic changes and the evolving expectations of voters-cum-consumers. Studies of stratification in former industrial regions of England found that class identity was waning during the 1990s and 2000s. These sentiments were accompanied by a notable widely felt mournfulness about the decline of community. Citizens sought to improve themselves, often identifying with the term 'aspirational' which entered common currency in the New Labour years. Aspiration became a meaningful concept people used to describe their own lives in a context where seemingly 'self-electing' careers and identities became a dominant experience.[57]

Blair's successor as the MP for Sedgefield, Phil Wilson, reflected in 2012 on what he saw as the misrepresentation of New Labour as an exclusively 'Islington dinner parties'–driven project, 'as if Tony Blair brought some new-fangled ideas to County Durham and told us this is what to believe'. Instead, Wilson insisted, 'globalisation, seemingly benign in so many ways, is welcomed into every home, every day, in every way' in the former Durham coalfields. Sedgefield voters worked for multinationals such as the Japanese Hitachi Trains and the Austrian Thorn Lighting, lived in bought former council houses they had built extensions for, and enjoyed increasingly varied and fancy restaurants more than working men's clubs.[58]

Wilson's observations were of a distinctively Blairite vintage. The unstoppable power of globalisation became a defining force in explanations for the declining agency of class-conscious politics, and of collectivist ambitions. Most prolifically, New Labour's favoured intellectual, sociologist Anthony Giddens, announced the 'Third Way' as the defining project of the twenty-first-century left. Giddens celebrated a 'new individualism' which centred on assertiveness and aspirations which were not confined to the selfishness of Thatcherism. He lionised the agency of empowered individuals to collaborate as well as compete in a world where conservative orthodoxies and hierarchies, including those of the traditional labour movement, were losing their social, economic and political power.[59]

Giddens loomed large over New Labour. In 1994, David Miliband, who served as a policy advisor to Blair before he himself became an MP, and subsequently a government minister, edited a volume of essays on *Reinventing the Left*. Miliband's father, the Marxist intellectual Ralph Miliband, was among the best-known theorists and critics of Labourism. David shared his father's view that Labourism was woefully insufficient for the 1990s, if from a radically opposed perspective. He underlined that 'the nation-state as a political community, the working class as a political movement, and the state as a political agency' had been swept away by 'globalisation' and atrophying centrifugal forces.[60] Alongside Giddens, one of the other contributors was Gordon Brown, the shadow chancellor. Brown praised Giddens in insisting that the 1990s was an era where 'individual aspirations are rightly greater than ever' and 'just about everyone has become a decision maker in his or her own right'. The role of 'the enabling state' lay in working with rather than against markets, prioritising efficiency, opposing monopoly power and primarily helping 'individuals' to 'have the opportunity to realize their potential to the full'.[61]

New Labour was persistently presented by its most zealous adherents as an adaptation to reality. The aftermath of the collapse of the Soviet Union, and the intellectual crisis which engulfed what remained of the left, certainly framed contemporary discourse around the 'Third Way' which came to justify the empowerment of employers, multinational capital and a highly liberalised financial sector as necessary for the greater good of society. Giddens's arguments chimed with a world-historical period where achieving significant structural reform of contemporary capitalism seemed deeply implausible. As we have seen, this discourse was also spurred by the domestic setting, following the bitter general election defeat in 1992. Giles Radice spelled out Labour's difficulties in an influential Fabian Society pamphlet, *Southern Discomfort*. Like Blair, Radice was a Labour MP in County Durham. His tract was focused on five bellwether seats Labour failed to win in the South of England: Gravesham, Harlow, Luton South, Slough and Stevenage.[62]

These areas had long been central to sociological inquiry concerned by the phenomenon of the 'affluent worker', and once again they were held to be at the apex of problematic societal shifts from a labour movement perspective.[63] Radice described the five constituencies as emblematic of larger changes in British political economy, characterised by 'suburban location, high home ownership and an above average population of white-collar and skilled manual workers'. Bluntly, he concluded that 'social change is a crucial factor in Labour's decline'. The people he spoke to were living well but crucially were not rich or from the established middle class, nor did they see themselves as such. They were instead described as 'upwardly mobile'. Male 'aspirants' were typically 'engineers, electricians, printers, salesmen, retail managers, clerks, painters and decorators and plumbers', while their wives were usually 'employed as shop assistants, typists, receptionists and hairdressers'. Crucially, this strategic constituency denied class as a meaningful political or economic agency: 'They believe that "class" no longer has much relevance to their own lives. They believe that they have "got on" by their own efforts and not with the aid of a group or class.'[64]

When Blair spoke to the aspirant southern voter, he was being pushed and advised by Philip Gould, a marketing executive turned arch New Labour moderniser. Gould's account of New Labour's electoral triumph, first published in 1998, begins with an autobiographical discussion of his own life in suburban Southern England. Far from embracing classlessness, Gould demonstrates an intricate awareness of social stratification and a powerful identification with the upwardly mobile working class:

> I learned my politics in an unexceptional suburban town where most people were neither privileged nor deprived, but nearly everybody was struggling to get by – which was not pretty and grew uglier – where people lived in unassuming council estates or in tiny semi-detached houses, where university was out of the question for most and where nearly everyone went to secondary-modern school.[65]

Gould in turn condemned what he saw as the dilettante stubbornness of the Labour Party. He exclaimed that left-wing party leader Michael Foot blamed *Sun* readers for the seismic defeat at the 1983 general election. Intellectuals and activists turned their noses up at the needs and wants of his old friends and neighbours:

> The party I love instinctively was to betray the people who lived here, its natural supporters: ordinary people with suburban

> dreams who worked hard to improve their homes and their lives; to get gradually better cars, washing machines and televisions; to go on holiday in Spain rather than Bournemouth. These people wanted sensible, moderate policies which conformed to their understanding and their daily lives.[66]

In the afterglow of the landslide 1997 general election victory which ushered in New Labour's thirteen years of government, Gould went so far as to condemn the history of the Labour Party itself. Not only was it 'too close to trade unionism; too obsessive about public ownership; too tied to myth; too rooted in its past', but Labour was in fact too marked by 'the culture and psychology of the British working class', which was combative, defensive and moulded by exploitation.[67] Blair shared this view in the late 1990s when he bemoaned the separation of 'democratic socialism and liberalism' in Britain during the early twentieth century.[68] Both Blair and Gould defined Labourism as narrow and limiting, aligning themselves with a broader rejection of working-class political representation. In the 1980s and 1990s, intellectuals such as David Marquand lamented the destruction of the 'progressive' coalition of Edwardian social reformers which had formed in the Liberal Party across class divisions.[69]

New Labour attempted to make good on the historical error of British working-class politics, using the novel means of late-twentieth-century media. Gould's combination of liberalisation and modernisation extended to Labour's means as much as its ends. He oversaw the shadow communications agency under Kinnock, and worked closely with Peter Mandelson, one of the three defining figures of the New Labour project along with Blair and his chancellor and then successor as prime minister, Gordon Brown. Mandelson's autobiography underlines the centrality of transformed means of communication, polling and centralising control of Labour's message to the tailored needs of distinct portions of the electorate. This was a transparently, even proudly, 'retail' offer, where election manifestoes may as well be one of any other tranche of consumer goods:

> I have no doubt that I would have been good at marketing breakfast food or baked beans – or even the Tories – but I could never have contemplated doing so. The tools of communication might be the same; the aim, the product and the driving political purpose were wholly different.[70]

Mandelson was revealingly cynical and honest about New Labour's approach to capital and economic power. He became notorious for having quipped in a fit of 1990s pique that 'we are intensely relaxed about people getting filthy rich as long as they pay their taxes'.[71] On a presentational level, New Labour's enthusiasm for 'Cool Britannia' celebrity kudos demonstrated the merger of media, politics and entertainment which was epitomised in the closeness between the government and the *Sun*.

Blair's urgent need to be seen as 'in vogue' was demonstrated in his maiden conference leader's speech in 1994, when he told delegates that 'switching on your computer to link up with work and education opportunities will one day be as natural as switching on your TV to watch a football match'.[72] This was a neat illustration of New Labour's preoccupations. Televised English league football was an occasional treat in the 1980s, confined to a handful of games per season.[73] It was only in 1992 that football truly entered its privatist era. Rupert Murdoch's BSkyB signed a landmark deal for over £300 million which granted his subscription channels the right to show up to sixty matches each season.[74] The sport formerly dominated by attending crowds characterised by geographical proximity to town and city grounds was now enjoyed instead by suburban television subscribers in the comfort of their own living room. A Ford Mondeo perhaps sat on the driveway complementing the satellite dish on the side of their owner-occupied house. Here was the full culmination of the shifts inaugurated by slum clearances and accelerated under Right to Buy. Even football matches were brought into line with the growing separation of work, residence and leisure, as they became increasingly removed from the communal gatherings which had sustained the spectator sport for a century.

New Labour celebrated these changes with an enthusiastic determinism. When he declared that class had ended in 1999, Blair made an appeal to Marxist phraseology to explain that his politics were merely catching up with the means of production in the cause of economic and social efficiency:

> A spectre haunts the world: technological revolution. Ten years ago, a fifteen year old probably couldn't work a computer. Now he's in danger of living on it. Over a trillion dollars traded every day in currency markets and with them the fate of nations. Global finance and communications and media. Electronic commerce. The internet. The science of genetics. Every year a new revolution scattering in its wake, security, and ways of living for millions of people. These forces of change driving the future.[75]

In 2005, Blair summarised this enduring perspective by exclaiming that he was simply an agent of history: 'I hear people say we have to stop and debate globalisation. You might as well debate whether autumn should follow summer.'[76] By claiming the mantle of historical necessity, New Labour in fact implemented a highly politicised agenda, one which aimed to accelerate the unmaking of the old collectivist and organised working class into more atomised pliant participants in the market economy. The task of New Labour was to forge the best new subjects that British society could offer to meet the challenge of the new liberalised era, using carrots and sticks alike.

Disciplining and punishing

In creating the new political, economic and social means for the age of globalisation, New Labour faced the challenge of how best to respond to the working-class constituencies facing impoverishment and evisceration through the destruction of manufacturing jobs and the proliferation of precarious employment. Gordon Brown became chancellor in 1997, having insisted that the new circumstances *empowered* labour – skilled 'human capital' – against the whims of footloose financial and industrial capital. In 1994, Brown warned that failure to embrace the globalisation agenda would mean a 'drift towards a low-wage, low investment, low skills economy'.[77] Brown had witnessed the long-running impact of industrial job losses in Scotland, centred on the experiences of mass unemployment in his Fife constituency, Dunfermline East, which bordered his hometown, Kirkcaldy. He first became an MP in 1983 after campaigning against pit and shipyard closures.[78] And yet New Labour not only sought to manage what it saw as inevitable economic change, including the ongoing haemorrhaging of industrial jobs; it also actively defended and extolled economic liberalisation and the growing dominance of the City of London over Britain's economy against calls for bailouts of manufacturing sectors such as carmaking and protections against outsourcing. Brown's prescriptions centred on making the worst effects of a low-waged and low-investment economy more palatable, along with disciplining those who did not grasp the offer.

The rewards of low-wage employment, such as they were, were increased by working tax credits. These additional benefits were significant and compensated for the relatively low level of the new minimum wage, which disappointed trade unionists. In effect, an emergent welfare system subsidised low-waged employment, which was increasingly feminised, precarious and concentrated in the service sector.[79] Defenders of New Labour's record point to the success in delivering low inflation (though this was an international trend), high growth (until the financial bubble burst in 2007–8) and a 'highly progressive' redistribution of income from the wealthy towards the poorest in society.[80] Researchers from the Institute for Fiscal Studies concluded after New Labour left office that poverty alleviation had been marked among families with children who had been the central beneficiaries of tax credits. By contrast, childless working-age people in low-waged employment had often languished and benefited the least. Most glaringly, the overall pattern of distribution was highly skewed in favour of the super-rich, meaning despite redistribution further down the income ladder, overall inequality marginally increased due to the largesse enjoyed at the very top.[81]

These outcomes tell a powerful story about the continued patterns of economic change in Britain over the late 1990s and 2000s. More than 1.5 million manufacturing jobs were lost between 1997 and 2009, as financial services and real estate became ever more dominant, and, relatedly, the geographical balance of the economy continued to tilt towards the South East of England.[82] By contrast, Fife, Durham and other former centres of heavy industry were increasingly dominated by low-waged and insecure work in call centres, supermarkets and warehouses.[83] The impact of these changes was self-reinforcing. Writing in 2011, Dan Corry, who had served as Gordon Brown's Downing Street policy chief, defended the record of 'supply side socialism', an agenda encouraging increased employment as a route out of poverty. This included the so-called New Deal, which was oriented towards the young unemployed. Blair summarised this policy and its success in 2004 as 'insisting on the responsibility to work if you could, as well as the right to help'.[84] The New Deal was funded through a one-off windfall tax on the utility industries privatised under the Tories. Here was New Labour in microcosm: accepting of the fundamental changes to Britain's economic structure instigated by Thatcher and Major, but using state means to offer some opportunities to help individuals better their position by becoming productive workers in a liberalised labour market.[85]

As its name suggested, the windfall tax was an exceptional measure. The New Labour government felt unable for most of its tenure to increase income taxes on the wealthiest. Corry reflected that Blair and Brown's governments had been spooked by 'a belief – probably well founded – that the nature of globalisation really does make capital mobile and creates certain limitations on how much one can improve regulations, forms of working and so on that add to business cost'.[86] By contrast, Corry was dismissive of Labour's historic trade union allies and their capacity to respond to the unfolding erosion of Britain's industrial base: 'Unions in general no longer had the capability or capacity to discuss intelligently industrial issues.'[87]

The ambitions for a progressive new model of British capitalism, which Brown had outlined earlier in the 1990s, were resultantly curbed. Talk of a recalibrated form of 'stakeholder capitalism' had grown in the middle of the decade following the publication of Will Hutton's book *The State We're In*. Hutton's visions appeared to be in sync with New Labour's aims, looking towards Germany and Japan's resilient industrial economies where shareholder value was not overwhelmingly dominant. In this alternative model, workers and managers cooperated to sustain innovative and more equitable enterprises.[88] Yet these hopes were dashed both by the historical intransigence of British management to sharing its workplace authority with its workforces and by the incoming government's unwillingness to pursue an agenda that questioned 'management's right to manage'.[89] Dan Corry ruefully reflected that there had been too much pride taken in how accepted New Labour was by financial and commercial interests, underpinned by the 'memory of the dark years where business was so hostile to Labour, influencing the public view of the party's economic competence'.[90] These ends also shaped the limited redistribution which Brown undertook. Technocratic measures were taken 'by stealth', threatening neither the economic nor the political interests of the globalised financial forces which now utterly dominated Britain's economy.[91]

By comparison, recalcitrant sections of the working class and those deemed further down the ladder, the lumpenised underclass, were far riper for disciplining. As early as his 1994 Labour Party conference leader's speech, Blair identified the criminality from the bottom end of the social spectrum as comparable to the threats workers faced from those at the top: 'The unemployed youngster has no right to steal your radio but let us be just as serious about catching the people in the City with an eye on your pension.'[92] Yet New Labour proved to be far less committed towards catching those at the top than the bottom, as the stark contrast between its laissez-faire approach towards financial markets and its more draconian crime and punishment agenda demonstrates. The prison population grew by two thirds between the mid-1990s and the late 2000s.[93]

Redrawing barriers between the rough and respectable was essential to defining who was and was not accepted as part of New Labour's Britain. These changes were part of a broadside which extended from anti-social behaviour orders to anti-terrorism legislation and growing hostility towards asylum seekers. Those who could or would not join the emergent affluent majority fell foul. In an increasingly disciplinarian environment marked by the demonisation of Muslim communities during the 'War on Terror', dimensions of class, race and nationality all came to undermine assumptions that Britain was becoming a more inclusive and egalitarian society.[94] The blaring sirens of the Green Goddess fire engines deployed to break the FBU strike in 2002, and the unprecedented scale of demonstrations against the Iraq War in 2003, were important indicators that New Labour was losing key components of the Labour Party's historic support base. Both these examples were strongly conditioned by opposition to the authoritarian nature of New Labour as well as the rightwards drift in policy.

Lewis Minkin, the leading historian of the Labour Party's internal workings, described Blair's 'supremacy' project as unfolding through 'a rolling coup', conditioned through domination of the party structures by 'a narrow base of committed supporters of his full political project'.[95] The violent ejection of an eighty-two-year-old delegate from the Labour Party conference in 2005 summarised these dynamics. Walter Wolfgang had first arrived in Britain as a young Jewish refugee from Nazi Germany in 1937 and was a long-standing peace activist. He was hauled out of the conference by stewards after he interrupted a speech by the foreign secretary, Jack Straw, to condemn British involvement in the invasion of Iraq. Wolfgang was then refused re-entry by police under the Terrorism Act, legislation passed by the New Labour government in 2000.[96]

A high-handed attitude towards people and organisations who could be considered allies, or at worst internal opponents within the labour movement, was a defining feature of New Labour. Approaches to the delivery of public services demonstrated similar mistrust through the philosophy of New Public Management. Under this direction, public services ought to be run based on principles governed by market logics, and where necessary simulated internal market models were constructed in place of real ones. Furthermore, unionised public sector workers were held in suspicion, as potentially nefarious 'producer' interests who were prone to the artificial creation of demand and the proliferation of jobs and functions.[97] Class tensions were stoked by these assumptions. Part of the solution was to demand 'efficiencies', as the firefighters faced, in return for any significant improvements in pay and conditions.

Ultimately, New Labour understood social progress through individual advancement within but preferably out of the working class, as exemplified by Blair's story of the evolving aspirations of his Sedgefield constituents between the 1940s and the 1990s. This left large sections of British society, particularly those broadly considered manual workers, in a denigrated position. Industrial action by a quite different group of workers revealed the profound contradictions at the heart of the 'human capital' agenda. In the spring of 2004, 5,000 Scottish nursery nurses went on an all-out strike against their local authority employers. This dispute was also a defining moment for the Labour-led Scottish Executive, the new government of the devolved Parliament first formed just five years before. The strike was the largest all-out dispute in Scotland for twenty years, since the 1984–85 miners' strike. Workers were angry about the meagre pay offers that they received despite the increasing demands which were being placed on them. They marshalled the case for the importance of childcare provision which New Labour administrations in London and Edinburgh proudly associated with their achievements in government. One Glasgow striker attended a demonstration with a homemade placard which read 'we don't just change nappies, we change lives'. Another nursery nurse who had been working in the sector for sixteen years when the dispute began told researchers Gerry Mooney and Patricia McCafferty that she worked in a 'professional service' which was increasingly developing 'a social work edge'.[98]

Early-years workers were expected to professionalise but not to demand commensurate improvements to their status and wages. Herein lay the tension between New Labour's promise to improve opportunities for women workers and its pledges to facilitate entry into the labour market by increasing childcare provision. The nursery strikers were in the relatively secure and well-paid section of the larger early-years workforce, which was increasingly characterised by a proliferation of less well-unionised private providers who were nonetheless sustained by public sector procurement.[99] Such workers were themselves likely beneficiaries of child tax credits, signifying the fragility of the improvements which New Labour offered along with the very real barriers to the classless and meritocratic society which supposedly characterised 1990s and 2000s Britain.[100]

'Chavs'

Revealingly, cultural depictions of the working class in New Labour Britain became defined by hostility and othering through their distance from the non-manual socially mobile norm. In *The Office*, one of the few contemporary popular television programmes to centre on a workplace, even the lowliest of the white-collar staff at a Slough paper merchants exhibit a sense of superiority towards the warehouse staff. The manual workers literally work beneath their clerical colleagues. They have the hallmarks of a crude culture which stems from their tougher, more physical jobs and entirely male workgroup. Warehouse workers also ration their effort and resist doing too much of what the softer office workers with managerial authority tell them to.[101] In a comical form, these depictions demonstrated the survival of manual and non-manual divisions in British views of class even in a society where the old forms of manual working-class power (real or imaginary) no longer posed a risk to middle-class sensibilities.

An entirely nastier and less sympathetic representation of the impoverished working class (or 'underclass') became the face of another 2000s BBC production. Vicky Pollard was a satire of the threatening tracksuit-wearing 'chav' in the flagship *Little Britain* sketch show which ran during the late Blair years, from 2003 to 2006. The Bristolian Pollard was portrayed variously as a pregnant teenager, a feckless mother and a malignant criminal whose very presence damaged the urban environments she inhabited. This is how she was described on the show's official website:

> Vicky Pollard is your common-or-garden teenage delinquent, the sort you can see hanging around any number of off licences in Britain, trying to persuade people going inside to buy them ten fags and a bottle of White Lightning.
>
> Whether nicking stuff from the supermarket or swapping her baby for a Westlife CD, Vicky reacts to any accusation with indignant outrage, while filling you in on 'this fing wot you know nuffin about'.[102]

Pollard was portrayed as a degenerate subject who needs disciplining, and a blight on social and economic progress. In a period where older meanings of working-class identity were falling into use as parts of biography and family histories rather than describing contemporary circumstances, Pollard held pernicious power. Depictions of the rougher-edged, less respectable working class gained a distinctly venomous quality in the 2000s.[103] They contrast with earlier more sympathetic comedic representations of the people who came to be labelled the underclass in the New Labour period. In the BBC's long-running comedy series *Only Fools and Horses*, which spanned seven series between 1981 and 1991, viewers were presented with the much more rounded lead character of Derek Edward Trotter – 'Del Boy' – the council flat tenant, small-time criminal and aspiring market trader who is constantly on the make. Unlike Pollard, Trotter is fundamentally empathetic as he tries to navigate a difficult changing world along with his brother, Rodney. Del Boy is ultimately just trying to get ahead in a shifting environment where he hopes his budding entrepreneurialism will eventually offer the Trotters the same rewards and living standards others managed to grab for themselves in Thatcher's Britain.[104]

Growing material differences were communicated through status divisions marked by the proliferation of consumption in an era when workers in full-time jobs generally experienced some extent of improvement in living standards. Distinctions between those languishing in the depths of exclusion and poverty and others hopefully heading towards middle-class stability and affluence were amplified financially by the growth of credit. While real-wage growth was comparatively limited, the availability of cheaper imported goods across a widening range of electronics and budget airline travel made workers and their families feel increasingly materially enriched. From Pizza Express to Disneyland, a hint of exclusiveness and affluence was held out to more and more people. Retail and culinary opportunities were backed up by the growth of consumer credit offers on items ranging from package holidays to cars to sofas.[105] Along with trips to retail parks and more flights abroad, rising house prices helped to reinforce this sense of new enrichment and opportunity, as detailed in the previous chapter.

New Labour was a response to the context of the late 1980s and 1990s, where the unmaking of the British working class had been considerably accelerated through the systemic weakening of key bastions of support. Trade union organisation, nationalised industries and council housing had all been diminished in the previous two decades. Within the Labour Party, the ascendency of New Labour was the culmination of a knowing compromise that ushered in major ideological changes. Fundamentally, these shifts rightwards centred on celebrating and advancing the prevailing political and economic dogma. On the one hand, this involved resituating formerly social-democratic politics to face the globalised liberal market economy. On the other hand, it also meant embracing the view that class-based and significantly redistributive politics, particularly at the level of power and wealth, were no longer plausible or desirable.

New Labour was alert to the nature of class in Britain and its retained sociological importance, as Philip Gould's carefully positioned analysis of his own upbringing in aspiring suburbia demonstrates. Labour's changing programme and presentation were justified based on a caricature of the party's previously limited appeal to a very narrow range of unionised, class-conscious manual workers. Within the context of the relatively stable economic conditions of the 1990s and 2000s, New Labour could reap electoral rewards and afford to use new state benefits to finance supplements for lower-paid workers, making work pay to some extent even where the benefits of security and unionisation were increasingly less likely to be available.

Similarly, the limited attempts to reform the British state represented difficult compromises which were most visible in devolution and the loosening of the Union in Scotland. These changes were confirmations of another important rift in the British working class which had been consolidated by electoral distinctions in the 1980s. It was further encouraged by the New Labour pivot towards what advisors such as Gould saw as the aspirations of South of England voters. While New Labour was often presented as an adaptation to changing circumstances, it should in fact be understood as a formative act of political agency. New Labour consolidated the defeat of collectivism and redistribution along with reinforcing the diminished faith in labour movement organisation which had accumulated during the 1980s and early 1990s. Growing dissatisfaction with New Labour was already apparent by the mid-2000s. Labour polled almost 4 million fewer votes in the 2005 general election than it did in 1997. Its working-class vote fell markedly, with support recorded as declining by a fifth among 'C2' skilled manual voters and a sixth of 'DE' unskilled manual voters in election studies by Ipsos.[106] Decreasing voter turnout and political disengagement only exacerbated these trends.

Many of those who had enjoyed relative stability and prosperity in the 1990s and 2000s saw it come crashing down after Britain was plunged into financial crisis over 2007 and 2008. The increasingly immaterial economy which New Labour had built left Britain uniquely exposed to the worst impacts of the crash. Reliance on international capital flows, the size of the financial sector and consumer indebtedness all became major barriers to recovery. In the meantime, New Labour could not even defend its own record. Labour was already struggling to marshal support before Brown's reputation for prudence and efficiency evaporated and the incoming Conservative–Liberal Democrat coalition swept away tax credits. The public sector was subject to a major attack, especially through the shrinkage of local government services and employment. These cuts left the poorest ever more vulnerable and dependent on the charity of food banks, which grew from a tiny presence to a major initiative sustaining millions of people where the state was failing them across the UK.[107] Meanwhile, the expectations of growing living standards which had buoyed Mondeo Man evaporated in a decade and a half characterised by stagnation. Political and economic tensions were clearly back on Britain's agenda by the late 2000s and into the 2010s, but New Labour had significantly weakened the labour movement in both its organisational and ideological capacity, even while it leant into authoritarianism. Forces on the right responded to the unmaking of Britain's economic, political and cultural working-class presence. They supplied an exclusionary combination of race and nationhood along with their own readings of class.

6

The White Working Class: 'British Jobs for British Workers'

Charles Swift was a formative figure in the development of Peterborough New Town during the 1960s and 1970s. With Swift as leader of the Labour council, Peterborough was a growing hive of young, go-getting people keen to better themselves and take advantage of Eastern England's booming economy. Peterborough was to be a town open to all who were willing to work and live respectably, enjoying the benefits of expanding car and home ownership. Swift opposed the racism instigated by the fascist National Front after his town welcomed Ugandan Asian refugees during the early 1970s, receiving death threats for making his stand.

Three and a half decades later, things had changed. Swift was still a councillor, but he no longer sat with the Labour group, and now he was leading protests against immigration to Peterborough, primarily from Poland and other Eastern European nations which had joined the European Union in 2004. In 2008, Swift appeared on a BBC documentary, *The Poles Are Coming!*, presented by Tim Samuels. Swift showed a camera crew around Lincoln Road, the main street in his ward, revealing the conditions of the overcrowded homes which the incoming Eastern European migrants were living in. He then pointed to houses marred by fly-tipping and gardens overflowing with rubbish, informing Samuels that 'these are all full of immigrants and people that have come'. While Swift blamed landlords, who he called exploitative 'speculators', the councillor also had a stern message for Gordon Brown's Labour government on the views of his constituents: 'They repeatedly say to you "enough is enough Charles. We've had enough of it."'[1]

In Peterborough, objections to New Labour's immigration policies combined socioeconomic discontent and nativist resentment. Swift was profiled in Samuels's documentary as a representative of a larger national trend held to be particularly visible in previously typically Labour-voting parts of England. Another Peterborough resident, Margaret Selway, was depicted as exemplifying these frustrations. The eighty-four-year-old fan of detective novels moved to Peterborough from London in the 1980s. 'I like juicy murders' is one of the quirky lines Margaret hits out with, but she did not like the changes on her doorstep: 'If I walk along, you don't see anyone that you know ... The English people all seem to be moving away ... We've got too much of an influx of them. I really do feel a foreigner in my own country.'[2]

Samuels's documentary was part of a larger political-cultural project of the 2000s which centred on portraying a disaffected white working class as the crucial protagonist in British society. While race as defined by skin colour was centrally important to the barriers of belonging implied by whiteness, it was not the only determining factor. Crucial overlaps of nationality and perceptions of cultural, ethnic and religious differences created a potent mix through which to demarcate a native British population from black and Asian Commonwealth migrants and their second- and third-generation descendants, as well as immigrants from Eastern Europe. Publicity for the BBC's 'White Season', which was broadcast in the spring of 2008, claimed:

> The White Season features a series of films that shine the spotlight on the white working-class in Britain today. It examines why some feel increasingly marginalised and explores possible reasons behind the rise in popularity of far-right politics in some sections of this community.[3]

The White Season was part of a larger trend in public discussion. A Google Ngram of British English publications reveals that use of the term 'white working class' approximately doubled in frequency between the mid-1990s and 2008. By contrast, discussion of the working class itself declined in frequency by around a quarter.[4] So while class itself was increasingly absent from public discourse, where class was invoked, it tended to be racialised.[5]

Race was the defining character of the white British working class, with class as the subordinate feature often defined in terms of poverty and ignorance to explain or excuse prejudice. Dilapidated council estates, tough city neighbourhoods or the rundown high streets of hard-up industrial and seaside towns were often closely associated with this constituency. The white working class was defined as having failed to meet the economic and cultural requirements of a globalising society. These were reactionary and backward elements who either could not or would not equip themselves to take part in a changing country or, put more simply, the ever-present 'great unwashed'.[6]

Marc Isaacs's film *All White in Barking* was another White Season documentary. It profiled tensions in outer East London. Isaacs filmed long-standing white residents discussing their objections to the smells of strange cooking brought by immigrants and showed the last trading days of a traditional butcher's before it closed down. In another scene, a married couple contemplated whether they would refuse to eat the food they were offered by their new Nigerian neighbours after accepting their invitation to a dinner party.[7] The reality of British cosmopolitanism was, in fact, disproportionately working-class across the twentieth and early twenty-first centuries, given the trajectories of immigration and population changes.[8] Middle-class viewers were nonetheless given the opportunity to affirm their own sense of accomplishment by drawing a contrast with those who had failed to make the grade.

A more politicised sense of the white working class as a dangerous residuum with the potential for political and social disorder was also present in Isaacs's film in the form of Dave, who viewers see canvassing for the far-right British National Party (BNP). In 2006, the BNP had won twelve councillors on Barking and Dagenham council, forming the main opposition to the Labour municipal administration.[9] Not long after *All White in Barking* was broadcast, the BNP's council group leader in Barking and Dagenham, Richard Barnbrook, was also elected to the Greater London Assembly, polling over 130,000 votes.[10] The next year, the BNP reached the pinnacle of its electoral success when party leader, Nick Griffin, and Andrew Brons were elected to the European Parliament as representatives for the North West of England and Yorkshire and the Humber respectively.[11] These successes consolidated the view that a far-right, racist and anti-immigrant current in British politics primarily emanated from predominantly Labour-voting constituencies suffering from the long-term impacts of factory and mine closures.

Barking and Dagenham loomed large in those depictions of 'white working-class' places, along with towns in the North of England. Sociologist Stephen Ashe completed a detailed study of Barking and Dagenham when the BNP made its electoral breakthrough. He concluded both that 'local history and the contours of place' were central to understanding the BNP's successes in mobilising significant minorities of the electorate but also in its ultimate political failure. Moreover, the designation of a place as of the 'white working class' was itself an act of historical and political construction. While Barking and Dagenham had long been considered a primarily white *and* working-class locality, its designation as a 'white working-class' one, with race coming first and class second, was more recent and involved the construction of a new sense of the locality and its residents. This designation combined an emphasis on racially and nationally conscious whiteness with a class descriptor which was primarily a filter for racialised resentment.[12] James Rhodes concluded from his study of the BNP's 2000s breakthrough in Burnley, a former cotton town in Lancashire, that the term white working class only tended to obscure class parameters in favour of racial and ethnic identity: 'The "whiteness" of the "white working class" continues to point to "race" as the primary basis of social identification, albeit with class now recognised as an additional organising dimension.'[13]

An angry fusion of national, racial and workplace politics was given a renewed prominence when hundreds of construction workers walked out on a wildcat strike at Lindsey oil refinery in Lincolnshire towards the end of January 2009. Lindsey is around a hundred miles to the north of Peterborough. It lies within the constituency which elected Andrew Brons to Brussels later in the year. The Lindsey strike was widely presented as an example of a backlash against immigration and the policies of the Labour government by white British workers in the context of rising unemployment following the onset of recession after the financial crash in autumn 2008. Press coverage of the dispute, which attracted large-scale illegal solidarity action among construction workers at other refineries and power station sites, framed the strikers as animated by demands for 'British jobs for British workers'. This was a slogan which the Labour Prime Minister Gordon Brown had taken up in 2007, but it was also used by the BNP. Reporting was accompanied by pictures of workers waving Union Jacks and St George's Cross flags.[14] The dispute was motivated by opposition to an Italian subcontracting firm, IREM, employing Italian and Portuguese workers on conditions below the agreed terms of the mechanical engineering construction sector. It was reported by BBC News in simpler terms, as a 'mass walkout over foreign labour'.[15] Members of the strike committee who led the Lindsey workers later distanced themselves from this reporting, underlining that they were engaged in a stoppage over conditions and fair access to jobs. The strikers had themselves included immigrant workers from Eastern Europe.[16]

Perspectives on the politics of the white working class were constructed from above, even where they received assent and garnered some mobilisation from below. Commentary on the Lindsey dispute was written less than a year after the fortieth anniversary of Enoch Powell's 'Rivers of Blood' speech, which had formed part of the pretext for the BBC's White Season. Powell's inflammatory April 1968 address to Conservative activists gathered at the Midlands Hotel in Birmingham consolidated an oppositional populist and racist politics centred on the supposed threat that growing Caribbean and Asian populations presented to the white British majority.[17] His demands for the repatriation of immigrants created a crucial opening for the neo-Nazi National Front, but it has also left an indelible mark on the Tory Party and on Labour.[18] Labour Prime Minister Keir Starmer echoed Powell as part of an immigration crackdown in May 2025 when he warned of Britain becoming an 'island of strangers'.[19]

In another of the White Season programmes, the documentary *Sign Zones: Rivers of Blood*, which was directed by Ashley Gething and written by Denys Blakeway, Powell's speech was singled out as a formative – and perhaps prophetic – moment in British political history. The narrator states that, forty years on, 'many are now asking, was not Enoch Powell right to predict disaster in his Rivers of Blood speech?'[20] Popular responses to Powell are discussed in terms of the support he received from 'white working people, traditionally Labour supporters', singling out images of London dockers and meat porters from Smithfield market who took strike action to support Powell. Archived footage includes a porter in white overalls declaring in highly emotive wartime terms that 'this race relations issue goes well beyond the field of politics and trade union matters. This is an issue of national importance. As important to us as Dunkirk.' Another extract from news reporting includes an interview with a man from Powell's Wolverhampton constituency in the West Midlands who concurred, stating that for 'the first time we've had someone speak up for what the working-class people think is right'.[21] Powell began his speech by declaring that he was speaking on behalf of concerned voters who had spoken to or corresponded with him. He claimed that his infamous line that 'in this country in fifteen or twenty years' time the black man will have the whip hand over the white man' were the words of 'a constituent, a middle-aged, quite ordinary working man employed in one of our nationalised industries'.[22] Yet Powell's speech was clearly an instance of a patrician Conservative claiming to speak for white plebeian interests. The title of the Rivers of Blood speech, taken from the Roman poet Virgil, was less ambiguously the work of the former classics professor and brigadier who now championed the British people against the liberal integrationist elite.

Since Powell, there has been a thread of far-right attempts to speak for a resentful British white working class across more than half a century. Barriers between the far right and the political mainstream have repeatedly been transgressed. Workplaces as well as the streets and housing estates have been crucial battlegrounds, along with the evolving political positions of the Labour Party and trade unions. The late 2000s was a crucial period. First, the Lindsey oil refinery strike was a rare instance of successful militant and even illegal union action which garnered an extent of tabloid sympathy on the grounds of its allegedly anti-immigrant stance. Second, the BNP breakthrough was marked by the party's claim that it represented an overlooked white constituency dissatisfied with the Labour Party. These advances were contextualised by New Labour's hostility towards the dangerous so-called 'underclass' who could not or would not take advantage of new economic opportunities, as discussed in the previous chapter. It was this lumpen constituency, whose political expressions were flag-waving nationalism and boneheaded racism, which were held to explain the electoral advances of the BNP.

The reality was a more complex picture of both class relations and support for the far right. Nonetheless, in the 2010s and 2020s, the perceived need to placate an aggrieved white working class came to hold a growing grip on British politics. This pivot was anchored in the form of the coalition which delivered Brexit but also in the rising electoral popularity of Nigel Farage's various electoral vehicles: the United Kingdom

Independence Party (UKIP), the Brexit Party and most recently Reform UK. While claims to represent a popular or working-class constituency were central to these challenges, they were also becoming ever more distant from a politics centred on mobilising class-based material interests.

From Powell to the BNP

Powell popularised a form of race politics centred on competition for resources as well as the looming threat he saw the growing black and Asian population posing to social order in Britain. His claim to speak on behalf of 'the working man' was accompanied by a disavowal of 'archbishops who live in palaces, faring delicately with the bedclothes pulled right up over their heads'. It was working-class people who experienced the influx of migrant families and competition for council houses, bore the brunt of growing hospital waiting lists and experienced wage compression or competition for manual jobs.[23] Secret Service reports compiled by MI5 on the strikes which followed Powell's sacking from the shadow cabinet underline that political activists were present in organising the walkouts. When strikers from the West India Dock rallied outside Parliament on 23 April 1968, their leaders included Harry Pearman, who was a Labour Party member but had previously been involved with the hardline anti-Communist group Moral Re-Armament. Communist Party members among the dockers had tried and failed to discourage the West India workers from striking.[24] The next day, the organisers of the protest by striking Smithfield market meat porters included Danny Harmston, who stood at the head of 'two orderly groups' of 300 porters. Harmston was a known fascist, having stood as a member of Oswald Mosley's Union Movement party in the South West Islington constituency at the 1966 general election, winning 816 votes.[25] The intelligence services detected minimal 'organised political action behind the demonstration', putting Harmston's role down to opportunism.[26]

This industrial action revealed, in the words of labour

historian Fred Lindop, 'no sense of a contradiction in calling on the tradition of workers' solidarity to exclude other workers on the basis of their skin colour or culture'. In Lindop's view, the striking dockers saw themselves as defending Powell's right to 'free speech' following his sacking from the Tory front bench, but they were also invoking a 'clannish' politics centred on their almost entirely white workplaces and adjacent communities in London's East End. As they rallied outside Westminster, the dockers harassed Ian Mikardo, the left-wing Labour MP for Poplar. Earlier in the year, the dockers' committee for London and the South East region of the Transport and General Workers' Union (TGWU) had also passed policy calling for immigration controls.[27]

The racist Cockney was a fixture of British television in the late 1960s through the character of Alf Garnett in Johnny Speight's BBC sitcom, *Till Death Do Us Part*. Garnett was portrayed by Warren Mitchell as a deeply reactionary patriarch who admired Powell and supported repatriating immigrants. His racist rants against what he saw as the growing, threatening presence of non-white people in London were combined with a deep unease about increasing cultural liberalism. Like the dockers who jeered at Mikardo, Garnett also had little time for socialists, whom he saw as both lazy and dangerously misguided. Garnett's influence was confined in the show to the burden he imposed on his long-suffering wife, Else, and daughter, Rita, along with her boyfriend, Mike, a left-wing Liverpudlian who bore the brunt of Alf's living-room rants.[28]

Strikes in support of Powell were not confined to London and extended to Powell's local base in the Midlands. Nor were they limited to workplaces marked by the presence of fascist activists. There were also stoppages by tanker drivers in West Bromwich and gas plant builders in Derbyshire. Shirin Hirsch's detailed history of the response to Powell in the West Midlands records that 1,000 workers at the Norton Villiers works in Wolverhampton finished early in a protest in support of Powell but then worked later the next day to avoid damaging production. Similar patterns were visible elsewhere, including at GKN in Bradley, Bilston, where the overwhelming majority of the 1,200 workers signed a petition. Workers at the HP Sauce factory in Birmingham left placards at the plant in support of Powell. As Hirsch highlights, these actions did not go unopposed. Asian and black workers and their communities organised through the Indian Workers' Association and the Black People's Alliance, the latter of which was formed in response to the displays of racism Powell inspired. Local Labour MPs Renée Short, who represented Wolverhampton North East, and Bob Edwards, the member for Bilston, who was also the general secretary of the Chemical Workers' Union, were vocal opponents of Powell. This level of committed opposition was, however, exceptional within the labour movement.[29]

Stoppages in support of Powell were relatively unusual invocations of worker mobilisation for an explicitly racist and politicised aim attached to a national figure. They do, however, fit into a wider pattern of racism in British workplaces and trade union history. These trends were marked in some of the areas that the BNP later experienced relative success in the 2000s. For instance, in the 1970s and 1980s there was an active National Front presence in Barking and Dagenham which overlapped with the large Ford factory in Dagenham, the area's main industrial employer. Stephen Ashe records that fascist activists, including National Front member Tony Lecomber, worked at Ford and that another far-right activist even became a TGWU steward at the plant. In 1999, a major compensation claim was won by Asian and black workers who had been excluded from employment in the truck fleet. Ford also apologised to another Asian worker, Sukhjit Parmar, following years of workplace racism and a violent assault. Following this, there was a walkout by white workers after an Asian worker punched a foreman.[30]

The 1999 payout came just three years after an apology by Ford for excluding black Dagenham workers from a picture for a company marketing poster in 1991. An 'ethnic-cleansed' version of the poster was produced for the 'everything we do is driven by you' advertising campaign. In 1996, Bill Morris, the general secretary of the TGWU, condemned the decision following the awarding of compensation, underlining that in the view of his union 'this is an appalling situation which reveals the depths of racist attitudes in our society'.[31] Morris was a first-generation Jamaican immigrant and the first black general secretary of a British trade union. He became involved in trade unionism while working as a municipal bus conductor in Wolverhampton, motivated by opposition to racism in the workplace but also by opposing discrimination within the labour movement.[32] The ascent of Morris to leadership of the TGWU was part of a lasting change in British trade unionism. By the 2020s, black workers were more likely to be members of a trade union than white workers, within a much-changed and smaller labour movement which primarily organised within public services.[33]

These shifts evolved over the prior half century through the recomposition of an increasingly multicultural working class. As discussed in chapter 2, the National Front's presence in West London was a major factor in perceptions of public order and disorder which contextualised the policing of the Grunwick dispute, following street battles between fascists and anti-racist protesters led by Asian youth in nearby Southall. These mobilisations came after a young Sikh man, Gurdip Singh Chaggar, was killed by racists in 1976. Southall had a longer history of far-right organising which stretched back into the previous decade when fascists had enjoyed some electoral success in opposing house sales to immigrant families and driving up concern over the changing racial makeup of school rolls.[34] A report on another landmark industrial dispute involving black and Asian women workers, the nearby strike for equal pay at Trico, also underlined the presence of the National Front. Gail Turner, writing for *Rank and File Contact*, a newssheet produced by left-wing activists in the electricians' union, reported that 'an electrician, who has now left the firm, a member of the National Front, made particular efforts to abuse the pickets' after crossing official picket lines mounted by the engineering union. This male worker was nominally motivated on gender rather than racial grounds, insisting that 'they felt there was no case for equal pay'.[35]

Conversely, trade union activism was also an important ground for challenging workplace racism. Jack Saunders' detailed history of workshop-level union organising in British car factories records that a 'very visible' black and South Asian presence among union representatives at Ford Dagenham contributed to a one-day strike against racist violence in the late 1970s along with later initiatives against workplace racism and sexism. Even around the peak of Powell's influence a decade earlier, Caribbean labourers had instituted an overtime ban at the Austin East Works in Birmingham. These mobilisations countered the trend of white shop stewards becoming involved in promoting patterns of racial discrimination and exclusion.[36]

Yet the structural nature of discrimination at Dagenham, inherent in Ford's payouts in 1996 and 1999, demonstrates the pervasive nature of racism, which cannot be confined to the violence of committed fascists alone. Similar practices were visible in other sectors, including in the Midlands. The iron-founding industry was marked by expanding production in the decades after the Second World War, driven in part by increasing demand for car parts. Indian workers came to swell the bottom rungs of the workforce as employers sought recruits to the lowest-paid and least-prestigious positions. They were confined to labouring jobs and often given segregated inferior facilities such as bathrooms, along with lower wages, piece rates and bonus or productivity payments. In the 1950s, unions, especially those which represented skilled workers, settled on a strategy of exclusion. This shifted as Indian workers responded by organising collectively and employing militancy, striking when shop stewards were dismissed at plants such as Dartmouth Auto Castings in Smethwick in 1959 and at Qualcast in Derby during 1965.[37]

A decade after Bill Morris found black workers were suffering from racial discrimination on the municipally owned buses in Wolverhampton, Sikh workers mobilised for their right to wear the turban as part of their uniforms. Powell's 1968 speech identified this organising with the looming threat of 'communalism'.[38] The ban was lifted the next year following a campaign led by Sikh bus workers with support from their community along with the Indian Workers' Association and Renée Short, who were noted local opponents of Enoch Powell. Conversely, the TGWU was largely absent and unsupportive while Powell continued to mobilise opposition.[39] When Powell's supporters rallied in Dudley after the Rivers of Blood speech, they booed and hissed at a black bus conductor. On 21 April 1968, the day after the speech, 800 members of the North Wolverhampton Working Men's Club also voted to retain a 'colour bar' policy. Frank Smith, who had previously served as the Labour Mayor of Wolverhampton, abstained on a second vote.[40] This pattern represented the narrowing of conceptions of British nationality on racial grounds which was consolidated in legislation passed by Conservative and Labour governments. The Commonwealth Immigrants Act 1968 restricted immigration rights to those who held a prior 'substantial connection' to Britain through family and birth. In effect this was a policy that debarred immigrants from the Caribbean, Africa and the Indian subcontinent while generally retaining freedom of movement for white Commonwealth citizens.[41]

Panics around waves of Indians arriving to Britain as refugees having been expelled from Kenya and Uganda were nevertheless seized upon by Powell and the National Front, but they only represented the exception to a pattern of diminishing immigration from the Commonwealth.[42] Growing support for the far right was particularly visible within the Pennine textile areas of Yorkshire and Lancashire when they were suffering from industrial depression in the early 1970s. National Front supporters advocated economic protectionism for textile interests, which they presented as threatened by both Jewish financiers and Asian immigrants. Jim Merrick, a dyer and Tory activist, founded the Yorkshire Campaign to Stop Immigration. At the Rochdale by-election in 1972, the year of hysteria about Ugandan Asian immigration, Merrick won 4,000 votes. Four years later, the National Front won two council seats in Blackburn and took almost a third of the vote across six wards.[43]

National Front electoral success was only ever fleeting. The Front's violent street presence was, however, a major threat faced by black and Asian communities. Sociological studies of the National Front suggest a party which had 'proletarian elements' within its ranks, numbering perhaps in the tens of thousands at their peak.[44] These included generally younger men who tended to be employed or self-employed as skilled workers.[45] Young members of the National Front such as Nick Griffin and his close ally Joe Pearce, took on a 'Strasserite' orientation to their activities, inspired by the 'left-wing' or 'anti-capitalist' strain of German National Socialism which had been led by Gregor Strasser. Graham Macklin points to younger men with few formal educational qualifications as having been central to the National Front, including through its integration with right-wing football hooligans in English cities. Yet while Pearce was a fascist from Barking who had led protests against 'red teachers', Griffin was a Cambridge law graduate whose father, Edgar, was a business owner and a Tory councillor.[46]

Tom Nairn, the Scottish New Left intellectual, understood that Powell was defined by his combination of anti-European, anti-imperial and racist British nationalism along with his defence of a capitalist market economy. Powell stood as a patrician defender of property and order, appealing 'to an even wider stratum of discontented middle-class and lower-middle-class natives'.[47] His establishment standing assisted Powell to legitimate a programme which built from cross-party support for immigration controls towards a more assertive and race-conscious authoritarian nationalism. Powell's call for a stable society unthreatened by challenges from alien migrants, greedy trade unionists, socialist radicals or the liberal establishment ultimately strongly influenced the politics of Thatcherism. The Conservative general election victory in 1979 legitimated core aspects of Powell's agenda, not in the guise of a working-class insurgency but on the back of a much more decisively middle-class orientation. Thatcher's Tories appealed to populism on the basis of nationhood and race but also through asserting the rights of management in no-nonsense terms as represented by the anti–trade union National Association for Freedom's campaign in support of the bosses at Grunwick explored in chapter 2. Under Thatcher, the Conservatives promised to restore domestic order and to further limit immigration. In 1978, as leader of the opposition, Thatcher affirmed that 'people are really rather afraid that this country might be rather swamped by people with a different culture'.[48] She was appealing to the Tory base as much as disaffected Labour voters. One of her ministers, Michael Heseltine, recalled in 2008 that Powell's speech had animated his constituents in true blue Devon as much as it had the West Midlands and London.[49]

'British jobs for British workers'

Projections of a nationalist working class aggrieved by the growing presence of foreigners were a significant feature of British politics the following year, when the unofficial strike action commenced at Lindsey oil refinery. The construction workers' objections exposed the limitations of Britain's liberalised labour laws after more than a decade of Labour government. Posted Worker Directives for migrant workers only secured legal minimums, meaning that the National Agreement for the Engineering Construction Industry (NAECI), known in the sector as the 'Blue Book', was not judged legally enforceable. Lindsey was only one of several building sites with similar tensions surrounding subcontractors using workforces exclusively recruited from Southern and Eastern Europe.[50]

Solidarity strikes were launched soon after at large energy sites including other refineries and power stations which cumulatively involved thousands of workers in England, Scotland, Wales and Northern Ireland.[51] Building workers were seen waving Union Jacks, calling for 'British jobs for British workers' and opposing the presence of foreign workers who were taking mechanical engineering construction jobs while British workers signed on the dole in the depths of the recession after the 2008 crash.[52] One worker was quoted by BBC News as saying, 'All we want is for Gordon Brown to fulfil his promise. He said British jobs for British workers.'[53] Phil Whitehurst, a plater and GMB trade unionist in his fifties, welcomed the pressure on the prime minister, telling the tabloid *Daily Star*, 'We have got Gordon Brown worried.' Whitehurst also thanked the *Star* for supporting workers engaged in an illegal industrial dispute.[54] It was highly exceptional for a British newspaper associated with the political right to adopt this position, but evidently the nationalist dynamics trumped any misgivings the *Star* may have felt over the class or trade union sentiment behind the strike in its reporting.

Brown was attending a meeting in Davos, Switzerland, when the strike began. There was a potent symbolism in the juxtaposition between the picket lines at Lindsey and the prime minister in dialogue with the World Economic Forum, attempting to rescue the global economy and preserve flows of commerce, investment and labour. He was quoted as saying, though, that he 'understood' the grievances felt by workers in difficult economic circumstances. Pat McFadden, Brown's employment minister, was somewhat more abrasive, condemning calls for 'protectionism' and defending the merits of 'international trade'.[55] McFadden also condemned irresponsible 'unofficial industrial action' in Parliament. Yet there was disquiet in the chamber on the government's benches. Austin Mitchell, the Labour MP for Greater Grimsby, not far from Lindsey, spoke in support of the strikers' grievances, arguing:

> [in considering] all the other jobs that will come into being with the contract for the closure and reconstruction of the Lindsey oil refinery, preference should be given to British workers, and to

> local workers, in an area of high unemployment where the skills are available.[56]

In a later debate, Shona McIsaac, the member for the Cleethorpes constituency, which included the refinery site, referred to

> a sense of injustice and anger on the part of unemployed construction engineering workers who saw people being brought in from Italy. They felt that they had the skills and the training to do the jobs on that construction project at the refinery, and what was happening seemed unfair to them.[57]

These terms of debate were given further succour in Parliament by comments from members who were uncomfortable about what they saw as the nationalist or racist direction of the strikes. Jeremy Corbyn, the Labour MP for Islington North, discussed 'some very nasty undertones to the discussions surrounding the disputes', underlining the danger of 'some turning against others on the basis of their passports or ethnicity'. Russell Brown, the Labour MP for Dumfries and Galloway, articulated a similar sentiment by evoking the danger of a repeat of the fascism which had taken place in Europe between the two World Wars. Brown warned trade unionists and workers not to 'play into the hands of and pander to the extreme right in any country'.[58] The concerns of Corbyn and Brown were likely heightened by reports of the BNP's support for and involvement in the dispute. The BNP announced its 'solidarity with the construction lads' soon after the walkout began.[59]

In 2009, David Owens was a recently elected BNP councillor in Boston, around fifty miles to the south of Lindsey. He was a self-employed construction worker himself, running his own bathroom-fitting firm. Owens told the *Financial Times* that the workplace conflicts appeared tailor-made for his far-right party:

> This situation is building support for us. The three main parties agree with handing control over immigration and the labour

market to Europe. We are the only party that is committed to change the law by taking us out of the EU.[60]

Two days after the walkouts began at Lindsey on 29 January, the *Guardian* reported that the BNP had sent 'a team of supporters' to join the pickets.[61] Tony Woodley, the joint general secretary of Unite, whose members were heavily involved in the walkouts, was also quoted as having alleged that 'the BNP are seriously and sizably involved, infiltrating meetings and posing as organisers'.[62] A report in the Trotskyist Socialist Workers Party's *Socialist Review* also alleged BNP involvement, including a van full of activists driving around picket lines and BNP supporters distributing leaflets to strikers.[63] Yet Woodley's co-general secretary, Derek Simpson, appeared to have fewer worries about associating himself with the nationalist framing of the strike. Simpson posed with two glamour models sent by the *Daily Star* decked out in t-shirts bearing the 'British jobs for British workers' slogan.[64]

The *Star* keenly claimed the mantle of the dispute's chief press backer. Its Saturday edition on 31 January 2009 reported on the three previous days of industrial action as a 'mass protest over jobs for migrants'. Journalist Gary Nicks wrote that the paper had played a crucial role in breaking the story around discontent at Lindsey before the strike began, and that it had been 'bombarded with messages from scaffolders, engineers, electricians, pipe-fitters, welders and steel erectors', fuelling the 'great British jobs revolt'.[65] These red-blooded men were gifted the same treatment as Derek Simpson: 'Page 3 babes Charlotte McKenna and Porchia Watson' were welcomed at Lindsey. Robert Robson, a twenty-six-year-old Glaswegian striker, reportedly said, 'Thanks for coming all this way girls. It's made our day.' On 6 February, strike leaders thanked the *Star* and its readership for helping them achieve an agreement which led to a hundred local workers being recruited at Lindsey, bringing an end to the walkout.[66]

Following this successful culmination of the dispute, the *Star* encouraged workers to capitalise on its success. The newspaper produced a poster which it asked groups of 'skilled Brit tradesmen' to pose with outside their workplaces. Construction workers in Birmingham and Newcastle were among those who took up the call. Pictures were accompanied by quotes from workers. Craig Meacham, a twenty-one-year-old from Stourport-on-Severn, said, 'We should be offered the jobs before foreigners.' Paul White, a forty-two-year-old street cleaner, claimed that 'the whole nation wants British jobs to go to British workers'.[67] White's comments and the 'British jobs for British workers' slogan begged rather than answered the question of who the British working class were in 2009. The answer provided by the *Star* appeared to be a highly exclusionary one: British-born white men who wear boiler suits and hi-vis jackets while working in tough conditions on building sites. Their enemies, it seemed, were incomers, unwelcome competition for jobs who lowered their standards of employment. This influential depiction helps explain the role of anti-immigration politics in the unmaking of the British working class, when even a rare instance of militant trade union mobilisation could be characterised as a xenophobic strike.

While these framings proved lasting and influential, they were far from representative of the more complicated dynamics behind the walkout at Lindsey and other large sites. Engineering construction workers are in fact highly skilled and mobile workers, used to working in itinerant contexts within the UK, and often abroad too. It was the extent of interconnection and activist networks, including online organising in internet forums, which made the scale of the strikes possible.[68] Paul Madden, a striker from Merseyside, explained:

> We would be hypocritical if we said foreigners could not work here. Eighty per cent of us have worked abroad. But we always do it for the same pay as the locals. We want transparency of wages to see if that is the case here.[69]

During the strike, the BBC was heavily criticised by trade unionists for misrepresenting another striker who was interviewed for television news. The man was quoted as saying, 'These Portuguese and Eyeties – we can't work alongside of them', but the context he provided afterwards was not given: 'We're segregated from them. They're coming in in full companies.'[70] Important dynamics of the dispute were therefore misrepresented, while chauvinistic undertones were accentuated and projected onto the workers and their spokespeople.

An article published by another Trotskyist group, the Socialist Party, whose activist Keith Gibson was a leading member of the strike committee, claimed that 'without any trade union resources to hand, a couple of strikers gave out posters brandishing [Gordon] Brown's statement ["British jobs for British workers"]'. Although 'the beginning of this leaderless unofficial strike had seen a few posters with the slogan "British jobs for British workers"', this did not extend to any truck with fascism: 'The far-right BNP, now emboldened by Brown's nationalistic slogan and whipped up in the media, made the mistake of visiting the picket line. The construction workers didn't waste time in enforcing their eviction notice!' Furthermore, the culmination of the dispute involved no repatriation or job losses among the migrant workers employed by IREM. These victories were defended in another round of strike action in the summer of 2009, following an attempt to impose redundancies on the Lindsey construction workforce.[71] There is corroboration for the claim that the BNP was turned away from the strike. Phil Whitehurst, another member of the strike committee, told the news website politics.co.uk on 3 February 2009 that he objected to 'people [who] have said it's racist. It's not. We're not part of the BNP. I've shunned the BNP away from here.'[72]

Workers who walked out at Lindsey did, then, contain elements of nationally aggrieved strikers who chose to present the dispute as a strike for 'British jobs for British workers'. These sentiments were visible on the internet forums which helped to collectivise and spread the dispute, as well as on the picket lines.[73] Yet in essence, Lindsey was a trade dispute, and its leaders sought and won a resolution which did not involve removing European subcontractors from British workplaces. The BNP, journalists, and politicians on the mainstream right, centre and left all assisted in ensuring it was projected primarily as a dispute between native and foreign workers – what the *Daily Star* commended as 'the great British jobs revolt'. This framing not only obscured the origins and nature of the arguments being put forward at Lindsey. It also reinforced the argument that the strike was part of a larger festering rebellion by a discontented and disenfranchised white working class. As Ince et al. stated in their analysis of the Lindsey dispute, labour conflicts are often 'contentious and ambiguous struggles'.[74] National affiliations, along with ethnic and racial dynamics, were hardly a recent introduction to British workplaces and trade unionism. Yet the Lindsey strike and the solidarity action it garnered was exceptional in its scale and its achievements as perhaps the largest unofficial strike in Britain in the twenty-first century which won significant concessions. In turn, these features meant its projection as a strike informed by anti-immigrant politics carried greater significance which was only reinforced by the context of growing electoral support for the BNP.

The rise of the BNP

The expectation that the BNP would gain from the Lindsey walkout was symptomatic of the party's increasingly established presence in British politics by the late 2000s. In its self-presentation, the BNP was not a party with strong roots in British fascism and neo-Nazism, but 'the Labour Party your grandfather voted for'. BNP candidates even engaged in stunts such as posing outside the former home of Clement Attlee, the leader who delivered Labour's heroic 1945 election landslide and head of the government which founded the National Health Service.[75] Party leader Nick Griffin exemplified this political strategy during the 2009 European elections while campaigning in Barnsley, a former coal mining town in South Yorkshire. *The Times* reported that Griffin addressed '300 white, working-class supporters'. He identified with the injustices Barnsley workers suffered during and after the 1984–85 miners' strike and linked these to current experiences of joblessness and recession, which he argued were propelled by mass immigration from Eastern Europe. Griffin's audience included former miners, the mother of two Iraq War veterans, and unemployed young workers. They were united in their disappointment with Blair and Brown's New Labour Party, which was seen as distant from their lives and failing to address distress in Barnsley.[76]

Griffin's eventual election to the European Parliament in May 2009 was the peak of a decade-long reorientation he instigated after winning the party's leadership in 1999 by promising to represent 'the neglected and oppressed white working class'. Analysis by John et al. in the mid-2000s pinpointed disaffection with the Labour Party in Outer London, Lancashire, Yorkshire and the West Midlands as fuelling support for the BNP. In Barking and Dagenham, voters viewed the BNP as a means to give Labour a 'kick up the backside', which helped to explain the party's success in local council elections. BNP voters were also, however, distinctive in how much they prioritised immigration. Further complicating straightforward links between class consciousness and support for the BNP, trade unionism remained a decisively anti-BNP force. A 2004 national opinion poll demonstrated that 80 per cent of trade unionists said they would 'never' vote for the BNP, which was considerably in excess of the population as a whole.[77]

The BNP thrived as Labourism atrophied. Its success can be understood as profiting from the conditions of labour movement de-organisation detailed in dwindling levels of trade unionism since the late 1970s. In 2005, historian Thomas Linehan argued that BNP successes were made possible in no small part because the labour movement was less able to both represent its traditional constituencies, including manual workers and public housing tenants, and effectively organise anti-fascist activity.

The BNP's electoral advances were closely associated with places where union organisation, power and authority had dwindled and where 'neighbourhood deterioration' was visible within 'areas which had undergone a degree of deindustrialisation'.[78] Contemporary academic research underlined the BNP's relative success among a white working-class constituency marked by disaffection from the Labour Party. Sociologists Nigel Copsey and David Macklin published a study in 2011 which identified the BNP's support as 'largely rooted in a politically abandoned and economically insecure (male) white working class'.[79] A separate study by then political scientist Matthew Goodwin found that the BNP appealed most to 'angry white men', who he defined as 'financially insecure working-class men, the unemployed and less well-educated'.[80] The simplistic picture drawn by Goodwin legitimated the disaffected white working class as a potentially dangerous but also sympathetic constituency. Goodwin subsequently went on a political 'journey' out of academia and into far-right politics. In the 2020s, Goodwin declared that he had joined a 'counter-revolution' being staged by the 'forgotten masses' and began presenting a regular television show on the right-wing GB News channel before standing as a parliamentary candidate for Nigel Farage's Reform UK on an anti-immigration ticket.[81]

Rising electoral support for the far right has been one of the prolonged costs of the unmaking of the British working class, but studies of localities where the BNP made its most sustained advances qualify this picture. They demonstrate the importance of a finer-grained analysis attentive to local political dynamics and their relationship with class structures. James Rhodes's analysis of Burnley reveals that the political mainstream made important space for the BNP. In Burnley, in the early 2000s, the former Labour council leader, Harry Brooks, led a group of independents who were the main opposition and articulated racialised objections to local spending. Brooks and his allies claimed council funds were funnelled towards predominantly Asian neighbourhoods at the expense of 'traditionally white working-class areas'.[82] Mike Makin-Waite, who was employed as a senior council official in Burnley during the 2000s, thoughtfully emphasises the importance of explaining how the effects of workplace closures and the disappearance of comparatively stable and well-paid industrial employment have been politicised in different localities: 'The decline in manufacturing provides an important backdrop to recent political developments in Burnley. But suggesting that far-right impulses were automatic in such circumstances is to accept as an explanation what has to be explained.'[83]

Pinpointing these explanations is particularly important given that the BNP's breakthroughs were confined primarily to some former industrial areas of England. By contrast, in some comparable locations, such as Scotland's former coalfields and steelmaking and shipbuilding areas, Labourism faced a different form of potent nationalist political challenge in the same period. In this context, it was the centrist or centre-left politics of the Scottish National Party which broadly supplanted the Labour Party at local, Scottish and UK elections between 2007 and 2015.[84] Both cases saw new parties profiting from the political effects of the unmaking of the British working class where Labourism had lost both its affective draw and its efficacy.

Interviews which Stephen Ashe recorded with BNP voters in Barking and Dagenham are important in revealing how they discussed and understood class and how it influenced their political outlook. Ashe found that his interviewees exhibited strong 'working-class identities and vocabularies of class'. Their narratives centred on themes of community 'fragmentation' since Right to Buy, high streets dominated by pound shops and the loss of neighbourliness. BNP voters rationalised their choice by pointing to the cumulative costs of the unmaking of the British working class. Ashe concluded that forms of class identification could be the basis for articulating support for the BNP or at least voicing the grievances which encouraged relatively large numbers of Barking and Dagenham voters to do so: 'a degree of working-class consciousness shapes political disillusionment rather than being an indicator of its erosion'. In Barking and Dagenham, BNP voters located class in personal experiences of employment as well as material deprivation. They retained enduring opposition towards the Tories but had also become hostile towards a Labour Party which was felt to take them for granted. Antagonistic feelings towards the Labour Party grew when Margaret Hodge became the MP for Barking. Hodge was the daughter of a steel magnate. Ashe reported she was not seen as strongly connected to the local area. Therefore, both 'class and racialised-nationalised lines' animated sympathy for the BNP. Familiar arguments over the allocation of public services and housing also contributed to immigrants being viewed as a threat.[85] The BNP encouraged this discontent by making 'bogus claims' that a scheme known as 'Africans for Essex' had led to the local council being paid to house immigrants by central government and that African migrants were being given £50,000 grants to relocate to Essex.[86]

Another important foundation of the BNP's advances in Barking and Dagenham cited by Ashe is the party's attempt to present itself as 'ordinary'. Richard Barnbrook, who became the opposition leader on the council and a Greater London Assembly member, was profiled as a respectable local man and a former Labour Party member.[87] These dynamics reveal the complicated textures which shape the intersections between the politics of class, race and place in pressurised local contexts. They also demonstrate the slipperiness of appeals to ordinariness. Social historians such as Jon Lawrence have underlined that ordinariness has often replaced class as a dominant identifier since the late twentieth century.[88] Florence Sutcliffe-Braithwaite developed this argument, tracing the working- and middle-class appeal of placing oneself within an 'ordinary' majority of unprivileged working citizens standing above an underclass residuum but below a privileged elite.[89] Definitions of ordinariness often align with those of respectability, as well as being open to politicisation on racial or ethnic terms. They can cross-pollinate with class, national and race consciousness rather than counteract them.

The class base of BNP support is complex when viewed in these terms. Opinion polling demonstrated that the party performed comparatively well among the 'C2' class group. This category incorporates skilled manual workers, including sole traders. James Rhodes's research in Burnley closely corresponded with these findings. He interviewed a self-employed tradesman and BNP voter who attacked benefit-dependent and unrespectable 'scruffy whites'. Other BNP voters articulated stigmatising comments towards poorer, primarily white neighbourhoods as well as areas associated with the town's Asian community.[90] Mike Makin-Waite's analysis of Burnley concurs, underlining that it was 'people who were anxious about what they had to lose, and wanted to erect barriers against perceived risks, who had returned the far-right councillors'. This was demonstrated on 2 May 2002 when the BNP won three council seats in Burnley. The first BNP councillor to be announced was elected in Cliviger with Worsthorne, which was the only ward on the local authority with below-national-average levels of deprivation. Nick Griffin commented, 'We did not expect to win here. It is such a middle-class area.'[91]

Along with the de-organised and disillusioned elements of the working class, the BNP also gained from the never-organised elements of the small business proprietors or insecure middle-class voters who had often been prominent in the social base of far-right politics. David Owens, the self-employed bathroom fitter who became a BNP councillor in Boston, can be seen as representative of part of the party's electoral base. Analysis of a national opinion poll commissioned by the Joseph Rowntree Foundation on BNP support in the mid-2000s found a concentration among 'C2' voters, or the skilled manual workers. Furthermore, the authors concluded that 'the BNP believe that it is the lower middle rather than the poorest social classes which are drawn to the far right'. BNP support was concentrated in relatively higher-waged areas with lower levels of benefit claimants but also comparatively low levels of formal educational attainment.[92] Daniel Trilling similarly emphasises that 'relatively well-off voters' were important to the BNP's successes in the 2000s, including men from occupational backgrounds such as 'builders, joiners, electricians, mechanics etc'. These voters included a significant minority who had usually supported the Tories rather than Labour. BNP successes in the North of England included winning councillors in areas of Halifax which usually returned Conservative candidates.[93] At the peak of its influence, the BNP also had representation in traditionally Conservative- and Liberal-dominated authorities in the South of England like Hertfordshire County Council and Three Rivers and Epping Forest District Councils.[94]

The BNP's own literature reveals these contradictions and tensions. Its general election manifesto from 2010, when Griffin stood in Barking aiming to become the BNP's first member of the House of Commons, demonstrates the party's claim to represent constituencies which the Labour Party now neglected: 'In pursuit of Labour's globalist ideals, the white working class has been abandoned, replaced and displaced by a new ethnic electoral power base.'[95] It put forward a broadly Powellite position of ending immigration, deporting illegal immigrants and 'voluntary repatriation', warning that Labour had already 'orchestrated mass immigration to change forcibly Britain's demographics and to gerrymander elections'.[96] However, although the BNP endorsed 'British jobs for British workers', its manifesto also asserted a position of 'workfare not welfare'. While this policy centred on removing the rights of asylum seekers and immigrants to access state benefits, the manifesto also discussed the problem of 'socialist state-induced dependency' which had inculcated a 'scrounger entitlement mentality'.[97] These policies were combined with a more esoteric position affirming 'the right to bear arms'. Other commitments demonstrated the retained influence of neo-Nazism in the party, including a 'proscription against the promotion of racial integration in schools and the media'.[98]

Such pledges perhaps demonstrate the limited achievements of Griffin's attempts to 'modernise' the BNP and present it as a respectable electoral force rather than a fascist one with a history in racist street politics.[99] Not long before the general election, the BNP had decided to admit non-white members on the pain of legal action by the Equality and Human Rights Commission. BNP spokesperson Simon Darby told the *Guardian* he hoped this marked the BNP's acceptance as 'a bona fide party'.[100] Yet by the end of the year the BNP was in turmoil. Griffin polled more than 6,600 votes in Barking at the general election but came third. The BNP were beaten in the context of a higher turnout mobilised by both a re-energised local Tory campaign and a much more active Labour one which succeeded in retaining the seat for Margaret Hodge. Labour's local canvassers built on the back of a broad anti-fascist campaign which went 'door-to-door' on the 'white estates' where the BNP were seen as the greatest threat.[101] Barking and Dagenham was symptomatic of a larger BNP failure in 2010. The biggest setbacks were 'in or nearby former industrial areas' where the party had been seen to be putting down roots. Only 2,500 party members even voted in a leadership challenge Griffin faced at the hands of fellow MEP Andrew Brons a year later. [102]

In the form of the BNP, the far right was defeated in 2010. However, the political agency attributed to a disgruntled white working-class constituency lived on and only grew considerably more potent in the 2010s and 2020s. In the aftermath of the general election, Morgan McSweeney and Jessica Studdert, political advisors to the Local Government Association Labour Group, reflected on challenging the BNP. Their argument rested on typifying BNP voters as middle-aged white working-class men 'characterised by having big dreams for their family. They play the lottery and watch X Factor.' These voters were susceptible to the rumours of service and housing provision being skewed towards immigrants which were spread by the BNP in 'highly fractured communities' where collectivism had long since ebbed away. McSweeney and Studdert struck a deeply pessimistic tone, noting core features of the unmaking of the

British working class which had unfolded in the preceding decades. Within the context of distrust and waning faith in the capacity of the Labour Party among groups it had previously regarded as core voters, canvassers were advised to 'look for agreement' and to avoid 'direct confrontation' on racism or immigration. An accepting approach was strongly advised in instances where local Labour councils were perceived as failing to take desired action against campsites frequented by Travellers.[103] McSweeney went on to become the chief advisor to Labour's next prime minister following the 2024 general election. He is credited with urging Keir Starmer to embrace the Union Jack and pivoting Labour towards an increasingly hostile and draconian stance on immigration as the subject came to dominate British political debate.[104] McSweeney resigned in February 2026 following the scandal surrounding Peter Mandelson's relationship with Jeffrey Epstein. Starmer resigned a few months later after Labour performed badly in local elections in England and devolved elections in Scotland and Wales, losing seats to the far-right Reform UK as well as the Scottish National Party, Plaid Cymru and the Greens.

The white working class redux?

A brief televised encounter between Gordon Brown and a voter in Lancashire made headlines during the 2010 general election as the previous Labour government's tenure came to a close. Gillian Duffy's father had sung 'The Red Flag' at Manchester's Free Trade Hall, and she was herself a retired former local authority worker. Duffy articulated her disappointment with Labour's record in office, centring on the exhaustion of public services, before asking Brown, 'All these Eastern Europeans what are coming in, where are they flocking from?' It was Brown's comment afterwards, when he thought his microphone had been turned off and journalists had moved on, which made sure the interaction left a lasting impact. Brown said that Duffy was 'just a sort of bigoted woman who said she used to be Labour'.[105]

Gillian Duffy became a minor celebrity who made media appearances at subsequent elections. Six years later, now in her early seventies, Duffy told the BBC that she intended to vote for Britain to leave the European Union at the referendum held in June 2016: 'I love being English and I don't want to be a European.'[106]

Duffy's insistence that she loved being English was perhaps revealing of the pressures facing political Britishness as it had defined the working class during the forward march of Labourism. In the mid-twentieth century, Britishness had been the overriding political national identity within Scotland, England and Wales. Important national and regional distinctions were generally subservient to Britishness, particularly as they structured orientations towards a Labour Party which embraced its standing as a part of the Union over and above its constituent nations. Duffy's confrontation with Brown, a Scotsman who was serving as a Labour prime minister, took place in a context whereby the territorial politics of the Union which had been formative to the making of the British working class were under strain. Brown's final major intervention in political life was championing a 'No' vote at the 2014 referendum on Scottish independence which recorded a 45 per cent vote in favour of breaking up the Union. A few months later, at the 2015 general election, Labour failed to poll the highest popular vote at a general election in Scotland for the first time since 1959 and its representation fell from forty Scottish MPs to just one, losing swathes of formerly safe seats to the Scottish National Party. Further territorial splits were demonstrated in the 2016 Brexit referendum, when the Leave vote was founded upon a concentration of Eurosceptic voters in the South of England. Yet former industrial settlements in the North of England and South Wales, areas like Duffy's hometown of Rochdale, were crucial in consolidating the electoral majority for Brexit and came to determine its political meaning.[107]

A redefined cultural politics of class and its symbiosis with English nationhood evolved over the 2010s. It was revealed through a relatively trivial spat in November 2014 during the Rochester and

Strood by-election in Kent. The election was called after Mark Reckless resigned as a Conservative MP to run for UKIP. Reckless won the seat, confirming the strength of the Eurosceptic and anti-immigration vote in his constituency. Labour's alleged distance from its traditional working-class base was affirmed during the campaign when Shadow Attorney General Emily Thornberry published a tweet which read 'image from #Rochester' above a picture of a white van parked outside a suburban home which was draped in two England flags. Thornberry subsequently resigned from the shadow cabinet after her social media comments were interpreted as demeaning, but not before she had come under fire for her derision towards hardworking patriots.[108]

The owner of the house, Dan Ware, became a hero in the tabloid press. The fawning over Ware can be read as a follow-up to the embrace of the Lindsey strikers by the *Daily Star*: a no-nonsense ordinary man standing against an effete left-wing politician. Ware was a car dealer who occupied a very different class position to unionised construction workers. He was later quoted as backing the Tories ahead of the 2015 general election on the grounds that they were good for small businessmen.[109] The embrace of Ware as an English everyman was representative of the remade politics of class. Old divisions from the 1980s and 1990s between the immiserated unemployed or precariously employed and the go-getting white-van men were papered over. Instead, emphasis lay on the distinction between cosmopolitan snobs who look down on white men grafting in tough times. Segments of the middle class facing downwards economic pressures became crucial to the dynamics of the political mainstream and far right. Often these voters have been integral to the cross-class coalitions which have supported the BNP and backed Brexit along with UKIP and later Reform UK, but they are legitimated through a language of ordinariness and have even been badged as plebeian or working-class.[110]

Months after the Brexit referendum, Theresa May claimed to speak for 'ordinary, working-class families'. The new prime minister announced that she was willing to say what her predecessors would not, emphasising that, while 'a lot of people don't like to admit' it, to 'someone who finds themselves out of work or on lower wages because of low-skilled immigration, life simply doesn't seem fair'. May's speech merged class and national grievances with ethnic and racial undertones. She attacked employers who chose to hire foreign workers over British ones. As May drew her dividing line between the loyal 'citizens of somewhere' and the globally oriented 'citizens of nowhere', it was metropolitan Britain which was the main target.[111]

Here lay the roots of a divide through which the right sought to reconstitute the meaning of class politics in Britain, redrawing the lines of place, nationhood and interest. There were echoes of Powell's denunciation of liberal-minded churchmen and Labour ministers as well as shimmers of the more recent advances of the BNP. Most of all, it was the more enduring vote for UKIP, which had polled almost 4 million votes in 2015, along with the vote for Brexit the next year, which informed the projection of a provincial majority. A decade later, Reform UK, Nigel Farage's post-Brexit successor to UKIP, had achieved electoral breakthroughs in local councils, regionally and at Westminster, including in Lincolnshire, where former Tory Minister Andrea Jenkyns became the mayor of Greater Lincolnshire. In 2025, another industrial crisis erupted at Lindsey refinery while Britain was again being governed by an increasingly unpopular Labour government. Ownership of the plant had passed from Total, a well-known oil major, to the less financially robust Prax Group. The company was privately owned by a husband-and-wife team, Winston and Arani Soosaipillai. Prax Group collapsed in the summer of 2025 amid reports of financial 'irregularities' related to a loan worth more than three-quarters of a billion pounds and an outstanding tax bill of £70 million.[112]

The closure of Lindsey was symptomatic of a larger manufacturing jobs crisis in Britain. Sectors such as refining, steel, and car and vehicle manufacturing suffered from spiralling energy costs but also from being subject to unreliable owners without firm commitments to their workforces. Unite responded by hosting a rally at Grimsby Town Hall demanding government intervention. Jenkyns was among the speakers, despite being on the record as stating 'I don't like trade unions' and 'I want workers to have rights, but it's got ridiculous now' in relation to modest proposals by Starmer's Labour government to roll back some of the excesses of Conservative anti–trade union legislation. Rather than irresponsible capitalists, Jenkyns spuriously blamed the modicum of intervention which the Labour government was pursuing in shifting Britain's economic base towards greener forms of manufacturing as having caused the closure of Lindsey.[113] In 2025, Reform UK enjoyed a base of support and legitimacy far in excess of the BNP a decade and a half earlier, and it was not as associated in the popular mindset with fascism or street thuggery. Jenkyns was welcomed on an official labour movement platform while campaigning around the same plant where the BNP was sent packing by unofficial strikers in 2009. Consistent disappointment with Labour governments to deliver in the face of eroding unionised employment and living standards conditioned this acceptance.

The unmaking of the British working class dented the nexus of trade union organisation and Labour Party linkages which had defined its political presence. A more widely felt social and cultural sense of affiliation among manual workers and their families had also frayed, in a context where they no longer made up a straightforward majority of British society. As these connections eroded, so too did the sense of a British nationhood defined by common investment in the state, industry and trade unions which had been integral to the articulation of a British working class during the height of its influence in the twentieth century. Class reappeared in the lexicon of mainstream politics during the 2010s in claims oriented towards legitimating, directing and controlling white working-class anger characterised by racial, cultural and national resentment. Often this case was made by politicians who overtly rejected class politics when it came to struggles for collective material improvements, organised labour or opposing immiserating austerity.

7

Essential Workers: 'The Working Class Is Back'?

Gagarin Way, Lumphinnans, West Fife, 24 May 2025. It was a sunny Saturday. We were on the trail of coal and communism and wondering what working-class politics meant now in one of its former strongholds. I was with Brendan Moohan, a sixty-year-old ex-miner. Brendan was one of the youngest victimised miners in Scotland. He was sacked from his job at Monktonhall colliery in Midlothian after being arrested picketing in the great strike which had ended in the spring forty years before. I got to know Brendan through involvement in socialist and trade union politics as well as by following Hibernian Football Club. We timed our trip for the Saturday after the league season ended and on the day of the Scottish Cup final, on account of Hibs' failure to achieve a shot at glory this time around. As we ventured down the Main Street in the former mining village, Brendan asked a passerby if he knew where Gagarin Way was. With a wry smile the man directed us to a housing scheme to the left, remarking as our conversation ended that Lumphinnans was known as a 'Little Moscow'.[1]

Gagarin Way is the only street in Britain named after a Soviet cosmonaut. Its lineage is closely associated with a time when Communist Party of Great Britain (CPGB) activists in collieries, workshops, dockyards, communities and council chambers articulated a belief in the coming socialist transformation of society by the politically conscious industrial working class. Some of their leaders are celebrated in the names of other streets nearby. Gagarin Way turns on to Gallacher Place which commemorates Willie Gallacher, the Red Clydeside engineering worker who met

Lenin in Moscow before he became the MP for West Fife when the Communists stood on an anti-fascist 'popular front' platform in 1935.[2] Moffat Crescent stands towards the eastern boundary of Lumphinnans where the village runs into the larger settlement of Lochgelly. Abe Moffat was a Lumphinnans-born-and-bred miner who became a prominent trade unionist and CPGB cadre after serving as an infantryman in the First World War. Having been repelled by the slaughter on the Western Front as well as the disregard shown for the lives of miners at home, Moffat played a leading local role in the 1926 General Strike and miners' lockout. He became president of the National Union of Mineworkers Scottish Area upon the union's formation in 1944, remaining in post until retirement in 1961 when he was succeeded by another Lumphinnans miner, his brother Alex.[3]

Later, when we were wandering through the Lochore Meadows (known locally as 'the Meedies'), Brendan brought the conversation through to his frustrations with the longer-term impacts of the defeats he lived through in the 1980s and their effect on how class and politics were commonly understood in Britain. The Meadows themselves are a testament to earlier pit closures, which were accompanied by the relatively positive experiences of social and economic reconstruction in the coalfields that I explored in the first chapter of this book. Former colliery land was reclaimed following pit closures in the 1960s to form an enduring community resource: a large park replete with an artificial lake. The concrete frame of the Mary colliery was left as a permanent reminder of the industry after it closed in 1966, sixty-two years after production at the site first began. It has now stood as a reminder of West Fife's industrial history for as long as miners worked the pit's reserve beneath the ground.[4] As we were heading towards the still-standing concrete headgear, Brendan reflected on enduring spells of unemployment between working on and off as a poorly paid labourer, first in the building trade and then in retail.

Yet it was the sense of having lost an ideological battle in popular understanding that had hurt most and lasted longest.

Brendan said he had 'lived through the abandonment of everything he had believed in'. He inferred that I was born in 1990. At this time, he had been struggling to implore disinterested fellow workers to keep or start paying union dues. Brendan's greatest condemnation was for the intellectuals he thought had abandoned the struggle when it needed them most. He singled out André Gorz among the 'French postmodernists' who had in his view done serious damage to the left. Gorz had bid *Farewell to the Working Class* in the title of his 1982 book, the year Brendan first went down Monktonhall.[5] Gorz's argument was that a working class empowered through and defined by its attachment to industrial jobs was fast becoming a thing of the past. The supposed 'interchangeability' of labour meant there was minimal differentiation between the experiences and outlook of workers making anything from ball bearings to sheet metals to fuels, which may have come as news to Brendan and his colleagues in the distinctive culture of the British deep coal mining industry. In Gorz's assessment, skilled workers marked by pride in their occupations had been replaced by a diffuse agent, the clunkily titled 'non-class of non-workers'. Gorz's message was posed as emancipatory: 'Work is not and should not be the centre of one's life.' Where the miners and their communities had rallied around the specificity of their jobs and the social structures built around them, the non-workers were defined by their antipathy and resistance to their miserable experience of employment and exclusion from 'decision or initiative'.[6]

Gagarin Way was an appropriate venue for the beginning of this conversation, because our dialogue followed in the wake of a dramatisation exploring the same themes. Gregory Burke's 2001 play – *Gagarin Way* – centres on the plight of two Fife electronics plant workers who turn to terrorism out of boredom, alienation and frustration that the industrial and political means their forebears had open to them were now closed for younger generations. Their attempt to kidnap a prominent American capitalist fast descends into farce when the consultant they have abducted turns out to be a man called Frank from

Leven, another former Fife coal settlement. Reality starts to dawn that the plan has been botched when Frank comes to, after having been knocked out by his assailants. Frank's accent is recognisably local. Before his kidnapping, Frank was trying to ply his way in a complex world of just-in-time production, flows of microchips and shifting multinational business interests. The Scottish factory had recently been transferred from American to Japanese owners, which the workers were not even aware of yet, but this change was likely to come with redundancies or even closure. In somewhat Gorzian terms, Frank insisted his job too was 'work . . . just work'. Burke's title was sardonic. Less than twenty years after the last national miners' strike, a younger cohort of workers could only see an impossible mantle of historic struggles. The street signs had become a taunt to contemporary ineptitude and burdens of past failures.[7]

Burke's play was prescient. Across the first half of the 2000s, a global microelectronics crisis led to the swift closure or downsizing of the manufacturing plants which had been seen as providing an economic future for Scotland's struggling former heavy-industry regions.[8] Britain's ex-coalfields are now increasingly centres for storing, moving and selling goods made elsewhere, and have become further relatively impoverished as a result. The most recent *State of the Coalfields* report published in 2024 found that if they were treated as a single region of Britain, the coalfields would have a population of around 6 million, home to almost one in ten Britons. Wages are lower than average and focused on routinised manual employment along with concentrations in public services such as health and social care. In other words, these are still working-class places. Warehousing is one of the leading sectors. It accounted for over 60,000 new jobs created in former mining areas between 2012 and 2022 alone. By then the sector employed 175,000 workers in the coalfields, roughly matching coal mining at the time of the 1984–85 strike.[9]

More than 6,500 Fife workers were employed in warehousing in the early 2020s. This transformation is epitomised by the huge Amazon distribution centre which opened in Dunfermline in 2011. A report for the *Scotsman* newspaper on the build-up to the festive order rush in 2023 described the facility as a technological phenomenon: 'a depot the size of seventeen football pitches with four miles of conveyor belts' which 'stretches over 1.5 million square feet'. The workforce nearly doubled in size to 2,200 on the back of 1,000 seasonal temps who were ingratiated into a highly industrialised form of delivering Christmas presents: 'Staff can be seen passing boxes along four miles of conveyor belts and moving orders from one area to another for processing, gift wrapping, and labelling, before packages are shipped straight to customers' doors.'[10]

Another major Amazon distribution centre is located in the former pit and power station settlement of Rugeley in Staffordshire. There are overlaps between the technical marvel associated with Amazon distribution and how Rugeley's modernised colliery and power station of the 1960s were described in chapter 1. Just as these had housed a remade working class fit for the rationalised coalfields, so a large concentration of workers is now employed at Amazon. In 2022, a strike broke out at Rugeley and other distribution centres. Amazon demonstrates the potential for a renewed workplace class politics, contesting conditions of employment and utilising modern means of communication. An anonymous Amazon worker reported for the *Notes from Below* project on how in August 2022 a wage strike spread via social media. Workers walked out at Tilbury in Essex as well as at Rugeley and Coventry in the West Midlands following the awarding of a paltry thirty-five-pence hourly pay rise in the context of rapidly mounting inflation. Amazon were flush with profits, bolstered by orders during the COVID-19 lockdown.[11]

Amazon featured prominently in efforts by *Notes from Below* to understand Britain's evolving 'class composition' through analysing changing sectoral balances, union organisation and forms of mobilisation.[12] This is a valuable means to assess shifting class relations in the 2020s. The Amazon dispute evolved in the context of the larger 'strike wave' of 2022–23.[13] This spike in workplace mobilisation was industrially but also politically defined by the clarion calls of Mick Lynch, the general secretary of the National Union of Rail, Maritime and Transport Workers (RMT). In a series of combative television interviews, and then at rallies across the country, Lynch memorably insisted that his members' strike action demonstrated that 'the working class is back'.[14] Lynch's popularity was testament to the potential for a materially grounded politics of class, one which collectivised economic grievances and trade union organising. The strike wave suggested that the basic traditions of collectively demanding material improvements which had fostered the powerful working-class politics of the twentieth century could have a future. More than 2.5 million working days were lost to strikes in both 2022 and 2023, a relative recovery in worker mobilisation by the standards of recent decades to levels not seen since the late 1980s.[15] Yet Lynch's appeal to 'the working class' also invites questions of who this refers to in contemporary Britain. It cannot be limited to the formally employed, typically white and male manual workers in industry and transport who traditionally dominated the labour movement but are now far fewer in number and less important to the British economy than they once were. Identifying the working class in the 2020s also requires analysis of institutional links between work, trade unions and party politics which were severed during the unmaking of the British working class. These changes are reflected in the fact the RMT is no longer affiliated to the Labour Party.

Picket lines at warehouses and railway stations provoke the question of whether a 'new working class' is emerging with new or revived forms of economic and political agency. Class has also re-emerged in the British political lexicon since the 2008 crash and the onset of austerity following the election of a Conservative-led government in 2010. Yet there appears to be a sharp tension between increasingly stark levels of poverty and inequality and the seemingly diminishing importance of conventionally understood class factors in explaining political outlooks and voting preferences. Patterns of voter 'dealignment' have deepened and the two-party system has become ever more strained. The COVID-19 pandemic and the strike wave which followed appeared to demonstrate and even reinforce the centrality of class to British society. First, the category of 'essential workers' emerged during the pandemic, revealing that workers in many occupations were far from interchangeable, then the strike wave demonstrated a popular basis for assertions of workers' collective interests. If a new working class is emerging, it is very much still in its early stages and its constituencies, boundaries and key expressions are yet to be determined.

Reinventing class in the twenty-first century

Class was back in the 2010s. The 'classless' pretensions of the 1990s and 2000s were rocked by the impact of the financial crash and the inequities made stark by the austerity measures adopted by the Tory–Liberal coalition government. The positive reception of Ken Loach's 2016 film *I, Daniel Blake* demonstrated shifting public perceptions about the inequities of an increasingly brutal welfare state. It followed the plight of a joiner from Newcastle, whom the film is named after. Blake is compelled by the social security system to seek employment even though he is patently too ill to work. He befriends Katie Morgan, a single mother from London who has been relocated to cheaper housing on Tyneside. Katie ends up working at a brothel to feed her family, while Daniel dies of a heart attack as he appeals for his right to sickness benefits. *I, Daniel Blake* marked a sharp distinction from the 2000s portrayals of the feckless underclass discussed in chapter 4.[16] These had reached a crescendo earlier in the 2010s when programmes which coincided with the coalition's attack on welfare recipients, such as Channel 4's *Benefits Street* and BBC Scotland's *The Scheme*, mocked and stigmatised the unemployed, long-term sick and council housing tenants for viewers' entertainment.[17] When *I, Daniel Blake* was broadcast by the BBC in 2019, it appeared to underline a significant shift in cultural perspectives. Tory politicians were forced on the defensive, attacking Loach as a partisan propagandist but losing face as welfare professionals, public sector trade unionists and claimants themselves championed his portrayal of Britain in the 2010s.[18]

While class may have returned to public consciousness, social scientists and broadcasters were eager to explore how it had in their view changed irrevocably from the traditional understandings which had dominated British perspectives on societal divisions and political identity. The notion of a relatively cohesive working class, and the dominance of employment or occupation in definitions of class, were both seen as old hat, or perhaps cloth cap. In 2011, the BBC launched a 'Great British Class Survey' which promised to engage large swathes of the public in reinterpreting the nation's evolving social structure. Prominent sociologists from the London School of Economics, Mike Savage and Fiona Devine, worked with a team of researchers to analyse over 160,000 responses. Their findings proclaimed out with the old and in with the new. To continue engaging obvious public interest, a 'class calculator' was launched. Individuals could use the indicator by answering a series of survey questions. Results then placed them in a new structure. Instead of relying on the 'traditional British social divisions of upper, middle and working class', which 'seem out of date in the twenty-first century, no longer reflecting modern occupations or lifestyles', Savage, Devine and their colleagues devised 'a new model made up of seven groups'.[19]

In descending order, respondents were situated on a gradient scale as either elite, established middle class, technical middle class, new affluent worker, traditional working class, emergent service workers or part of the insecure precariat residuum dependent on insecure marginal economic activity or state benefits. These groups reflected different balances of economic resources, including property ownership, savings and income, with social and cultural categories. Within the social section, respondents were asked who they associated with, discriminating for instance between those with friends who work as shop assistants or lorry drivers and others whose acquaintances were university lecturers or lawyers. The cultural component probed recreational activities, asking respondents whether they listened to rock, hip hop or classical music, if they watched sports, went to the theatre or visited art galleries, or enjoyed excursions to stately homes. The calculator was a hit. It had been completed by more than 7 million people when Savage published a book exploring *Social Class in the 21st Century* in 2015.[20] Savage and his collaborators clearly succeeded in striking a popular note. He concluded that 'social class is now a very powerful force in the popular imagination once again. People in Britain are aware of and interested in and also upset about class.'[21]

Moreover, the survey and resultant typology was clearly responsive to important trends which were observable in Britain and in other former industrial economies in Europe and North America. The context of an increasingly inegalitarian society was emphasised by Savage, who underlined Britain's 'hierarchical class order'.[22] The significance of a growing gulf, particularly towards the top, was emphasised by the attention Savage paid to the elite in place of what he saw as the earlier tendency of sociologists to fixate on the boundaries between the working and middle classes. The elite accounted for just 6 per cent of the population. They are a larger section of society than the 'super-rich' or the '1 per cent' but are marked nevertheless by being 'massively advantaged over the rest' in their mutually self-reinforcing command of wealth, income and social networks.[23]

Nearly three decades earlier, Savage had published a study exploring the history of working-class politics in the Lancashire town of Preston. Then he had differentiated between housing activism organising tenants, industrial workers forming trade unions opposed to their employers in privately owned industry, and a growing Labour Party electoral machine active in municipal and parliamentary elections. These distinctive spheres of housing mobilisation, workplace trade unionism and party politics each cohered through a unifying labour movement.[24] The conceptualisation of political mobilisation which Savage drew on in 2015 was much thinner than in 1987. In and of itself, this perhaps demonstrates the unmaking of the British working class in action, given the weakening of activity across the three areas and their seeming divorce from one another. Savage's 2015 analysis is largely confined to electoral preferences, drawing on that year's general election. He concluded that evidence pointed towards 'the end of old-fashioned class politics'. Previously strong alignments between manual workers and Labour voting on the one hand, and between business owners, the self-employed and managerial employees and the Conservative Party on the other, had weakened considerably since the 1980s.[25]

These trends continued in subsequent elections. A markedly declining 'class gradient' was evident at the 2017 general election when both the Conservative and Labour vote increased proportionately and in terms of total votes cast. The Labour vote ranged from 36 per cent among managerial and professionals to 43 per cent among semi-skilled and unskilled manual workers.[26] Research by the polling agency YouGov suggested that the heavy setback Labour suffered at the 2019 general election only compounded these trends. Not only did the Tories win across all social classifications polled, but their majority over Labour was also higher among manual workers – a fifteen-point gap of 48 per cent to 33 – than it was among non-manual and professionals, who broke 43 per cent to 33 per cent. Broadly, Labour's vote held up best among better-educated and younger voters.[27]

The 2019 general election result also encapsulated a larger trend towards volatility and vacillation in electoral alignments. In 2015, the pro-independence Scottish National Party replaced Labour as the dominant party among Scottish working-class voters, as it won all but three of fifty-nine constituencies in Scotland at the general election. Geoffrey Evans and James Tilley's study of the shifting role of class in British politics emphasised that 60 per cent of the working-class electorate voted for the Nationalists. The Eurosceptic and anti-immigration United Kingdom Independence Party (UKIP) also polled well in England and Wales. Its advances included a concentration of working-class support, anticipating the 'Leave' vote at the following year's 'Brexit' referendum on Britain's membership of the European Union.[28] In 2017, Labour struggled in certain ex-industrial constituencies even as it gained votes across the country. The Tories succeeded in overturning Labour majorities in former manufacturing and mining seats like Walsall North, Mansfield and Stoke-on-Trent South in the Midlands. Labour had also barely hung on in other comparable seats such as Ashfield in Nottinghamshire.[29]

England's former coal mining regions provided further cataclysmic moments in two subsequent general elections. During the early hours of 13 December 2019, Ian Levy was announced as the new Conservative MP for the Northumberland constituency of Blyth Valley. It signalled the beginning of a rout. Dennis Skinner, the iconic ex-coal miner and member for Bolsover, was among the Labour MPs who fell to defeat at the hands of the Tories. Skinner features in chapter 4 of this book as one of the leaders of the Clay Cross councillors who refused to implement rent increases legally mandated by Edward Heath's Conservative government in the early 1970s. He was also a prominent supporter of the 1984–85 miners' strike. The ouster of Skinner was widely reported as symbolic of the wider setback Labour suffered across 'Red Wall' constituencies in former industrial regions of England and Wales.[30]

The Tories also took Ashfield, where their candidate was another former miner and an ex-Labour councillor. Lee Anderson defected to the Tories in 2018 after he was suspended by the Labour Party for hiring a bulldozer and erecting boulders to stop Travellers from staying in his ward.[31] Anderson became an enduring symbol of a rightwards-moving angry and nationalist white provincial English working-class segment in the 2020s. Having risen to vice chair of the Conservative Party,

Anderson was again reprimanded, this time for referring to London's Labour mayor, Sadiq Khan, as an 'Islamist'.[32] In March 2024, Anderson jumped ship again, joining Nigel Farage's far-right Reform UK. He became the party's first MP. Anderson presented himself as leading a movement of the disaffected, declaring, 'All I want is my country back', and defining himself and the people of Ashfield against the effete 'liberal elite' who he alleged dominated the Tories and Labour.[33] Anderson held his seat as one of five Reform MPs elected at the general election four months later.[34] Reform's best performances included coastal constituencies but also formerly strongly Labour-voting areas in Yorkshire and the Midlands.[35] YouGov polling also suggested the Reform vote had been bolstered by working-class support, with manual grades around twice as likely to vote Reform as non-manual workers and professionals, while social renters were the housing tenure most likely to vote Reform.[36]

Following the 2024 general election, the rise of Reform continued in parliamentary and council by-elections across diverse constituencies in England, Wales and Scotland. The party grew in strength as it claimed to speak for the politically disenfranchised mass of British people and in opposition to immigration. Figures such as Anderson drew dividing lines between the interests of predominantly white provincial towns and villages on the one hand and cosmopolitan large cities on the other. Reform focused its ire on the university-educated middle classes and especially the political class, which largely comes from this background, denigrating them as snobbish and out of touch with plebeian 'common sense'. Labour and Scottish Nationalist as well as Tory governments were slated for having been profligate with scarce public resources which ought to be redirected to their constituents but are instead being misspent abroad or on asylum seekers.

A potent mix of political appeal with roots in varied geographical class positions amalgamates in Reform. It combines an apparent investment in obtaining just rewards for British workers with a highly libertarian perspective on the rights of capital and the movement of money. In April 2025, Nigel Farage championed the nationalisation of Scunthorpe steel works in Lincolnshire as the Labour government was dithering, before it eventually did take over the plant from its Chinese owners to stop them from closing it down.[37] Yet he was no new-found convert to public regulation or national ownership of essential goods. A few months later, Farage promoted cryptocurrency as 'the ultimate freedom: being in control securely of your own money, making your own decisions, free from authoritarian government'.[38] These contradictions have been at least temporarily navigable or even beneficial for Reform, held together by the appeal of nationhood, loathing for discredited established parties and the ability to blame immigration and the malice or incompetence of governments of varying political stripes for Britain's problems.

The version of history, class and nationhood which Reform draws together was exemplified in the recent unveiling of the restored Silverhill colliery winding wheel in North Nottinghamshire in September 2025. Local campaigners were unable to raise the funds required, but Lee Anderson ensured a local property developer, who is affiliated with Reform, paid for most of the restoration. Silverhill was a victim of the pit closure programme announced under John Major's government in 1992 as the coal industry was prepared for privatisation in 1994. Yet when Farage was interviewed next to the proudly restored winding wheel following its unveiling, he blamed imported Polish coal for making good Nottinghamshire miners unemployed.[39]

Social researcher Sacha Hilhorst has commented on the appeal of these narratives in Nottinghamshire mining villages, underlining growing distrust in the Labour Party but noting tensions between the outlooks of Reform voters. The men and women she interviewed include former canning and textile workers. As comparatively secure and well-rewarded industrial jobs disappeared, they have been replaced by the demands of greedy '24/7' employers: the relentlessness of work at Sports Direct's massive warehouse at Shirebrook along with the emotional demands and low wages afforded to women in social care or as teaching assistants. Hilhorst spoke to former Labour voters who backed Reform hoping for taxes on the rich and redistribution towards poorer people like themselves. Their outlook is wildly at odds with Farage's crypto backers and likely also clashes with the large number of Tory-to-Reform switchers propelling the party's popularity.[40] Reform's polling success is accompanied by a shift of left-wing voters away from Labour towards the Greens, Plaid Cymru and Scottish National Party, who have been fuller-throated in their opposition to the resurgent far right. Labour is mired in ever-growing difficulties when it comes to sustaining a coalition or presenting a programme around delivering incremental material improvements for workers and their families.

Yet in spite of these important contingencies, analyses of the political meaning of class and its electoral significance in Britain often blandly restate a dated differentiation between manual and non-manual workers. Furthermore, they tend towards understanding class as a gradient or form of stratification but not as a relationship which holds out a potential for organising political agency. In the aftermath of the 2019 general election, reporting on Northern English voters who had abandoned their seemingly generations-long tribal affiliation with the Labour Party reached fever pitch but was also met by polemical responses on social media. These portrayals revealed the endurance of highly static identity-driven understandings of class, often connected to family or place rather than contemporary economic activity, social relationships or political consciousness. Research by sociologist Kirsteen Paton on political representations of class in Britain highlighted the example of Helen Pidd, the *Guardian*'s North of England editor. Pidd wrote a feature on the Lancashire constituency of Leigh in June 2020 after it had voted Conservative for the first time in a century at the general election the previous December. She profiled a pizza restaurant owner, Andrew Twentyman, who slammed Labour's direction under Jeremy Corbyn's left-wing leadership between 2015 and 2019. Critics pointed out that Twentyman was far from a traditional Labour supporter, given that he was a business owner rather than a worker. They also drew attention to his brother, who was a property developer. Pidd, though, defended her coverage, insisting that 'you can be working class and run a restaurant – or indeed be a property developer'.[41]

Savage's approach to class is certainly significantly more attuned to the distinctions in economic power and status implied by property ownership than Pidd's appeared to be. However, it is also open to the criticisms that it is 'gradational, not relational'. In other words, the fundamental structuring role of conflictual relationships *between* classes is not apparent in his schema. Furthermore, a definition of the working class or plebeian groups emerges which is primarily determined by deprivation. Harriet Bradley's critique of Savage's model argues that it defined its working-class categories primarily by absence and lack of resources rather than by exploring 'the distinctive nature of working-class cultural life'.[42] Daily life in Britain has remained fundamentally marked by the contours of social class in the view of Bradley and Paton. Life at work and home, as well as expectations of how we are understood by others and treated by those in positions of authority, are all moulded by class. These are fundamentally *relational* experiences, and class is made, remade and contested in these interactions but also consequently reimagined through them. Class is therefore considerably less elective than is suggested by a survey which figures 'turning off the Beatles and turning on to Beethoven' as a potentially significant shift in social standing.[43]

These critical readings hold out the potential for an alternative understanding of the dynamics of class in the 2010s and 2020s centred on a reconstituted or new working class. In the early 2010s, Guy Standing influentially formulated the 'precariat' to describe what he viewed as a distinctive dislocated social layer forming beneath the traditional working class in the social hierarchy. These workers were defined by their precarity. Whether they worked driving taxis or as freelance web designers, it was their lack of permanence and secure occupational grounding which most characterised the precariat. They were a 'dangerous class' more prone to explosive protests than sustained institution-building.[44] Savage used the same term to define his bottom class, explicitly drawing on Standing to define Britain's 'invisible people' subsisting on the edge of society, the economy and the welfare state.[45]

Yet writing in the aftermath of the 2017 general election, political blogger and academic Phil Burton-Cartledge suggested a rather different reading whereby a similar constituency had in fact been galvanised by seemingly more traditional forms of politics. Labour's popularity among younger voters could be explained by an emergent subject he termed 'the socialised worker'. Corbyn's pledge to stand for 'the many not the few' had included promises around housing and employment as well as public ownership of key industries. They appealed to socialised workers who are products of an information society, often educated to degree level with aspirations for professional and white-collar jobs. Even where they found such work, the socialised workers were often marred by precarity. Downwardly mobile graduates also often found themselves dependent on jobs in sectors like hospitality, social care or retail.[46]

The hopes and potential of this coalition were perhaps demonstrated in two moments at music festivals. During the summer of 2017, Jeremy Corbyn rallied supporters at Prenton Park on Merseyside. Weeks before the general election, he appeared after Sheffield rock band Reverend and the Makers, known supporters of campaigns for justice for miners victimised by political policing in the 1984–85 strike, and ahead of the Libertines. A few weeks later, Corbyn was one of the unlikely star acts at the Glastonbury festival in Somerset.[47] Grime artist and Corbyn supporter Stormzy spoke out after the horrific death of seventy-two people in a West London council tower block fire which had shocked the nation in the aftermath of the general election.[48] Divides of geography and race, as well as between older and more emergent forms of the British working class, were being navigated in these moments, but they ultimately proved too brittle to survive tumultuous political conditions.

Following the 2019 general election, Burton-Cartledge chided Ben Bradley, the new self-described 'blue-collar Conservative' MP for Mansfield, after he gloated about his win in the former North Nottinghamshire coalfields. Bradley, he argued, ought instead to have had his attention on the draconian conditions of the warehouses built atop former collieries in his constituency.[49] The scourge of landlordism and dependency on the private rented sector is another defining feature of the new working class. It is mostly agglomerated in the large cosmopolitan cities which in England continued delivering big Labour majorities under Corbyn, even in the context of the major national setback which brought Bradley and Anderson to Westminster.[50] In the early 2020s, despite the thorough defeat of the Labour left as represented by Corbyn, a new agenda of trade union politics was at least momentarily galvanised by the language of class conflict. It was one that seemingly provided a bridge between at least some sections of the older and newer working class.

Essential workers

Jacky Yuill trembled as she spoke to a room of attentive listeners. It was 10 November 2021, and Glasgow was hosting the COP26 climate summit. World leaders were whizzing in and out of town, including US President Joe Biden. But more than one hundred people crowded into the Gal Gael centre in Ibrox, on the southern banks of the Clyde, to hear from a very different set of speakers. Among the most powerful was Jacky, a short blonde middle-aged Glaswegian woman. Jacky's story came from working in a care home during the COVID-19 pandemic. She and her colleagues had been told that they were 'key workers' or 'essential workers' by both the UK and Scottish governments. They had been obligated to attend work as usual, risking their life and health for the sake of elderly residents and still earning meagre wages. Usually more privileged white-collar workers were able to work from home, while others had been 'furloughed' – earning most of their wages while idle.

During the summer of 2020, Jacky submitted her reflections to the Workers' Stories Project which I was involved in running along with trade unionists, socialists and artists, Suki Sangha, Ruth Gilbert, Hailey Maxwell and Megan Park. Our aim was to provide a platform for workers to narrate their experiences of the pandemic.[51] Jacky's written account powerfully brought home the injustices of work in a care system which routinely takes advantage of the better nature of women such as herself. This time she had been pushed too far. In the early period of the lockdown, the virus swept through Jacky's care home. Ten residents died, while two of her colleagues fell seriously ill. Jacky herself caught the virus and was off work but confined to statutory sick pay of just £95 per week, which compelled her to go back to work earlier than she should have. The tipping point for Jacky, though, came when a small company bonus was announced, but from which she was excluded due to having been absent:

> No. I was not accepting this. I immediately joined a union. I think I should have joined earlier but I always felt it was a lot of money to pay, while in a job just over minimum wage. However, this showed me that it was important I had the defence if needed and somewhere I can go to seek advice. Surely, they cannot do this with the bonuses? At this point I didn't care if it was £10 or £100. It was the principle. I risked my life to come to work, and this is how I have been treated. I told the manager that I would be contacting the union about this.[52]

There were few dry eyes left in the busy room when Jacky was given the platform to share her story at a gathering of contributors to our project the following autumn. By then, Jacky had lost her job for her brave stand, but she did not regret it, instead imploring the audience to join a union if they had not done so already. Jacky subsequently found work in a supermarket, another hive of poorly rewarded key workers. She recorded her story for an archive hosted by the Open University which placed her within a historical trajectory of working-class women activists.[53]

It was an opportune moment for the message. One of Jacky's fellow speakers at Gal Gael was Chris Mitchell, the firebrand Glasgow City Council cleansing-workers convener. In the autumn of 2021, Mitchell had emerged as a social media sensation in the build-up to and during strike action that coincided with the international climate summit. He was best known for his catchphrases 'I'm Chris Mitchell from the GMB trade union' and 'the camaraderie and the solidarity is only getting bigger and bigger' but also for galvanising groups of colleagues to join him in shouting 'Stand with us! Not against us!' Days before his speech at Gal Gael, Mitchell had spoken at a rally with famed teenage Swedish climate activist Greta Thunberg, after she invited the striking workers to join young activists demanding environmental change.[54]

Both Jacky's refusal to be cowed any further, and the picket lines outside lorry depots and refuse tips formed by GMB members in Glasgow, were a sign of things to come across Britain during the months which followed. A movement that was unlike any seen before in the twenty-first century was forming in workplaces across Scotland, England and Wales. The strike wave of 2022 and 2023 was galvanised by mounting inflation, which was already gathering pace before the new year but accelerated even further after the Russian invasion of Ukraine in February 2022. Energy and food prices shot up. Inflation had hit double digits by the summer. There had been no precedent for a loss of purchasing power on this scale in around forty years.[55] Workers who had been told they were essential were now being asked to sacrifice all over again just as lockdown restrictions began to be fully lifted. In total, there were more than 10 million essential workers in the UK. They had been concentrated in the poorest half of earners. Along with health and social care, education and childcare, the distribution of food and necessary goods as well as public transport were among the leading sectors by numbers in employment.[56]

Workers withdrew their labour at schools and colleges and universities but also at key centres of logistics and distribution like ports and warehouses. Construction and maintenance workers at oil refineries and petrochemicals plants and even offshore North Sea platforms joined the demand for inflation-matching wage rises. Two large, long-running disputes in the postal service and on the railways proved central to defining the wave and in allowing Mick Lynch to play the role of an iconic leader with appeal far beyond the ranks of the RMT membership or even unionised workers at large. Lynch helped to generalise the objectives of the dispute, accompanying his bold declaration that 'the working class is back' with a robust follow-up: 'We refuse to be poor anymore.'[57]

While they were far from the most significant disputes in terms of the days lost to action, victories obtained, disruption caused or the high-profile leaders they produced, the Amazon strikes discussed earlier in this chapter were important for other reasons. A strategic and growing section of the workforce was beginning to engage in significant forms of collective action in Britain for the first time. This was not for lack of trying on the part of trade unions. More than twenty years earlier, an attempt to form a union at Amazon's warehouse in Milton Keynes had ended in a humiliating and overwhelming defeat at a recognition election. Company managers wore t-shirts 'telling the union to get back in the history books' as fewer than one in five workers voted in favour of recognition.[58]

Discontent among Amazon warehouse workers was a response to both the conditions in the workplace and the meagre rewards on offer. An Amazon worker writing anonymously for *Notes from Below* on 5 August 2022 explained the background to the evolving strike action: 'Everyone I know has had to work hard and been pushed to their limit every day.' The trigger came in the form of a tiny pay rise after the company had racked up huge profits during the pandemic, when retail outlets had closed while Amazon kept delivering. Warehouse workers were facing rent, food and energy bill rises too, but their wages were less and less able to meet them, despite the demanding conditions they worked under.[59] Another report by an Amazon worker from Coventry was published two days later. It underlined that they had worked through the pandemic, 'including the lockdowns', having been judged as essential workers.[60] Amazon workers had faced the dangers of the pandemic to deliver goods to households experiencing the comparative safety of working from home or furlough but were only receiving a major cut in their living standards in return. Callum Cant mapped the spread of Amazon industrial action for *Notes from Below* later in the month. The action had begun when workers downed tools at Tilbury on the Thames Estuary and went to the canteen, refusing work following the announcement of the pay offer. Eventually it spread across eleven sites.[61]

These actions built on the atmosphere of frustration and resistance which Cant and his fellow editor, Jamie Woodcock, had recorded over the previous decade. Woodcock's research into call-centre employment drew on working 'undercover' as a sales rep on the phones. He emphasised how just as Amazon replicated industrial processes of old, call centres subjected workers to 'computerised Taylorism', requiring them to follow the lead of a computer server and robotically recite a script while also maintaining a charming manner to please customers. Workers found ways to resist through forms of 'refusal to work' which were rarely collectivised beyond adding in nonsensical but amusing terms to scripts for the entertainment of coworkers.[62] Woodcock underlined the retention of antagonistic workplace relationships and collective sentiment in the precarious workplaces of twenty-first-century Britain.

Cant told a more developed story of mobilisation when he worked as a cycle courier for Deliveroo, one of the 'platform' firms which mushroomed in Britain by employing labour on highly flexible terms through mobile-phone applications. Deliveroo recruited a workforce numbering in the tens of thousands in the second half of the 2010s. Dangerous conditions on the streets, ranging from cycle thieves to delivery riders being targeted in acid attacks, became important instigators of worker organising. So too were intermittent earnings, poor wages and being treated shoddily by the company managers and restaurant owners who exercised employer power over the riders, along with the relentless algorithm itself. In the autumn of 2018 industrial action spread from Deliveroo to involve workers at another platform, Just Eat, and extended from the smaller 'independent' unions who first organised workers at Deliveroo to involve larger 'mainstream' unions like Unite, the Bakers, Food and Allied Workers Union and the GMB. Industrial action was supported by rallies in towns and cities in Scotland, England and Wales, while other workers in 'gig economy' jobs like taxi drivers at Uber organised strikes too.[63]

Despite this build-up, the strike wave of 2022 and 2023 did not lead to a larger generalised sustained upsurge of trade unionism. Density in fact fell year on year to leave just over a fifth of British workers as union members in 2024. Although union membership in the public sector grew, it continued to fall in the private sector, likely connected to ongoing changes associated with the downsizing of older established manufacturing industries and the growth in the numbers of the very 'new economy' workers who activists hoped they could convince to organise.[64] Amazon workplaces were mired in controversy as workers and trade unions alleged that fulfilment centres were risky places to work. In spring 2023, amid another strike at Amazon in the Midlands, Maria, a Romanian worker at Rugeley, summarised how English and migrant staff alike were battling for basic human recognition and dignity. She told left-wing journalist Taj Ali that her discontent came from visible dangers at work. Maria joined the strike fuelled by rage at the attitude of managers who 'act like they are superior to us'. One of Maria's colleagues, Ian, also spoke to Ali. As a local miner's son, he pointed to the experience of the long struggle for safety and economic security in the British coal industry as inspiring his decision to picket his distribution centre.[65]

These parallels between conditions below and above ground included the shared risks of dangerous workplaces. In August 2024, the *Guardian* reported that ambulances had been called to Amazon facilities in the UK 1,400 times in the previous five years. At Dunfermline, in the vicinity of the former Fife coalfields, there was an eerie recalling of industrial conditions past, with more than fifty call-outs related to chest pain along with others for breathing problems. At Mansfield in Nottinghamshire, more than fifty call-outs were for serious incidents including life-threatening heart attacks or strokes. Pregnancy-related conditions and miscarriages but also more specific workplace hazards such as exposure to acid, electrocution and burns were also reported.[66]

Amazon had defied a unionisation drive at its Coventry distribution centre the month before, but it was a far narrower victory than the trouncing at Milton Keynes in 2001. The GMB was defeated by twenty-nine votes, with just shy of half of workers voting in favour of a union and marginally more against.[67] Towards the end of the year, trade unions gained some measure of recompense when senior Amazon managers floundered before the House of Commons Business and Trade Committee. Stuart Morgan, the Amazon Logistics Human Resources Director, attempted to excuse the firm's record of ambulance callouts by first claiming that most were for health conditions unrelated to work but then pointing to the size of his company's workforce. Liam Byrne, the committee's chair and the Labour MP for Birmingham Hodge Hill and Solihull North, pointed out that the Palace of Westminster receives 50,000 visitors each day, a figure equivalent to Amazon's entire UK workforce, without any comparable record of people requiring medical attention. Byrne also raised the case of a worker who, according to testimony from the GMB, had lost 80 per cent of his sight following his exposure to chemicals at work at an Amazon depot. He referred to allegations that management had refused to phone an ambulance due to being under pressure to reduce call-outs, which resulted in the man's loss of sight being made permanent. Byrne then put the question of exploitation forward bluntly, asking 'are you basically profiteering from the hard work of employees and not giving them the full measure of their reward?'[68]

Worker disempowerment and ongoing union non-recognition at Amazon in Rugeley can be contrasted with the unionisation and collective action achieved at both Lea Hall colliery and Rugeley power station, which were explored in chapter 1. In the early 1970s, powerful organised workforces used workplace mobilisation and parliamentary mechanisms to win meaningful improvements in pay and conditions. If a new working class is forming in Britain in the 2020s, it is still in its preliminary phases. Yet there are signs of a renewed politicisation of work and employment, along with moments of assertiveness, sometimes from quarters which had previously been written off by resigned, defeated trade unionists. At least for a time in 2022 and 2023, there was also a popular generalisation over the return of the organised working class to political relevance. These sentiments were bolstered by renewed trade union mobilisation and reinforced by the moral argument that socially necessary jobs in 'essential' occupations ought to sustain a commensurate standard of living. It was far from the case that the British working class was 'back' in any enduring form, and trends towards the fracturing of the labour movement continued. The apparent popularity of the view that irresponsible employers and exploitative landlords should not be able to profit from backbreaking labour, dangerous conditions or the better nature of caring people like Jacky Yuill at least demonstrates the latent potential for a new working-class politics.

Conclusion

Class Politics After the British Working Class

In October 2023, less than a year before he became prime minister, Keir Starmer was challenged as leader of the Labour Party to define what it meant to be working class by the LBC radio station journalist Nick Ferrari. Starmer retained an emphasis on class as Labour leader even as he was seen to move the party rightwards, distancing himself from the more radical programme Labour had adopted under Corbyn. He often discussed class in no small part through his own life story and family. Starmer presented himself as a representative of working-class interests based on growing up as the son of a father who was a skilled manual worker, a toolmaker, while his mother was a nurse who worked in the National Health Service. The answer he gave Ferrari was far from certain or convincing:

> Working-class families have the ordinary hope to get on in life. People will say to me, well look Keir, you've come a long way. But that is the ordinary hope of the working class. To have a decent education, to get a decent secure job, to get a car, to have a nice holiday.[1]

Starmer was questioned further by Ferrari, who pointed out that plenty of middle-class people have similar aspirations. The Labour leader resorted to discussing how he and many others had been on 'a life journey from what you might call working class to middle class'.[2]

Starmer's definition is symptomatic of the depoliticisation of class in twenty-first-century Britain. Rather than class being conceived in terms of exploitation, distribution or conflict, it is personal life journeys and identities which are often at the heart of public debate surrounding the topic. While it is easy to lampoon the facileness of Starmer's answer, it could also be countered that it is unlikely that earlier Labour leaders would necessarily have offered a more sophisticated perspective. Class is notoriously difficult to pin down, especially in the British context, where economic and political interests coincide with lingering dimensions of status and hierarchy. Often, these have been joined by cultural habits and consumption patterns. Perhaps most importantly, though, these signifiers have become increasingly detached from the social relationships and affinities they once more meaningfully represented.

This book began from the thesis that the British working class was present at its own unmaking, reapplying Edward Thompson's maxim that the English working class was present at its making in the late eighteenth and early nineteenth centuries.[3] In the second half of the twentieth and early twenty-first centuries, as in the context of an industrialising England that Thompson explored, the working class was subject to economic and political power in what was always a highly asymmetrical setting. Nonetheless, working-class people acted even as they were acted upon. There is a complex history of varied responses that range from the spirited defence of the coal industry and legitimate trade union power in the 1984–85 miners' strike, to the sinking of redundancy payments into Right to Buy mortgages and subscriptions, to the public offerings made by newly privatised companies. These actions were often seemingly contradictory. Former striking miners commonly enough also bought their council houses.

Another crucial feature of the unmaking is its decades-long nature. This is not a story that can be neatly summarised by the Thatcher years alone. Closures of mines, docks and railway lines, along with the clearance of slum neighbourhoods in the cities and industrial towns where Labourism had its origins, conditioned the unmaking and began much earlier. Union battles such as the Grunwick strike also demonstrate that the success of intransigent employers who were intent on exploiting precarious workers, particularly women and immigrant workers, was also apparent before 1979. Furthermore, the unravelling continued long afterwards, unfolding in the twenty-first century through New Labour's explicit rejection of class politics and then the assertion of racist British nationalism on the right which was branded as speaking for the disenfranchised white working class. Working-class people were part of these changes, in their workplaces, at the housing offices and building societies, and at the polling booths. They deserve a rich history attentive to dynamics on the picket lines and the assembly lines as well as the pubs, clubs, football terraces, community centres and kitchen tables.

Across most of the period that this book addresses, there was a vocal public conversation about the shifting contours of class. From the 1950s into the 1990s, academic social researchers, journalists and politicians engaged in debates over the meaning of growing working-class incomes and homeownership. These discussions included intellectual arguments over affluent workers and whether the working class had or had not been bourgeoisified. They also fed into New Labour's realignment with what its key political strategists saw as the new political terrain marked by aspirational service-sector workers in a globalising economy. There was a contradictory twist to this analysis: although New Labour arguments appealed to a material analysis with class implications, its adherents also announced the political death of class. In the years of New Labour government, when class was thought to be a settled issue, this conversation became quieter. The debate on class as it has since re-emerged has been less convincingly invested in connecting questions around ways of living and social relationships with political affiliations and economic conflict. Class has been understood in more elective forms, as a cultural inheritance or as a more crudely socioeconomic feature without organisation or mobilisation at its heart.

The British working class emerged and then matured as a

powerful social and political agent in the late nineteenth century and first half of the twentieth century. Its collectivist culture linked the home and the workplace to local and national politics, most strongly in the large cities and the industrial regions of Scotland, England and Wales. These connections shaped the sense of shared interest which formed class consciousness. In the mid-twentieth century, the British working class reached the peak of legitimacy, power and cultural recognition, but it was challenged and then ultimately fractured and dissipated in the decades which followed. Labourism, the key expression of British working-class politics, was founded upon connections between trade unionism, industrial communities and the Labour Party. This political culture was threatened by transformations which in many cases had origins in policies embraced by Labour governments. Shifts towards a more affluent, suburban and homeowning working class along with the rundown in employment in traditional industries were followed by a more generalised deindustrialisation from the late 1960s. Yet, as chapter 1 explored, Labourism was adaptive to this environment too, and union strength increased for another decade, particularly within growing public services. While deindustrialisation and de-organisation unfolded together, the latter began more than a decade after the former was already a marked national trend. A confident labour movement pushed forward towards newer constituencies, especially women employed in the public sector, in the 1970s.

The changing composition of Britain's working class was marked by trends such as expanding women's employment and post-war Commonwealth immigration. Chapter 2 explored these shifts through the context of the iconic strike at the Grunwick photo-processing plant. Grunwick exposed the limits of union power even when most workers in Britain were covered by collective bargaining and a majority were union members. A titanic effort to secure union recognition at a relatively small firm failed in the face of determined intransigence by management and the political and policing support which the employer came to enjoy. Massive mobilisations of Metropolitan Police resources kept the plant open each working day during a two-year strike, even in the face of mass pickets which demonstrated the breadth of support from trade unionists across Britain. Yet Grunwick's management won the dispute because most of the Grunwick workforce kept working, and they were willing to be driven through picket lines on the ageing buses which the company bought specially for the purpose.

While trade unionists castigated Grunwick as an archaic firm intent on resurrecting Victorian master and servant relationships, it was in fact a sign of things to come. Met officers dealt out similar blows on picket lines in the coalfields and then on the other side of London at the Wapping print-works in the 1980s, as the bastions of stalwart trade unionism that had supported the Grunwick workers were in turn broken. As chapter 3 explored through the closure of Cardowan colliery in Lanarkshire, unions and workforces were isolated and targeted industrially and politically. In the 1980s, unlike in the 1970s, coal miners found that they could not rely on the support of power station workers whose assistance had been important in helping to deliver their wage strike victories the previous decade.

British workplaces have been reconstructed in the image of the managerial authority which triumphed at Grunwick rather than that of the strongly embedded traditions of union recognition that the publicly owned coal industry developed at Cardowan. Union membership has plummeted since the 1980s, falling to below half of the 13 million peak achieved in the late 1970s.[4] Fewer than a quarter of British workers were members of a trade union in the early 2020s.[5] These are important indicators, but they fail also to capture the diminishing standing unions exercise even within organised workplaces along with their reduced place in the life and worldviews of workers in contemporary Britain. Another demonstration of declining levels of union activity is that from 1990 to 2021 the total number of days lost annually to industrial action never surpassed the level of 2 million, which it frequently had done over the 1950s, 1960s,

1970s and 1980s.[6] If anything, those figures understate the extent of change, given that in the earlier period brief workplace stoppages were frequent but tended to go unreported. This is not to exaggerate the predominance of strikes in the past, with most factories remaining strike-free, at least at the level of recorded disputes, in most years.[7] Most significantly, though, as the 'Affluent Worker' study of car workers concluded in the 1960s, and as demonstrated in the industrial action of miners and power workers explored in chapter 1, trade unionism was understood by workers as an effective collective means for realising improved living standards.[8]

The declining efficacy of workplace organisation and waning belief in the capacity of trade unionism have powerfully shaped the unmaking of the British working class. These changes have also encouraged shifts in predominant economic identities. The Thatcherite attack on unions in the 1980s was combined with the promotion of 'enterprise culture'. Under New Labour, workers were encouraged to invest in themselves: human capital perspectives underlined that workers were their own main asset, individually in competition with others in the growing global labour market. One symptom of these circumstances is the growth of self-employment. In the first two decades of the twenty-first century, recorded self-employment in Britain grew by two-thirds, from 3 million to 5 million.[9] The number of businesses, which are overwhelmingly small enterprises, also grew from 3.5 million to 6 million over the same period.[10]

Dan Evans has persuasively argued that the expansion of the traditional petty bourgeoisie of sole traders and small business owners is a leading factor in contemporary British class relations, along with the growth of a 'new petty bourgeoisie' of graduate professionals. The former, in Evans's view, also overlap significantly with landlords.[11] One in twenty-one adults was a landlord in Britain in the mid-2020s.[12] They were overwhelmingly minor rentiers, with around eight in ten English landlords letting fewer than five properties in 2024.[13] Landlords are at the apex of the larger change in housing which was pivotal in the unmaking of the British working class, as explored through Right to Buy council house sales in chapter 5. Homeownership has become a dominant economic identity; bricks and mortar are foundational to narratives of social mobility. Since the 1980s, the state provision of expanding council housing for a large swathe of the working class has been replaced with increased rates of owner-occupation underlined by the promise of ever-rising house prices. An enduring legacy of Right to Buy is the retreat of the local state from housing provision along with the strong links (and sometimes conflicts) it created between tenants and Labour Party councillors.[14]

Council housing has become residualised. Public tenants have been stigmatised as the denizens who failed to equip themselves for prosperity through asset ownership. As explored in chapter 5, in the New Labour era the underclass emerged as the counterpart of the aspirational agents of human capital. Reprising older notions of the 'rough' working class, these were the feckless, crime-ridden, work-resistant menaces to British society who needed tough love to become functional and productive. Politically, the underclass fed into the projection of a racist white working class concentrated in depressed mill towns and less salubrious London suburbs suffering from factory job losses.

In the discussion of the rise of the British National Party (BNP) during the 2000s in chapter 6, a more nuanced reality was identified. BNP electoral support was not confined to generally Labour-voting former industrial settlements in Yorkshire and Lancashire, and, moreover, the electoral base was more complex than the underclass picture suggests too. There was indeed a marked tendency for 'skilled workers' or 'C2' voters, including self-employed tradesmen, to back the BNP, which conformed to a larger history of links between this grouping and support for fascism. Whether referred to as 'C2' or skilled or better-off, the upper sections of the working class are a key feature of its unmaking. They were central to debates over affluence in the 1960s and 1970s before becoming the tenants most likely to buy their council homes in the 1980s and then emerging as Blair's sought-after 'Mondeo Man' voters of the 1990s.

The unmaking of the British working class unfolded in the reshaping of relationships which moulded the lives of workers and their families, along with how they understood their position in society: work and employment, communities and housing, along with their connections to formalised politics. Industrial towns and cities dominated the analysis in this book along with the coalfields: Scotland's Central Belt, London, the Midlands and North West and North East of England, Yorkshire and South Wales. Nationhood and territorial politics are another crucial dimension. The British working class was marked by an attachment to forms of organisation and consciousness which reinforced a British national affiliation across Scotland, England and Wales even where it accommodated regional and national distinctions. The British state, nationalised industries and trade unions which organised workers across Scotland, England and Wales were all formative. In the 2020s, the Union is significantly weaker than it was in the 1950s and 1960s where this history begins. This is most immediately visible in the continued high levels of support for Scottish independence. It also reverberates in the weakening of attachments to Britishness defined by Union in the context of devolution in England and Wales, along with increasingly assertive appeals to an insurgent Englishness on the political right.[15]

Class has also been reinvigorated as a source of political inspiration on the British left and centre as well as the right, including in parliamentary discussion. The former Scottish National Party First Minister, Nicola Sturgeon, quipped during a Scottish Parliament debate in 2023, 'I do not come from a deprived background. I come from a working-class background.'[16] Establishing this distinction was significant to Sturgeon. It was a marker of respectability and status which had clear overlaps with twentieth-century working-class politics in Scotland and Britain. As with the quote from Keir Starmer above, it serves as a comment on a personal journey of social mobility. The return of class in the 2010s and 2020s has often been through analyses which underline the value of gradations between socioeconomic groupings rather than economic or political conflict. Both Starmer and Sturgeon appear to legitimate this perspective, underlining their biographies and family stories through status distinctions but also aspirations for mobility and meritocracy.

The year before Sturgeon's remark, in the context of the beginning of Britain's 'strike wave', a different more assertive appeal to class was made by Mick Lynch, the straight-talking general secretary of the National Union of Rail, Maritime and Transport Workers (RMT). As discussed in the previous chapter, Lynch's declaration that 'the working class is back' suggested potential for a more collectivist form of working-class mobilisation rooted in workplace and community sensibilities but also ultimately grounded in a perspective which viewed workers as engaged in legitimate battles with their employers.[17] Yet while Lynch's rallying cry held out hope, at least for a moment, it also underlined the distance which had been travelled. Appeals to the working class in the 2020s required a more assured recasting of the boundaries of British society on terms which could begin to more certainly identify and mobilise an evolving constituency. Starmer's stuttering answer to Ferrari was structural as well as personal. If the working class is back, then there is still much to be achieved in re-establishing its presence on terms which are readily understood by the working class itself as well as its allies and enemies. This is urgently required in an era when the political purchase of appeals to class has grown but when competing definitions of class are put forward on the right as well as the left.

The unmaking of the British working class was a decades-long experience and the consequences are still reverberating in British society and politics. In the 1960s, the working class had achieved the peak of its cultural influence and political and economic power. Even as the slums were cleared and people tuned in to watch televised dramatisations of the industrial communities they had left behind in their suburban homes, trade unionism and collective organisation remained important to structuring political consciousness and living standards. The defeat of organised labour started in the setbacks of the 1970s when employers such as George Ward at Grunwick were able to begin halting the advance of trade unions with the support of the Tory opposition. In government, senior Labour figures such as Prime Minister Jim Callaghan and Chancellor Denis Healey tasked themselves with disciplining and coercing trade unions which increased the tensions between the political and industrial wings of the labour movement. In the process, they aided the rising Thatcherite right by discrediting the view that a union–Labour Party alliance could deliver a more prosperous and less conflict-ridden country.

Grunwick was formative not only because it was an attempt by unions to organise among a predominantly Asian and black workforce, but because it was a firm in a consumer-facing service sector and a relatively small employer on the outskirts of London. While unions had weathered the initial wave of deindustrialisation by expanding membership in the growing public sector, their strength was eroded thereafter. The violent policing of Grunwick anticipated what was to come through the press offensive and the intense anti–trade union politics adopted by the Conservative Party first in opposition and then in government. In the 1980s, these conditions were generalised, made most visible in the arrest of thousands of miners during the pivotal 1984–85 miners' strike. Trade unions were defeated not just industrially but politically and ideologically, as their members were criminalised during industrial action. Collectivism was forced onto the defensive and increasingly viewed as antiquated. Unionisation survived in redoubts within the remainder of the public sector following the onslaught of privatisation. Workplace organisation was still disproportionately concentrated in the former heavy-industry regions, but it remained weakest in the new economy, particularly in the booming service sectors of the South East of England.[18] A similar fate met council housing, which became seen as embarrassingly archaic at best and a marker of poverty and social failure at worst. Powerful changes acted in combination. Building society memberships and mortgage payments displaced union cards and dues, shifting how people identified politically and who they saw as their fellows.

These shifts were not just happening outside of the labour movement or to those who had abandoned it. They fundamentally altered the weakened trade unions and the Labour Party. New Labour was characterised by the party leadership self-consciously distancing itself from its trade union affiliates through appeals to a classless future based on individuals rising or falling based on their own worth. Diminished social safety nets provided inducements to take up precarious and low-paid jobs. But in the context of accelerating deindustrialisation, public sector outsourcing and the touting of a 'flexible labour market', New Labour marked a further significant denting of what remained of Labourism. While New Labour's partisans often claimed they were merely responding to societal and economic change, and embracing the necessity of globalisation, it was in fact a deeply ideological tendency which politically consolidated the defeats that the labour movement had experienced in the preceding decades.

The underclass became a crucial face of the working class in this period, increasingly stigmatised as unwilling or unable to take up new opportunities and wedded to the most reactionary and backward parts of British culture, from alcoholism to crude racism. Class returned to British politics in this image in the early twenty-first century, often in far-right guises. During the late 2000s, the BNP, a party with its roots in neo-Nazism, claimed to speak for the 'white working class', promising to prioritise white British claims to housing, public spending and 'British jobs for British workers'. While the BNP imploded following electoral failure in the early 2010s, a disenfranchised white plebeian nationalist constituency was projected through the Brexit vote, and the rise of Reform UK along with the reshaping of the politics of immigration, race and nationhood in a thoroughly nativist direction. In an increasingly ill-divided society where the politics of both housing and work are renewed flashpoints, a more traditional politics of class made itself felt episodically in the 2010s and 2020s. To succeed, that politics will need to cast an image of a new working class which resonates with unionised care and cleansing workers, striking Amazon warehouse staff and organising tenants who are unwilling to go on being exploited by landlords, as their forebears were a century before.

At root, the unmaking of the British working class is a story of how ordinary people have understood themselves, their families, their work and their relationships to their neighbours, employers and those they consider either socially above or beneath them. It has been dictated by where they felt they could or could not affect power and a loss of collective affinity. Centrally, the unmaking eroded an affiliation between manual employment and labour movement politics, but it was steeped in the broader communal culture of industrial society at work and home. These were not relations men and women entered of their own volition, but their individual and collective agencies reforged and ultimately unmade them. The unmaking was dictated by ministerial decisions, corporate boards, police batons and press barons, but it was also shaped in workplace conversations, union meetings, collective demands for new public houses and desires to buy them. Cumulatively, the unmaking is the impact of these changes on the consciousness and actions of tens of millions of people.

Acknowledgements

This book began life in a conversation on a chilly evening walk through Scarborough in February 2016. I first set out the unmaking thesis immediately following the 2019 general election in an article published by the *New Socialist* website. *An Injury to All* is a far more ambitious history of the transformations to British society and politics since the middle of the twentieth century than I was able to set out in a short essay which traced the long-term dynamics behind Labour's defeat and increasing electoral instability. While this book is my solo-authored work, it would not have been possible without the support and friendship of colleagues, comrades and confidantes. Readers should consider them to have a share of either the praise or the blame.

John Merrick first broached developing a book project with Verso and patiently guided and encouraged me through forming my initial ideas into a chronological history based around studies of formative transformations to work, housing and party politics. When John moved on to pastures new, Tom Hazeldine carried on in the same stead and gave me the valuable guidance of an experienced editor.

I continued to benefit from the advice of my former PhD supervisor, Jim Phillips, who generously read a full draft of my book. Henry Bell did the same. Ruth Gilbert, James Bowness, Hamish Kallin, Satnam Virdee, Stewart Maclennan, Scott Lavery and Jack MacGregor all kindly read draft chapters or sections of my work. Stephen Ashe selflessly shared his PhD thesis with me, which was invaluable for writing the sixth chapter. Thanks also to Daniel Trilling and Dan Evans for discussing reading and sources.

Unite gave me permission to use the image from *Contact* which appears in chapter 5. Thank you to Joan Francis, Siobhan Endean and Jim Mowatt for their help as well as to Liz Wood at the Modern Records Centre. Many more archivists assisted me in the research for this project. Many other people also shared their life stories and memories with me in the oral history interviews referenced in this book. I cannot thank them all here, but I would like to thank three interviewees who extended friendship and camaraderie as I was writing this book. In September 2023, Willie Doolan gave me the honour of speaking at the Auchengeich Miners' Memorial Service in Moodiesburn, which commemorates the forty-seven miners who were killed in an underground fire in 1959. I regularly met Brendan Moohan before Hibs matches, which was an opportunity to discuss our respective writing commitments, and we wandered around West Fife on a sunny day in May 2025. Danny Carrigan kindly donated documents related to the history of the electricians' union after sharing his memories of work on the tools and as a full-time official.

Friends asked how the book was coming along and listened to me wittering on about parts I was struggling with or enthused by. Thanks especially to Valerie Wright, Jenny Morrison, Stephen Mullen, Dominic Hinde, Diarmaid Kelliher, Dave Featherstone, Conrad Landin, Hailey Maxwell, Rosie Hampton, Sean Kippin, Jack Taylor, Duncan Hotchkiss, Oliver Melling, Elliot Ross, Maha Athal, Lorcan Mullen, Jack MacGregor, Ewan Kerr, Kirsteen Paton, Patrick Orr, Tom Montgomerie and Coll McCail for making this a less lonely mountain to climb.

Laura Dover read chapters, entertained my musings and was a supportive and loving partner. She was part of the discussion in Scarborough that this book originates from. More importantly, we lived together in the Gorbals as it finally took shape.

A Note on Oral Histories and Presentation

Oral testimonies from former workers, members of their families and trade union officials appear in this book. They were recorded between 2014 and 2023 on a range of labour history research projects. Where participants have consented to be named in publication, I have given their full names. Elsewhere, I have referred to some participants by a single name to indicate that this is a pseudonym which has been adopted to protect their identity.

Notes

Introduction

1. Jimmy Hood, interview with author, South Lanarkshire Council offices, Lanark, 4 April 2014.
2. National Coal Board, *Review*, newsreel, 32nd year, no. 1 (1978).
3. Neighbouring Mansfield was largely represented by former miners from the 1920s to the late 1980s and remained a Labour seat before it fell to self-described 'blue-collar Conservative' Ben Bradley in 2017.
4. For an account sympathetic to the striking minority, see Harry Patterson, *Look Back in Anger: The Miners' Strike in Nottinghamshire 30 Years On* (Nottingham: Five Leaves, 2014). The strike-breaking perspective is put forward in David Amos, 'The Nottinghamshire Miners, the Union of Democratic Mineworkers and the 1984–85 Miners' Strike: Scabs or Scapegoats?' (PhD thesis, University of Nottingham, 2012).
5. Peter Wilsher, *Strike: Thatcher, Scargill and the Miners* (London: Coronet, 1985), p. 117.
6. Tam Dalyell, 'Jimmy Hood', *Independent*, 13 December 2017.
7. These differences crystallised in the distinct patterns of voting recorded between Clydesdale and Nottinghamshire at the Brexit referendum, when over 60 per cent of South Lanarkshire voters backed Remain and in Sherwood the same proportion supported Britain leaving the European Union.
8. E.P. Thompson, *The Making of the English Working Class* (Middlesex: Pelican, 1968).
9. Eric Hobsbawm, 'The Forward March of Labour Halted', *Marxism Today*, September 1978, pp. 279–86.
10. Eric Hobsbawm, *Worlds of Labour: Further Studies in the History of Labour* (London: Weidenfield and Nicolson, 1984), pp. 185–6.
11. Avner Offer, 'British Manual Workers: From Producers to Consumers, c.1950–2000', *Contemporary British History* 22 (2008), pp. 539–40.
12. Priyamvada Gopal, *Insurgent Empire: Anticolonial Resistance and British Dissent* (London: Verso, 2019), pp. 209–78.

13. Jack Taylor, *Oil, Nationalism and British Policy in Iran: The End of Informal Empire, 1941–1953* (London: Bloomsbury, 2023).
14. Ralph Miliband, *Parliamentary Socialism: A Study in the Politics of Labour* (London: Merlin Press, 1991).
15. Tom Nairn, 'The Nature of the Labour Party', *New Left Review* 1, no. 27 (1964), pp. 38–9.
16. David Edgerton, *The Rise and Fall of the British Nation: A Twentieth-Century History* (London: Penguin, 2018), p. 281.
17. Robert Garner and Richard Kelly, *British Political Parties Today* (Manchester: Manchester University Press, 1993), pp. 238–40.
18. Jon Lawrence, 'Class, "Affluence" and the Study of Everyday Life in Britain, c.1930–64', *Cultural and Social History* 10, no. 2 (2013), pp. 273–99.
19. Data from Bank of England, 'A Millennium of Macroeconomic Data', and Office for National Statistics publications.
20. Department for Business and Trade, 'Trade Union Membership, UK, 1995 to 2024: Statistical Bulletin', 22 May 2025, gov.uk.
21. Hobsbawm, 'The Forward March of Labour Halted'.
22. Selina Todd, *The People: The Rise and Fall of the Working Class, 1910–2010* (London: John Murray, 2010).
23. Selina Todd, 'Class, Experience and Britain's Twentieth Century', *Social History* 39 (2014), pp. 489–508.
24. Thompson, *The Making of the English Working Class*, p. 13.
25. Perry Anderson, 'Origins of the Present Crisis', *New Left Review* 1, no. 23 (1964), pp. 26–53.
26. Thompson, *The Making of the English Working Class*, p. 9.

1. The New Working Class

1. Ken Rochester, remote interview with author, 14 March 2022.
2. Quoted in Julia Mitchell, 'Farewell to "Cotia": The English Folk Revival, the Pit Elegy, and the Nationalization of British Coal, 1947–70', *Twentieth Century British History* 25 (2014), p. 598.
3. Mike Savage, 'Working-Class Identities in the 1960s: Revisiting the Affluent Worker Study', *Sociology* 39 (2005), pp. 929–45; Jack Saunders, *Assembling Cultures: Workplace Activism, Labour Militancy and Cultural Change in Britain's Car Factories, 1945–82* (Manchester: Manchester University Press, 2019), pp. 4–5.
4. Huw Beynon and Terry Austrin, 'The Performance of Power: Sam Watson: A Miners' Leader on Many Stages', *Journal of Historical Sociology* 28 (2015), pp. 458–90.

5. Quoted in Mitchell, 'Farewell to "Cotia"', p. 598.
6. Alf Robens, *Ten Year Stint* (London: Cassell, 1972).
7. Department for Energy Security and Net Zero, Historical Coal Data: Coal Production, 1853 to 2024, 31 July 2025, gov.uk.
8. Alex J. Robertson, *The Bleak Midwinter, 1947* (Manchester: Manchester University Press, 1987).
9. Department for Energy Security and Net Zero, Historical Coal Data.
10. Vaclav Smil, *Energy Transitions: History, Requirements, Prospects* (Westport, CT: Praeger, 2010), pp. 79–81.
11. Department for Energy Security and Net Zero, Historical Coal Data.
12. Rochester, interview.
13. 'Largest Cooling Tower', *Birmingham Post*, 26 January 1962, National Archives, Kew (hereafter TNA), Ministry of Power (hereafter POWE), 14/1058.
14. Secretary, Central Electricity Authority, to Secretary, Ministry of Power, 6 February 1957, TNA, POWE 14/1058.
15. Rochester, interview.
16. Rugeley B Generating Station: State of Technical and Other Particulars, 20 November 1963, TNA, POWE 14/1488.
17. The publicly owned electricity industry in Great Britain was reorganised in 1957, which led to the BEA being replaced. In England and Wales, generation and transmission were separated from supply with the formation of a national Central Electricity Generation Board as distinct from regional boards concerned with supply. The South of Scotland Electricity Board and North of Scotland Hydro Electricity Board continued as unitary boards. From 1957, a separate Electricity Council stood above these administrative units.
18. Walter Citrine, *Men and Work: An Autobiography* (London: Hutchinson, 1964), pp. 46–7.
19. Andrew Taylor, *What About the Workers?: The Conservative Party and the Organised Working Class in British Politics* (Liverpool: Liverpool University Press, 2021), p. 80.
20. Walter Citrine, *ABC of Chairmanship* (London: National Council of Labour Colleges, 1952).
21. Keith Jeffery and Peter Hennessy, *States of Emergency: British Governments and Strikebreaking Since 1919* (London: Routledge and Kegan Paul, 1983), pp. 210–17.
22. Lord Citrine to Hugh Gaitskell, subject: London Power Station Strike, 23 December 1949, TNA, Prime Minister's Office 8/1290.
23. T. Buchanan, 'Citrine, Walter McLennan', *Oxford Dictionary of National Biography* (2008).

24. Leslie Hannah, *Engineers, Managers and Politicians: The First Fifteen Years of Nationalised Electricity Supply in Britain* (London: Macmillan, 1982), p. 8.
25. Department for Energy Security and Net Zero, Historical Time Series of Electricity Supply, Availability and Consumption, 31 July 2025, gov .uk.
26. Central Electricity Generating Board (CEGB), *Power and Progress*, annual report, vol. 9 (London: CEGB, 1967); National Grid, 'History of the Supergrid', nationalgrid.com.
27. Ewan Gibbs, *Coal Country: The Meaning and Memory of Deindustrialization in Postwar Scotland* (London: University of London Press, 2021), pp. 38–9.
28. South of Scotland Electricity Board, 'Energy and Electricity in Scotland' (1976), National Records of Scotland, Edinburgh, Scottish Office Industry Department 14/1553.
29. Mark Wilson and John Wilson, interview with Ewan Gibbs, residence, Dunfermline, 22 April 2022.
30. Rochester, interview.
31. John Harvey, 'A Different View on Coal'. Written testimony sent to the author in correspondence in 2022 and used with permission.
32. Joe Bell, interview with author, residence, Whitehaven, 29 March 2022.
33. Fiona Bowler, '"Sacrificed on the Altar of Progress and Science": Early Cases of Disputed Disease Among British Nuclear Test Veterans', *Contemporary British History* 39 (2025), p. 425.
34. Lorna Arnold, *Windscale 1957: Anatomy of a Nuclear Accident* (Houndmills: Macmillan, 1995), p. 70.
35. Ibid.
36. '£40 A Week Men Work to Keep Away Boredom', *Sunday Express*, 18 February 1951, TNA, Atomic Energy Authority, 16/82.
37. E. Rees, 'Television, Gas and Electricity: Consuming Comfort and Leisure in the British Home, 1946–65', *Journal of Popular Television* 7 (2019), pp. 127–43.
38. Selina Todd, *The People: The Rise and Fall of the Working Class, 1910–2010* (London: John Murray, 2010), p. 9.
39. Jim Tomlinson, *Managing the Economy, Managing the People: Narratives of Economic Life in Britain from Beveridge to Brexit* (Oxford: Oxford University Press, 2017), p. 38.
40. 'Behind the Scenes on the Coronation Street Set', *Guardian*, 14 March 2018.
41. BBC, 'The Morecambe and Wise Show: 2 September 1968', History of the BBC, bbc.co.uk.

42. W.W.J. Knox and Alan McKinlay, *Jimmy Reid: A Clyde-Built Man* (Liverpool: Liverpool University Press, 2019), pp. 147–8.
43. John Goldthorpe, David Lockwood, Frank Bechhofer and Jennifer Platt, *The Affluent Worker: Industrial Attitudes and Behaviour* (Cambridge: Cambridge University Press, 1968), p. 98.
44. Jon Lawrence, *Me, Me, Me?: The Search for Community in Postwar England* (Oxford: Oxford University Press, 2019), p. 105.
45. Tony Roper, *The Steamie* (Kirkintilloch: Field Illeray Productions, 1987); Tony Roper and Duncan Haldane, *The Steamie*, broadcast on Scottish Television, 31 December 1988.
46. Richard Hoggart, *The Uses of Literacy: Aspects of Working-Class Life* (London: Penguin, 2009).
47. Eric Hobsbawm, 'Society: New and Old', *New Left Review* 142 (2023), pp. 104–5.
48. Quoted in Lawrence, *Me, Me, Me?*, p. 138.
49. Florence Sutcliffe-Braithwaite and Natalie Thomlinson, 'Vernacular Discourses of Gender Equality in the Post-War British Working Class', *Past and Present* 254 (2022), p. 279.
50. Jörg Arnold, *The British Miner in the Age of De-Industrialization: A Political and Cultural History* (Oxford: Oxford University Press, 2023), p. 104.
51. Matthew Day, 'The Short Happy Life of the Affluent Working Class: Consumption, Debt and Embourgeoisement in the Age of Credit', *Capital and Class* 44 (2020), p. 317.
52. Peter Hennessy, *Having It So Good: Britain in the Fifties* (London: Penguin, 2006), p. 283.
53. Jim Phillips, Valerie Wright and Jim Tomlinson, *Deindustrialisation and the Moral Economy in Scotland since 1955* (Edinburgh: Edinburgh University Press, 2021), ch. 5.
54. Moodiesburn focus group with retired miners' group, the Pivot, Moodiesburn, 25 March 2014.
55. NUMSA, Minutes of Executive and Special Conferences, 12 June 1961 to 6/8 June 1962, pp. 502, 509, National Mining Museum of Scotland, Newtongrange.
56. J.C.H. Mellanby Lee, Operational Research Executive (Scotland), 'A Paper for Consideration by the Scottish Area Monday and Friday Absence Committee', 8 August 1973, TNA, Coal 101/488.
57. Ibid.
58. Karel Reisz, *Saturday Night and Sunday Morning* (Bryanston Films, 1960).
59. EETPU, *Abridged Report of the National Conference for the Electricity Supply Industry, Pier Ballroom Hastings, 2–3 April 1974* (Glasgow: Civic Press, 1974), p. 60.

60. EETPU, *Abridged Report of the National Conference for the Electricity Supply Industry, Pier Ballroom Hastings, 18 and 19 May 1968* (Bromley: EETPU, 1968), p. 70.
61. Report of the Royal Commission on Trade Unions and Employers' Associations, cmnd.3623 (London: HMSO, 1968).
62. Saunders, *Assembling Cultures*, p. 35.
63. Arthur Marwick, *British Society Since 1945* (London: Penguin, 1996), p. 111.
64. Christopher Harvie, *Scotland and Nationalism: Scottish Society and Politics, 1707 to the Present* (London: Routledge, 2004), p. 85.
65. Stuart Jeffries, 'Britain's Most Racist Election: The Story of Smethwick, 50 Years On', *Guardian*, 15 October 2014.
66. Fred Lindop, 'Racism and the Working Class: Strikes in Support of Enoch Powell in 1968', *Labour History Review* 66 (2001), pp. 79–100.
67. EETPU, *Abridged Report: National Conference for the Electricity Supply Industry, the Spa, Scarborough, 9 May 1978* (Glasgow: Civic Press, 1978), p. 47.
68. Electricity Supply Industry – Court of Inquiry – Statement of the Trade Union Side of the National Joint Industrial Council, January 1971, TNA, Ministry of Labour (hereafter LAB) 112/4.
69. 'Power Workers' Inquiry: Chapple at Court', *Contact* 3, no. 1 (1971), p. 18, Modern Records Centre, Warwick, records of the Electrical Trades Union (hereafter, ETU), P/3/1.
70. Rochester, interview.
71. Ross McWhirter, London, to Wilberforce, 15 January 1971, TNA, LAB, 112/4.
72. Matt Myers, *The Halted March of the European Left: The Working Class in Britain, France, and Italy, 1968–1989* (Oxford: Oxford University Press, 2025), pp. 126–7.
73. G.W. Searle, Edgware, Middlesex, to Wilberforce, 16 January 1971, TNA, LAB, 112/4.
74. 'Monkeying with Wages', *Economist*, 13 February 1971, TNA, POWE 14/2413.
75. John Torode, 'The Power Court Jesters', *Guardian*, 25 January 1971, MRC, Frank Chapple archive, MSS 387.6.CH/105.
76. Ibid.
77. In February 1974, following the beginning of the second miners' strike, Chapple sent a circular out to all electricity supply industry shop stewards confirming that, as in 1972, 'no action should be taken which could be detrimental to the miners' strike', before outlining details on the boycott of fuel deliveries: Frank Chapple, Electricity Supply Industry: Mining Dispute, circular, 15 February 1974, MRC, ETU,

Circulars, Box 61, MSS.387/2000/61. See also Diarmaid Kelliher, *Making Cultures of Solidarity: London and the 1984–5 Miners' Strike* (London: Routledge, 2021), ch. 1.

78. John North and Derek Spooner, 'The Great U.K. Coal Rush: A Progress Report to the End of 1976', *Area* 9, no. 1 (1977), p. 15.

2. Grunwick

1. Jack Dromey, 'Jayaben Desai Obituary', *Guardian*, 28 December 2010.
2. Linda McDowell, Sundari Anitha and Ruth Pearson, 'Striking Narratives: Class, Gender and Ethnicity in the "Great Grunwick Strike", London, UK, 1976–1978', *Women's History Review* 23 (2014), p. 598.
3. Jayaben Desai, interviewed by Chris Thomas, 2007, Modern Records Centre (hereafter MRC), University of Warwick, 803/20A.
4. Ibid.
5. Report of a Court of Inquiry Under the Rt Hon Lord Justice Scarman, OBE, into a dispute between Grunwick Processing Laboratories Limited and members of the Association of Professional, Executive, Clerical and Computer Staff, cmnd.6922 (London: HMSO, 1977), p. 15.
6. Joe Rogaly, *Grunwick* (London: Penguin, 1977), pp. 11–14.
7. Ibid.
8. Ibid., pp. 12–20.
9. MendezMedia, 'Jayaben Desai Documentary – Featuring Jeremy Corbyn and Bob Crow', YouTube, 24 December 2015.
10. Jack Dromey, interviewed by Chris Thomas, 2007, MRC, 803/00.
11. Dromey, 'Jayaben Desai'.
12. Amrit Wilson, *Finding a Voice: Asian Women in Britain* (London: Virago, 1978), pp. 57–9.
13. Sarah Cox, 'Tom Durkin', *Socialist Worker*, 18 January 2003; Durkin features in archive footage in Chris Thomas, *The Great Grunwick Strike 1976–1978 – A History* (2007) hosted on the Modern Records Centre website.
14. Satnam Virdee, *Racism, Class and the Racialized Outsider* (Basingstoke: Palgrave Macmillan, 2014), pp. 124–37.
15. Sundari Anitha and Ruth Pearson, 'Striking Women – Striking Out', *Feminist Review* 108 (2015), p. 61.
16. McDowell, Anitha and Pearson, 'Striking Narratives', p. 612.
17. A. Sivanandan, 'UK Commentary', *Race and Class* 19, no. 1 (1977), p. 72.
18. A. Sivanandan, *A Different Hunger: Writings on Black Resistance* (London: Pluto, 1982), p. 136.

19. Duncan Needham, 'Goodbye Great Britain? The Press, the Treasury, and the 1976 IMF Crisis', in Steve Schifferes and Richard Roberts (eds), *The Media and Financial Crises: Historical and Comparative Perspectives* (London: Routledge, 2014), pp. 261–6.
20. Colm Murphy, 'The Political Crisis of British Keynesianism, 1973–1983', *Past and Present* (2025), gtaf012.
21. Jim Callaghan, Leader's Speech, Labour Party Conference, Blackpool, 28 September 1976.
22. Colin Hay, 'Trade Unions and the "Winter of Discontent": A Case of Myth-Taken Identity', *Historical Studies in Industrial Relations* 36 (2015), pp. 191–2. For a more extensive history of wage strikes in 1978 and 1979, see Tara Martin López, *The Winter of Discontent: Myth, Memory, and History* (Liverpool: Liverpool University Press, 2014).
23. Colin Hay, 'Narrating the Crisis: The Discursive Construction of the "Winter of Discontent"', *Sociology* 30 (1996), pp. 253–77.
24. HC Deb 14 July 1977, vol. 935, c. 760.
25. Ibid., c. 761.
26. Jim Phillips, 'Industrial Relations in the "Golden Age" in the UK and the USA, 1945 to 1980', in Bradley Bowden and Adela McMurray (eds), *The Palgrave Handbook of Management History* (Basingstoke: Palgrave Macmillan, 2019), p. 833.
27. Andy Beckett, *When the Lights Went Out: What Really Happened to Britain in the Seventies* (London: Faber and Faber, 2009), p. 391.
28. David Miller, interview with Chris Thomas, MRC, 803/23 and 803/00A.
29. Grunwick Strike Committee bulletin no. 23, 25 January 1977, MRC, Records of Frank Chapple, MSS/387/6/CH/17.
30. HC Deb 4 November 1976, vol. 918, c. 1660.
31. See Tim Strangleman, *Voices of Guinness: An Oral History of the Park Royal Brewery* (Oxford: Oxford University Press, 2019).
32. Ruth Dukes and Wolfgang Streeck, *Democracy at Work: Contract, Status and Post-Industrial Justice* (Cambridge: Polity Press, 2023), pp. 67–8.
33. Mary Irwin, 'The Rag Trade: "Everybody Out!" Gender, Politics and Class on the Factory Floor', in Jürgen Kamm and Birgit Neumann (eds), *British TV Comedies: Cultural Concepts, Contexts and Controversies* (London: Springer, 2016), pp. 66–79.
34. Wolfgang Ochel, 'Collective Bargaining Coverage in the OECD from the 1960s to the 1990s', *CESifo Forum* 2, no. 4 (2001), p. 63.
35. Bob Mason and Peter Bain, 'The Determinants of Trade Union Membership in Britain: A Survey of the Literature', *Industrial and Labor Relations Review* 46 (1993), p. 333.

36. Alan Tuckman, 'Then and Now: Vulnerable Workers, Industrial Action, and the Law in the 1970s and Today', *Historical Studies in Industrial Relations* 41 (2020), p. 254.
37. Jonathan Moss, *Women, Workplace Protest and Political Identity in England, 1968–85* (Manchester: Manchester University Press, 2019), pp. 82–100.
38. Ibid. For an overview of US multinationals closing branch factories, see Andy Clark, *Fighting Deindustrialisation: Scottish Women's Factory Occupations, 1981–1982* (Liverpool: Liverpool University Press, 2022).
39. Jack Dromey and Graham Taylor, *Grunwick: The Workers' Story* (London: Lawrence and Wishart, 1978), p. 23.
40. Chris Wrigley, 'Women in the Labour Market and the Unions', in John McIlroy, Nina Fishman and Alan Campbell (eds), *British Trade Unions and Industrial Politics: The High Tide of Trade Unionism, 1964–79* (Aldershot: Ashgate, 1999), p. 56.
41. Beckett, *When the Lights Went Out*, p. 402.
42. David McKittrick, 'George Ward: Grunwick Owner Whose Strike Battle Set the Scene for Thatcher's Union Reforms', *Independent*, 1 May 2012. This is further confirmed by Companies House records which demonstrate that Bonuspool Limited, which was first incorporated as Grunwick in the 1960s, was dissolved in 2014.
43. Les Levidow, 'Grunwick: The Social Contract Meets the 20th Century Sweatshop', in Les Levidow and Bob Young (eds), *Science Technology and the Labour Process* (London: Black Rose Press, 1981), p. 141.
44. John Cooper Clarke, 'Majorca', *Où est la maison de fromage?*, track 4 (Rabid, 1978).
45. George Ward, *Fort Grunwick* (London: Maurice Temple Smith, 1977), p. 14.
46. Ibid., pp. 25–30.
47. Rogaly, *Grunwick*, pp. 34–44.
48. HC Deb 30 June 1977, vol. 934, cc. 597–601.
49. 'Asians at Grunwick', *Spectator*, 25 June 1977, pp. 15–16.
50. Peter Paterson, 'Grunwick Revisited', *Spectator*, 22 October 1977, p. 10.
51. Robert Taylor, 'Grunwick: A Tale of Two Freedoms', *Observer*, 26 June 1977, pp. 14–15.
52. Matthew Cole, 'Unionising Amazon', *Tribune*, 13 May 2023.
53. Stuart Hall, *The Hard Road to Renewal: Thatcherism and the Crisis of the Left* (London: Verso, 2021), p. 29.
54. David Pallister, 'Tory Mouth for Grunwick Head', *Guardian*, 25 June 1977, p. 2.

55. Paul Blyton and Peter Turnbull, *The Dynamics of Employee Relations* (Basingstoke: Palgrave Macmillan, 2004), pp. 294–6.
56. James Vernon, 'Heathrow and the Making of Neoliberal Britain', *Past and Present* 252 (2021), p. 225.
57. Eric Hobsbawm, 'The Forward March of Labour Halted', *Marxism Today*, September 1978, p. 284.
58. Correspondence with Mark Perryman who kindly shared his memories of the event with me, 21 March 2024.
59. Dromey and Taylor, *Grunwick*, pp. 122, 173.
60. *NUM Scottish Area Executive Committee Minutes, 27th June 1977 to 14th–16th June 1978*, p. 648, National Mining Museum of Scotland, Newtongrange (hereafter NMMS).
61. Concord Media, 'Look Back at Grunwick', YouTube, 12 November 2015.
62. Taylor, 'Grunwick'.
63. Mahmood Ahmed, interview with Chris Thomas, MRC, 803/01A.
64. Vipin Magdani, interview with Chris Thomas, MRC, 803/20.
65. Miller, interview.
66. Dromey and Taylor, *Grunwick*, p. 145.
67. House of Commons Employment Committee, The Legal Immunities of Trade Unions and Other Related Matters, Minutes of Evidence, 27 February 1980, HC 462-ii, p. 36.
68. Dromey and Taylor, *Grunwick*, pp. 14, 140.
69. Diarmaid Kelliher, 'Class Struggle and the Spatial Politics of Violence: The Picket Line in 1970s Britain', *Transactions of the Institute of British Geographers* 46 (2021), pp. 22–3.
70. ITN News, 'Grunwick Dispute', 18 May 1977; posted by Steven Bainbridge on YouTube, 17 December 2012.
71. 'MP Convicted of Obstructing Police Outside Grunwick Plant', *Guardian*, 18 March 1978, p. 3.
72. Stephen Kelly, 'Eye-Witness at Grunwick', *Tribune*, 24 June 1977, pp. 1–2.
73. David Pallister, 'Grunwick Strike Leader Freed After Court Battle over Bail', *Guardian*, 16 June 1977, p. 22.
74. Ahmed, interview.
75. Albert Booth, interview with Chris Thomas, MRC, 803/04A.
76. Julia Langdon, 'Albert Booth Obituary', *Guardian*, 10 February 2010.
77. Albert Booth, interview.
78. Report of a Court of Inquiry Under the Rt Hon Lord Justice Scarman, pp. 6–13.
79. Nikki Knewstub, 'Migrants' Grunwick Lesson', *Guardian*, 19 June 1977, p. 3.

80. Report of a Court of Inquiry Under the Rt Hon Lord Justice Scarman, pp. 21–3.
81. Ian Aitken and David Pallister, 'Ministers Seek Guidelines for Police and Pickets', *Guardian*, 23 June 1977, p. 1.
82. Tony Benn, *Conflicts of Interest: Diaries, 1977–80* (London: Hutchinson, 1990), p. 289.
83. Ibid., p. 176.
84. Christopher Andrew, 'The Threat of Subversion', mi5.gov.uk.
85. Matt Myers, *The Halted March of the European Left: The Working Class in Britain, France, and Italy, 1968–1989* (Oxford: Oxford University Press, 2025), pp. 146–7.
86. Albert Booth, interview.
87. HC Deb 7 November 1977, vol. 938, c. 422; Dromey and Taylor, *Grunwick*, p. 176.
88. HC Deb 7 November 1977, vol. 938, c. 322.
89. HC Deb 11 July 1977, vol. 935, c. 31.
90. Malcolm Sutton, *An Index of Deaths from the Conflict in Ireland 1969–1993* (Belfast: Beyond the Pale, 1993), pp. 195–206.
91. David Pallister, 'Picket Line Peace Plan as Grunwick Violence Grows', *Guardian*, 24 June 1977, p. 1.
92. Dromey and Taylor, *Grunwick*, p. 125.
93. *Workers' Action*, 1–8 July 1977, pp. 1, 3.
94. Thomas, *The Great Grunwick Strike*.
95. Ann Field, interview with Chris Thomas, MRC, 803/12.
96. 'Grunwick Accused "Not the Attacker"', *Guardian*, 28 March 1979, p. 6.
97. John Ezard, 'Grunwick Attacker Gaoled for Two Years', *Guardian*, 30 March 1979, p. 30.
98. House of Commons Employment Committee, The Legal Immunities of Trade Unions and Other Related Matters, Minutes of Evidence, 27 February 1980, HC 462-ii, pp. 41–2.
99. David Downes and Tim Newburn, *The Official History of Criminal Justice in England and Wales: Volume IV: the Politics of Law and Order* (London: Routledge, 2022), p. 189.
100. 'In Pictures: "Strikers in Saris" Mural Unveiled in Birmingham', BBC News, 23 October 2023, bbc.co.uk.
101. Paul Gilroy, *There Ain't No Black in the Union Jack* (London: Routledge, 2002), pp. 84–9, 257.
102. David McNee, Report of the Commissioner of Police of the Metropolis for the Year 1977, cmnd.7238 (London: HMSO, 1978), p. 5.
103. Liam Turbett, *Glasgow 1975* (Glasgow: Scottish Labour History Society, 2025).

104. McNee, Report of the Commissioner of Police, pp. 5, 25.
105. Ralph Miliband, 'The New Revisionism in Britain', *New Left Review* 150 (1985), pp. 16–17.
106. Rogaly, *Grunwick*, p. 106.
107. Ward, *Fort Grunwick*, pp. 1–2.
108. 'Letters to the Editor: Grunwick and the Association with Freedom', *Guardian*, 30 June 1977.
109. 'Dummy Run', *Guardian*, 3 September 1977, p. 1.
110. 'Grunwick: Scarman Report (Court of Inquiry Report)', Margaret Thatcher Foundation, 26 August 1977, margaretthatcher.org.
111. Margaret Thatcher, *The Path to Power* (London: Harper Collins, 1995), pp. 397–9.
112. Beckett, *When the Lights Went Out*, p. 377.
113. David Pallister, 'Tory Mouth for Grunwick Head', *Guardian*, 25 June 1977, p. 2.
114. Thatcher, *The Path to Power*, p. 399.
115. Rogaly, *Grunwick*, p. 35.
116. David Howell, 'Defiant Dominoes: Working Miners and the 1984–5 Strike', in Ben Jackson and Robert Saunders (eds), *Making Thatcher's Britain* (Cambridge: Cambridge University Press, 2012), p. 157.
117. Ward, *Fort Grunwick*, pp. 61–6; R. W. Apple Jr, 'Pivotal Strike in Britain', *New York Times*, 19 November 1977, p. 7.
118. Ward, *Fort Grunwick*, pp. 94, 116.
119. Ibid., pp. 70–6.
120. Taylor, 'Grunwick', pp. 14–15.
121. Jack McGowan, '"Dispute", "Battle", "Siege", "Farce"? – Grunwick 30 Years On', *Contemporary British History* 22 (2008), p. 399.
122. 'PO Union Fines Workers over Grunwick', *Guardian*, 23 December 1977, p. 2.
123. Jayaben Desai, interview.
124. Mahmood Ahmed, interview.
125. Debt Justice, 'The Grunwick Strike', YouTube, 21 January 2014.
126. Diarmaid Kelliher, 'Thatcherism and the Picket Line', *English Historical Review*, 2026, ceag005.
127. 'Bristol Bus Boycott Pioneers Honoured', Unite Live, 1 May 2025, unitelive.org.
128. Graham Taylor, 'Jayaben Desai and the ILP Tradition', Independent Labour Publications, 30 August 2016, independentlabour.org; Laura Schwartz, *Feminism and the Servant Problem: Class and Domestic Labour in the Women's Suffrage Movement* (Cambridge: Cambridge University Press, 2019), p. 6.

3. Closing Cardowan Colliery

1. Margaret Wegg and Jerry Wegg, interview with author, residence, Stepps, 17 November 2014.
2. Cardowan focus group, St Joseph's Catholic Church, Stepps, 11 May 2023.
3. Wegg and Wegg, interview.
4. 'Fatal Accidents in British Coal Mines: 1874 to 1920', *Monthly Labour Review* 15 (1922), p. 199.
5. John Singleton, 'Origins of Disaster Management: The British Mine Rescue System, c.1900 to c.1930', *Business History* 65 (2023), pp. 983–1004.
6. Ewan Gibbs and Jim Phillips, 'Remembering Auchengeich: The Largest Fatal Accident in Scottish Coal Mining in the Nationalised Era', *Scottish Labour History* 54 (2019), pp. 47–57.
7. Willie Doolan, interview with author, the Pivot, Moodiesburn, 14 June 2019.
8. Cardowan focus group.
9. Doolan, interview 2019.
10. Peter Payne, *Growth and Contraction: Scottish Industry c.1860–1990* (Glasgow: Economic and Social History Society of Scotland, 1992), p. 17.
11. *Census of Scotland 1921*, vol. 1, part 22, *County of Lanark* (Edinburgh: HMSO, 1922), table E, p. 1139.
12. Richard Leonard, 'Socialism: More than a Creed', in Pauline Bryan (ed.), *What Would Keir Hardie Say?* (Edinburgh: Luath, 2015), p. 28.
13. Ewan Gibbs, 'Michael "Mick" McGahey: Miner, Communist and Trade Union Leader', *Twentieth Century Communism* 23 (2022), pp. 4–34.
14. Doolan, interview 2019.
15. Ewan Gibbs and Jim Phillips, 'Who Owns a Factory? Caterpillar Tractors in Uddingston, 1956–1987', *Historical Studies in Industrial Relations* 27 (2018), pp. 111–37; John Foster and Charles Woolfson, *Track Record: The Story of the Caterpillar Occupation* (London: Verso, 1988).
16. John Slaven, interview with author, STUC Building, Woodlands, Glasgow, 5 June 2014.
17. The Pattern of Output of Coal for Electricity Generation in the 1970s from the Scottish Coalfields, Lauriston House, Edinburgh, 22 June 1967, National Archives, Kew, London (hereafter TNA), National Coal Board (hereafter Coal) 31/120.
18. Miles Oglethorpe, 'Glasgow, Stepps, Cardowan Colliery', event reference: 851449 (2006), trove.scot.

19. Jim Phillips, Valerie Wright and Jim Tomlinson, *Deindustrialisation and the Moral Economy in Scotland Since 1955* (Edinburgh: Edinburgh University Press, 2021), pp. 83–112.
20. Oglethorpe, 'Glasgow, Stepps, Cardowan Colliery'.
21. David Stewart, 'Fighting for Survival: The 1980s Campaign to Save Ravenscraig Steelworks', *Journal of Scottish Historical Studies* 25 (2005), pp. 42–3.
22. *Census 1961 Scotland Occupation and Industry County Tables: Glasgow and Lanark* Leaflet no. 15 (Edinburgh: HMSO, 1966), table 3; and *Census 1971 Scotland Economic Activity County Tables Part 2* (Edinburgh: HMSO, 1976), table 3.
23. Anthony Rooney, interview with author, Morrison's Café, Bellshill, 24 April 2014.
24. Assistant Area Manpower Officer, Glasgow to James Tennyson, NUM District Secretary, Hamilton, 6 February 1964, National Records of Scotland, Edinburgh (hereafter NRS) Coal Board (hereafter CB), 219/14/1.
25. Rooney, interview.
26. The Proclaimers, *Letter from America* (Chrysalis, 1987). See Andrew Perchard and Keith Gildart, '"A Dying Mutual Friend": Popular Music and the Politics of Deindustrialisation in Scotland in the Long 1980s', *Contemporary British History* 39, no. 3 (2025), pp. 486–518.
27. Minutes of Special Meeting of Gartshore 9/11 Colliery Consultative Committee held in Grayshill Office, 18 January 1968, NRS, CB, 300/14/1.
28. Moodiesburn focus group, the Pivot, Moodiesburn, 25 March 2014.
29. Manpower Branch, NCB, Glasgow to Legal Department, NCB, Edinburgh, Background note: what happened at Gartshore 9/11 closure? (1968), NRS, CB, 300/14/1.
30. Ibid.
31. Ibid.
32. Ibid.
33. Nicky Wilson, interview with author, University of Glasgow, 10 February 2014.
34. J.W. Anderson, Coking Coal Suppliers, 22 April 1969; Scotland Coal Division, Cardowan and Kingshill No.3 Collieries, 20 May 1969, both in TNA, POWE, 52/305.
35. Scottish Office, NCB Colliery Closure Programme: Proposed Closure of Cardowan, April 1969, TNA, POWE, 52/402.
36. Ibid.

37. J.W. Anderson, Note for the Record: Cardowan, 21 August 1969, TNA, POWE, 52/402.
38. David Murray, 'Cardowan Coking Coal in Context', *Glasgow Herald*, 1 December 1969, TNA, POWE, 52/402.
39. G.C. Sheppard, NCB, London to Lawrence Daly, NUM, Edinburgh, subject: Cardowan Colliery, 7 July 1970, TNA, Coal, 89/103.
40. J.B. Burton to D.J. Nisbet, Memorandum: Cardowan, 9 March 1971, TNA, Coal, 89/103.
41. Minutes of Meeting with Representatives of the Trade Unions, 28 June 1972, The Whins, Alloa, TNA, Coal, 89/103.
42. Andrew Perchard and Keith Gildart, 'Managerial Ideology and Identity in the Nationalised British Coal Industry, 1947–1994', *Economic and Industrial Democracy* 44 (2023), p. 234.
43. Meeting held at 11am on Wednesday 25 February 1981, Thames House South, London, TNA, Coal, 31/135.
44. Jim Phillips, *Scottish Coal Miners in the Twentieth Century* (Edinburgh: Edinburgh University Press, 2019), p. 222.
45. Charles McGuire, '"Going for the Jugular": The Steelworkers' Banner and the 1980 National Steelworkers' Strike in Britain', *Historical Studies in Industrial Relations* 38 (2017), pp. 97–128.
46. Dominic Sandbrook, *Who Dares Wins: Britain, 1979–1982* (London: Penguin, 2019), pp. 138, 184.
47. Big Country, 'Steeltown', *Steeltown*, track 3 (Mercury, 1984).
48. William Ashworth, *The History of the British Coal Industry*, vol. 5, *1946–1982: The Nationalized Industry* (Oxford: Clarendon Press, 1986), pp. 399–404.
49. Wilson, interview.
50. Keith Harper, 'Ministers and NCB Give Way to Miners', *Guardian*, 19 February 1981, pp. 1, 15.
51. Peter Jones, Internal Tactics, 12 January 1981, TNA, Coal, 31/134.
52. Jim Phillips, *Collieries, Communities and the Miners' Strike in Scotland, 1984–5* (Manchester: Manchester University Press, 2012), p. 43.
53. Huw Beynon and Ray Hudson, *The Shadow of the Mine: Coal and the End of Industrial Britain* (London: Verso, 2021), p. 91.
54. Phillips, *Collieries, Communities*, p. 43.
55. John North and Derek Spooner, 'The Great U.K. Coal Rush: A Progress Report to the End of 1976', *Area* 9, no. 1 (1977), pp. 17–19.
56. *NUM Scottish Area Executive Committee Minutes July 1982 to June 1983*, pp. 696–7, National Mining Museum of Scotland, Newtongrange (hereafter NMMS).
57. Ibid., pp. 702–3.
58. Ibid., pp. 632–3.

59. Quoted in Robert Gildea, *Backbone of the Nation: Mining Communities and the Great Strike of 1984–85* (New Haven, CT: Yale University Press, 2023), pp. 35–9.
60. M.H. Butler and M.J. Parker, Revised Projection to 1987/88 Memorandum, 15 February 1983, TNA, Coal, 31/135.
61. Meeting Between Officials from the Department of Energy and the NCB, 28 February 1983, TNA, Coal, 31/135.
62. Ibid.
63. Note of a meeting held in Mr Cowan's Office at 2.30pm on Tuesday 7 June 1983, TNA, Coal, 31/135.
64. Miles Oglethorpe, 'Bo'ness, Kinneil Colliery', Event reference: 855826 (2006) trove.scot.
65. NUMSA, *Executive Committee Minutes, July 1982 to June 1983*, p. 336, NMMS.
66. Jim Phillips, 'Workplace Conflict and the Origins of the 1984–85 Miners' Strike in Scotland', *Twentieth Century British History* 20 (2009), pp. 152–72.
67. National appeal meeting, Cardowan colliery, 16 August 1983, Appendix 1: special extended CCC meeting held in the Parochial Hall, Stepps, 13 May 1983, FC/3/2/3/2, NMMS.
68. Ibid.
69. Peter Dorey, 'Weakening the Trade Unions, One Step at a Time: The Thatcher Governments' Strategy for the Reform of Trade-Union Law, 1979–1984', *Historical Studies in Industrial Relations* 37 (2016), pp. 174–5.
70. Wilson, interview.
71. Tommy Canavan, interview with author, residence, Kilsyth, 19 February 2014.
72. Cardowan focus group.
73. Martin Gostwick, 'Miners Win Unanimous Backing', *Morning Star*, 26 May 1983, TNA, Coal, 89/103.
74. 'Scargill Accuses NCB as Miners End Dispute', *Guardian*, 21 June 1983, TNA, Coal, 89/103.
75. Background Brief for National Appeal Meeting on Cardowan Colliery, 1983, NMMS, FC/3/2/3/2.
76. Jim Phillips, *Coalfield Justice: The 1984–85 Miners' Strike in Scotland* (Edinburgh: Edinburgh University Press, 2024), p. 154.
77. Willie Doolan, interview with author, the Pivot, Moodiesburn, 12 March 2014.
78. Wilson, interview.
79. Cardowan Colliery National Appeal Meeting Minutes, 19 September 1983, NRS, CB, 256/14/1.

80. Ibid.
81. 'Scargill Raps NCB Tactics on Cardowan Pit', *Morning Star* cutting from June 1983, TNA, Coal, 89/103.
82. Cardowan Colliery National Appeal Meeting Minutes, 19 September 1983, NRS, CB, 256/14/1.
83. Bill Magee, 'Cardowan Ballot Results', NCB Press Office, Edinburgh, 26 August 1983, TNA, Coal, 89/103.
84. Doolan, interview 2014.
85. Tony Lane, 'Foreign Fuel, Foreign Ships and Disorganised Trade Unionism: An Alternative Interpretation of the Defeat of the Miners in 1984–5', *Work, Employment and Society* 10 (1996), pp. 57–84.
86. Phillips, *Collieries, Communities*, pp. 53–80.
87. Estimates vary, but see figures quoted in Huw Beynon, introduction to Huw Beynon (ed.), *Digging Deeper: Issues in the Miners' Strike* (London: Verso, 1985), p. 17; and in Diarmaid Kelliher, *Making Cultures of Solidarity: London and the 1984–5 Miners' Strike* (London: Routledge, 2021), p. 70.
88. Kelliher, *Making Cultures of Solidarity*, chs 4 and 5.
89. Phillips, *Coalfield Justice*, p. 122.
90. Department for Energy Security and Net Zero, Historical Coal Data: Coal Production, Availability and Consumption, 31 July 2025, gov .uk.
91. Jonathan Davis, 'Lawson Puts the Final Cost at £2,500 Million', *The Times*, 20 March 1985, p. 7.
92. HC Deb 31 July 1984, vol. 65, c. 307.
93. Quoted in Peter Dorey, '"It Was Just Like Arming to Face the Threat of Hitler in the Late 1930s": The Ridley Report and the Conservative Party's Preparations for the 1984–85 Miners' Strike', *Historical Studies in Industrial Relations* 34 (2013), p. 173.
94. William McIlvanney, *The Big Man* (London: Hodder & Stoughton, 1985).
95. David Leland, *The Big Man* (Universal Pictures, 1990).
96. Gildea, *Backbone of the Nation*, pp. 332–5.
97. Florence Sutcliffe-Braithwaite and Natalie Thomlinson, *Women and the Miners' Strike, 1984–1985* (Oxford: Oxford University Press, 2023), pp. 232–3.
98. Cardowan focus group.

4. Right to Buy

1. 'The Working Class Lives On Says Judge', *Guardian*, 27 November 1990, p. 8.
2. Ibid.
3. M.A. King, E. Fairbairn and A.B. Atkinson, 'Housing Policy, Taxation and Reform', *Midland Bank Review*, spring 1980, p. 9.
4. 'Keir Starmer's Speech at Labour Conference', Labour Party, 10 October 2023, labour.org.uk.
5. Norman Ginsburg, 'The Privatization of Council Housing', *Critical Social Policy* 25 (2004), p. 117.
6. Alan Murie, *The Right to Buy?: Selling Off Public and Social Housing* (Bristol: Policy Press, 2016), pp. 2, 33–8; Alex Diner and Hollie Wright, *Reforming Right to Buy: Options for Preserving and Delivering New Council Homes for the Twenty-First Century* (London: New Economics Foundation, 2024), p. 10; data from Mark Stephens, John Perry, Peter Williams and Gillian Young (eds), *UK Housing Review 2025* (Coventry: Chartered Institute of Housing, 2025), table 17b.
7. 'Location, Location, Location' and 'Relocation, Relocation', channel4.com.
8. Chris Allen, *Housing Market Renewal and Social Class* (London: Routledge, 2008), pp. 61–75.
9. Stephens et al., *UK Housing Review 2025*, table 17a.
10. Richard Ronald, *The Ideology of Home Ownership: Homeowner Societies and the Role of Housing* (London: Palgrave Macmillan, 2008), p. 12.
11. 'Bridget Phillipson: Can We Save Britain's Schools?', *The Rest Is Politics* podcast, 17 June 2024.
12. Dan Evans, *A Nation of Shopkeepers: The Unstoppable Rise of the Petite Bourgeoisie* (London: Repeater, 2023), p. 234.
13. Nick Bano, 'The End of Landlords', *Guardian*, 19 March 2024.
14. Guy Ortolano, *Thatcher's Progress: From Social Democracy to Market Liberalism Through an English Town* (Cambridge: Cambridge University Press, 2019), p. 217.
15. Sex Pistols, 'Anarchy in the UK', *Never Mind the Bollocks, Here's the Sex Pistols*, track 8 (Warner Records, 1977).
16. Matt Weaver, 'Rotten to the Core', *Guardian*, 8 October 2003.
17. James S. Foreman-Peck, 'The Appraisal of Sales of Local Authority Rented Accommodation: A Comment', *Urban Studies* 19 (1982), p. 80; Murie, *The Right to Buy?*, p. 65.
18. Ibid.

19. Stephens et al., *UK Housing Review 2025*, table 17b.
20. Richard Disney and Guannan Luo, 'The Right to Buy Public Housing in Britain: A Welfare Analysis', *Journal of Housing Economics* 35 (2017), p. 53.
21. Diner and Wright, *Reforming Right to Buy*, p. 22.
22. HC Deb 15 May 1979, vol. 967, cc. 410–11.
23. John Boughton, *Municipal Dreams: The Rise and Fall of Council Housing* (London: Verso, 2018), p. 66.
24. Tracy McVeigh, '30 Years On, the Right to Buy Revolution that Still Divides Britain's Housing Estates', *Observer*, 6 December 2009.
25. Christopher Warman, 'GLC Tories to Allow Council House Sales', *The Times*, 26 March 1976, p. 6.
26. David Behrens, 'Social Housing Crisis Has Its Roots in This Key Ceremony, 40 Years Ago', *Yorkshire Post*, 3 January 2020.
27. Lynsey Hanley, 'From Thatcher to Johnson: How Right to Buy Ruined British Housing', *Guardian*, 29 June 2022.
28. Lee-Ann Richards, 'Harold Hill Council House, that Launched Magaret [*sic*] Thatcher's Right to Buy Scheme Is Sold for 20 Times Its Original Value', *Romford Recorder*, 20 April 2013.
29. Ibid.
30. Dominic Sandbrook, *Who Dares Wins: Britain, 1979–1982* (London: Penguin, 2019), pp. 485–92.
31. McVeigh, '30 Years On'.
32. Ibid.
33. Christopher Warman, 'Opposition to Homes Plan Grows', *The Times*, 10 October 1980, p. 2.
34. John Carvel, 'Campaign on Sales of Council Homes', *Guardian*, 12 September 1984, p. 3.
35. Richard Smith, producer at Central Office of Information, 'Right to Buy – TV Commercial', YouTube, 29 July 2022.
36. *Your Right to Buy Your Home: A Guide for Council, New Town and Housing Association Tenants* (London: Department of the Environment and the Welsh Office, 1984).
37. Ibid.
38. Andy Beckett, *Promised You a Miracle: UK, 80–82* (London: Penguin, 2015), p. 223.
39. Hamish Kallin and Tom Slater, 'Activating Territorial Stigma: Gentrifying Marginality on Edinburgh's Periphery', *Environment and Planning A* 46 (2014), p. 1362.
40. Seán Damer, *Scheming: A Social History of Glasgow Council Housing, 1919–1956* (Edinburgh: Edinburgh University Press, 2019), p. 7.
41. HC Deb 14 January 1980, vol. 976, cc. 1249–51.

42. Marion Kerr, *The Right to Buy: A National Survey of Tenants and Buyers of Council Homes* (London: HMSO, 1988), p. 3.
43. Ibid., pp. 4–14.
44. David Walker, 'The Right to Buy 2', *The Times*, 30 October 1984, p. 4.
45. 'House Proud Politics', *The Times*, 30 May 1982, p. 11.
46. Tom Freeman, '"Tenement Tory" Teddy Taylor Dies Aged 80', *Holyrood*, 21 September 2017, holyrood.com.
47. William Knox, *James Maxton* (Manchester: Manchester University Press, 1987), p. 43; Gordon Brown, *Jimmy Maxton* (Edinburgh: Mainstream, 1986), pp. 133–4.
48. Iain McLean, *The Legend of Red Clydeside* (Edinburgh: John Donald, 1983), pp. 18–26, 234–6.
49. HC Deb 17 May 1979, vol. 967, c. 458 and c. 1327.
50. HC Deb 14 January 1980, vol. 976, c. 1298.
51. Ned Donaldson and Les Forster, *Sell and Be Damned: The Glasgow Merrylee Housing Scandal of 1951* (Glasgow: Scottish Labour History Society, 2022), pp. 41–52.
52. Austin Mitchell, 'Clay Cross', *Political Quarterly* 45 (1974), pp. 165–78.
53. 'Risk of Creating Housing Monoliths', *The Times*, 23 March 1976, p. 6.
54. Guy Ortolano, 'Begrudging Neoliberalism: Housing and the Fate of the Property-Owning Social Democracy', in Aled Davies, Ben Jackson and Florence Sutcliffe-Braithwaite (eds), *The Neoliberal Age?: Britain Since the 1970s* (London: UCL Press, 2021), p. 322.
55. HC Deb 17 May 1979, vol. 967, c. 499. My emphasis.
56. Harold Carter, 'From Slums to Slums in Three Generations: Housing Policy and the Political Economy of the Welfare State, 1945–2005', University of Oxford Discussion Papers in Economic and Social History no. 98, May 2012, p. 2.
57. Alistair Kefford, 'Housing the Citizen-Consumer in Post-War Britain: The Parker Morris Report, Affluence and the Even Briefer Life of Social Democracy', *Twentieth Century British History* 29 (2018), p. 251.
58. Cater, 'From Slums to Slums', p. 26.
59. Housing Policy: A Consultative Document, cmnd.6851 (London: HMSO, 1977), p. 22.
60. Martin Pawley, *Home Ownership* (London: Architectural Press, 1978), pp. 1–2, 113–17.
61. Housing Policy, cmnd.6851, pp. 10–11.
62. Avner Offer, 'British Manual Workers: From Producers to Consumers, c. 1950–2000', *Contemporary British History* 22 (2008), p. 544.
63. Ben Jones, *The Working Class in Mid-Twentieth Century England* (Manchester: Manchester University Press, 2012), p. 104.

64. David Gee, *Shelter Report on Slum Clearance* (London: Shelter, 1974), pp. 12–23.
65. Jeff Torrington, *Swing Hammer Swing!* (New York: Vintage Classics, 2015).
66. Jimmy Reid, *Alienation* (Glasgow: University of Glasgow Publications, 1972), p. 10.
67. David Griffiths and Chris Holmes, 'To Buy or Not to Buy . . . Is that the Question?', *Marxism Today*, 8 May 1984, p. 8.
68. Jim Phillips, *Scottish Coal Miners in the Twentieth Century* (Edinburgh: Edinburgh University Press, 2019), p. 60.
69. Sam Wetherell, *Foundations: How the Built Environment Made Twentieth Century Britain* (Princeton, NJ: Princeton University Press, 2020), pp. 93–102.
70. Charles Johnstone, 'The Tenants' Movement and Housing Struggles in Glasgow, 1945–1990' (PhD thesis, University of Glasgow, 1992), p. 92.
71. Gerry Mooney, 'Living on the Periphery: Housing, Industrial Change and the State' (PhD thesis, University of Glasgow, 1988) pp. 407, 248, 670.
72. Valerie Wright, '"Housing Problems ... Are Political Dynamite": Housing Disputes in Glasgow, c. 1971 to the Present Day', *Sociological Research Online* 26 (2021), pp. 251–2.
73. McLean, *The Legend of Red Clydeside*, p. 236, quoted in Robert J. Morris, 'Review of Iain McLean, *The Legend of Red Clydeside*', *Scottish Economic and Social History* 4 (1984), p. 90.
74. Charles Pattinson, *Our Friends in the North* (BBC, 1996).
75. Alex Niven, 'The Socialism of T. Dan Smith', *Tribune*, 18 May 2019.
76. Andrew O'Hagan, *Our Fathers* (London: Faber, 1999).
77. Housing Policy, cmnd.6851, pp. 8, 14, 50.
78. Ibid., p. 68.
79. The Jam, 'Saturday's Kids', *Setting Sons*, track 8 (Polydor, 1979).
80. Mick Brown, 'Paul Weller: Changing Man', *Telegraph*, 8 May 2008.
81. Ray Forrest and Alan Murie, 'Residualisation and Council Housing: Aspects of the Changing Social Relations of Housing Tenure', *Journal of Social Policy* 12 (1983), p. 455.
82. Evans, *A Nation of Shopkeepers*, pp. 231–2.
83. Sandbrook, *Who Dares Wins*, pp. 229–45.
84. Style Council, 'The Lodgers', *Our Favourite Shop*, track 10 (Geffen Records, 1985).
85. Ortolano, *Thatcher's Progress*, p. 212.
86. Style Council, 'Welcome to Milton Keynes', *Our Favourite Shop*, track 3 (Geffen Records, 1985).
87. Jon Lawrence and Florence Sutcliffe-Braithwaite, 'Margaret Thatcher and the Decline of Class Politics', in Ben Jackson and Robert Saunders

(eds), *Making Thatcher's Britain* (Cambridge: Cambridge University Press, 2012), pp. 143–5.

88. Robert Garner and Richard Kelly, *British Political Parties Today* (Manchester: Manchester University Press, 1993), pp. 238–40.
89. Margaret Thatcher, *The Downing Street Years* (London: Harper Collins, 1993), pp. 39, 279.
90. Margaret Thatcher, Speech to Conservative Conference, 9 October 1987, Margaret Thatcher Foundation.
91. Alice Tihelková, 'Brick and Mortar Dreams and Nightmares: A Historical Look at the Role of Home Ownership in Britain', *American and British Studies Annual* 12 (2021), p. 145.
92. Hamish Gray, *The Cost of Council Housing* (London: Institute for Economic Affairs, 1968), pp. 9, 25, 36, 41.
93. Aled Davies, '"Right to Buy": The Development of a Conservative Housing Policy, 1945–1980', *Contemporary British History* 27 (2013), p. 429.
94. Arthur Osman and Simon de Bruxelle, 'Paying the Price of an Ideal Home of Your Own', *Observer*, 22 June 1986, p. 4.
95. Davies, '"Right to Buy"', p. 435.
96. 'Council House Sales Help the Tory Vote', *The Times*, 3 June 1983, p. 5.
97. Forrest and Murie, 'Residualisation and Council Housing', pp. 435, 455–7.
98. John Carvel, 'Where a House Is Not a Vote', *Guardian*, 23 May 1983, p. 3.
99. Richard King, *Brittle with Relics: A History of Wales, 1962–97* (London: Faber and Faber, 2022), p. 381.
100. Evans, *A Nation of Shopkeepers*, pp. 231–2.
101. Cardowan focus group, St Joseph's Catholic Church, Stepps, 11 May 2023.
102. Ellis, remote interview with author, 18 April 2023.
103. W. W. Knox, *Industrial Nation: Work, Culture and Society in Scotland, 1800–Present* (Edinburgh: Edinburgh University Press, 1999), p. 262.
104. North Lanarkshire Council, House Condition in North Lanarkshire: Local Housing Strategy 2021–2026 Evidence Paper (2021), p. 7.
105. Valerie Wright and Alistair Fair, 'The Opportunity and Desire to Buy: Owner-Occupation in Scotland's New Towns, c. 1950–80', *Contemporary British History* 38 (2024), p. 237.
106. Michael Jones, 'The Tories: Bringing the House Down', *Marxism Today*, May 1980, p. 10.
107. Peter Saunders, *A Nation of Homeowners* (London: Unwin Hyman, 1990), p. 228.

108. Ibid., pp. 233–6.
109. Anthony Bevins, 'Kinnock Lines Up Against Militant', *The Times*, 12 July 1983, p. 2.
110. 'Shift on Right to Buy', *Guardian*, 2 October 1984, p. 4.
111. David Walker, 'The Right to Buy', *The Times*, 29 October 1984, p. 4; Roger Penn, 'Britain in 1984: A Dual Crisis for Labour', *Berkeley Journal of Sociology* 30 (1985), pp. 10–11.
112. 'Tenants' Right to Buy Backed', *Guardian*, 30 September 1986, p. 4.
113. Jim Phillips, *Collieries, Communities and the Miners' Strike in Scotland, 1984–85* (Manchester: Manchester University Press, 2012), pp. 119–24.
114. Ash Sarkar, 'We Have to Vote Labour', Novara Media, 19 June 2024, novaramedia.com.
115. Gregor Gall, *Mick Lynch: The Making of a Working-Class Hero* (Manchester: Manchester University Press, 2024), pp. 54–5.
116. Statista, 'Household Debt to Income Ratio in the United Kingdom (UK) from 1st quarter 2000 to 1st Quarter 2023', statista.com; Lewis Kirkham and Stephen Burgess, 'A Question of Interest: Is UK Household Debt Unsustainable?', *Bank Underground*, 17 January 2019, bank underground.co.uk.
117. Meg Bartley, 'The Number of Homeowners Who Own Their Home Outright Has Increased over the Last Ten Years, According to New Data', *IFA Magazine*, 24 January 2024.
118. Marc Schoffman, 'Housing Affordability Ratio More than Doubles Since 1970s – Research', Estate Agent Today, 5 July 2023, estateagent .co.uk.
119. Statista, 'Ratio of Household Rent to Income in the United Kingdom (UK) as of April 2022 and April 2023, by Region', statista.com.
120. Ewan Gibbs, 'Refusing to Be Poor Anymore? British Trade Unionism in the 2020s', Institut Montaigne, 14 August 2023, institutmontaigne.org.
121. Richards, 'Harold Hill Council House'.
122. Murie, *The Right to Buy?*, pp. 40–8.
123. Ginsburg, 'The Privatization of Council Housing', pp. 121–3.
124. 'Right to Buy Ends in Scotland', Scottish Government, 30 July 2016, gov.scot.
125. 'Right to Buy to End in Wales This Month', Welsh Government, 9 January 2019, gov.wales.
126. Rupert Jones, '"Time Is Right" for Mortgage Relief to End', *Guardian*, 10 March 1999.
127. King, Fairbairn and Atkinson, 'Housing Policy', p. 8.
128. *Spitting Image*, series 13, episode 1, broadcast on ITV, 4 October 1992.

5. New Labour

1. 'A Moment Anchored in History', BBC News, 1 July 1999, bbc.co.uk.
2. Stuart Hall, 'New Labour's Double Shuffle', *Review of Education, Pedagogy and Cultural Studies* 27 (2006), p. 322.
3. Ewan Gibbs, 'Michael "Mick" McGahey: Miner, Communist and Trade Union Leader', *Twentieth Century Communism* 23 (2022), pp. 4–5.
4. Frank Burchill, 'The UK Fire Service Dispute, 2002–2003', *Employee Relations* 26 (2004), pp. 404–21.
5. Jim Phillips, *Collieries, Communities and the Miners' Strike in Scotland, 1984–85* (Manchester: Manchester University Press, 2012), p. 117.
6. Martin Childs, 'Leo Blair: Barrister Who Began as a Conservative but Followed His Son into the Labour Party', *Independent*, 19 November 2012.
7. Ewan Gibbs, 'Socialism in a Cold Climate', in Gerry Hassan (ed.), *The Story of the Scottish Parliament: The First Two Decades Explained* (Edinburgh: Edinburgh University Press, 2019), pp. 189–98.
8. Alfie Steer, '"Keep the Party Labour": The Grassroots Alliance and Activist Opposition to New Labour, 1994–2007', *Modern British History* 37 (2023), p. 226.
9. Tony Blair, Leader's Speech, Labour Party conference, Blackpool, 1 October 1996.
10. Eric Shaw, *Losing Labour's Soul: New Labour and the Blair Government, 1997–2007* (London: Routledge, 2007), pp. 153–4.
11. Bob Jessop, 'From Thatcherism to New Labour: Neo-Liberalism, Workfarism and Labour-Market Regulation', in Henk Overbeek (ed.), *The Political Economy of European Employment* (London: Routledge, 2003), p. 139; Peter Kilfoyle, *Labour Pains: How the Party I Love Lost Its Soul* (London: Biteback, 2010), p. 44.
12. 'Tony Blair's speech to the IPPR and Demos at Beveridge Hall, University of London', BBC News, 11 October 2004, bbc.co.uk.
13. Labour Party, *New Labour: Because Britain Deserves Better* (1997), labour-party.org.uk.
14. Tony Blair, *Tony Blair in His Own Words* (London: Politico, 2004). On *Marxism Today*, see pp. xvii, 40–9.
15. Geoff Andrews, *Endgames and New Times: The Final Years of British Communism* (London: Lawrence and Wishart, 2004), ch. 6.
16. Blair, *Tony Blair*, pp. 187–92.
17. Martin Jacques and Stuart Hall, 'The Election: Blair Is He the Greatest Tory Since Thatcher?', *Observer*, 13 April 1997, p. 31.

18. Willie Thompson, *The Long Death of British Labourism: Interpreting a Political Culture* (London: Pluto, 1993), pp. 5–6.
19. Ibid., p. 158.
20. Ibid., p. 144.
21. Eric Hobsbawm, *Politics for a Rational Left* (London: Verso, 1989), p. 288.
22. Tudor Jones, *Remaking the Labour Party: From Gaitskell to Blair* (London: Routledge, 1996), pp. 6, 130.
23. Stephen Brooke, 'Revisionists and Fundamentalists: The Labour Party and Economic Policy During the Second World War', *Historical Journal* 32 (1989), pp. 157–60.
24. Neil Kinnock, Leader's Speech, 29 September 1987, Brighton.
25. Colm Murphy, *Futures of Socialism: 'Modernisation', the Labour Party and the British Left, 1973–1997* (Cambridge: Cambridge University Press, 2023), pp. 5–7.
26. Jim Tomlinson, 'Deindustrialisation and "Thatcherism": Moral Economy and Unintended Consequences', *Contemporary British History* 35 (2021), p. 623.
27. For an account produced by key participants, see London Edinburgh Weekend Return Group, *In and Against the State: Discussion Notes for Socialists* (London: Pluto, 1980); For a history of an important example, see Daisy Payling, *Socialist Republic: Remaking the British Left in 1980s Sheffield* (Manchester: Manchester University Press, 2023).
28. Florence Sutcliffe-Braithwaite, 'Discourses of "Class" in Britain in "New Times"', *Contemporary British History* 31 (2017), p. 306.
29. Kinnock, Leader's Speech, 1987.
30. Ken Coates and Tony Topham, *The Making of the Labour Movement: The Formation of the Transport and General Workers' Union, 1870–1922* (Nottingham: Spokesman, 1994), pp. 51–77.
31. Peter Turnbull and Victoria Wass, 'The Greatest Game No More: Redundant Dockers and the Demise of "Dock Work"', *Work Employment and Society* 8 (1994), p. 499.
32. Harry Enfield, *Loadsamoney (Doin' Up the House)* (Mercury, 1988).
33. Arun Starkey, 'Why the Harry Enfield Character in "Loadsamoney" Is More Important than Ever', *Far Out Magazine*, 4 December 2022, faroutmagazine.co.uk.
34. Diarmaid Kelliher, *Making Cultures of Solidarity: London and the 1984–5 Miners' Strike* (London: Routledge, 2021), p. 151.
35. Eric Hammond, *Maverick: The Life of a Union Rebel* (London: Weidenfeld and Nicolson, 1992), p. 73.
36. Helena Chmielewska-Szlajfer, *(Not) Kidding: Politics in Online Tabloids* (Leiden: Brill, 2024), pp. 13–14.
37. John Lloyd, *Light and Liberty: The History of the Electrical, Electronic,*

Telecommunication and Plumbing Union (London: Weidenfeld and Nicolson, 1990), pp. 650–62.

38. Staff Attitude Survey – September 1989, Modern Records Centre, University of Warwick (hereafter MRC), Central Electricity Generating Board, 959/6.
39. John Daly to Secretaries of NALGO Electricity Branches, 1 December 1988, Privatization: Future of the Negotiating and Consultative Machinery, MRC, NALGO, MSS 389/2004/18.
40. Fact Sheet 8 (1987), National Library of Wales, Aberystwyth (hereafter NLW), GB 0210 WALTUC Wales TUC Cymru Archives (hereafter WTUC), G 4/1/2.
41. Simon Beavis, 'Power Unions in Disarray on Privatisation Plans', *Guardian*, 1 November 1988, cutting, NLW, WTUC, G 4/1/2.
42. Tim Jones, 'Laird Share Plea Splits Unions Fighting Sell-Off', *The Times*, 1 November 1988, cutting, NLW, WTUC, G 4/1/2.
43. Martin Adeney, 'Sir Gavin Laird Obituary', *Guardian*, 12 November 2017; Hammond, *Maverick*, p. 28.
44. EETPU, Abridged Report of the National Conference for the Electricity Supply Industry held at Norbreck Castle Hotel Blackpool from Sunday 20 May to Monday 21 May 1990, p. 1.
45. Danny Carrigan, interview with author, residence, Cumbernauld, 27 September 2022.
46. Ewan Gibbs, 'Refusing to Be Poor Anymore? British Trade Unionism in the 2020s', Institut Montaigne, 14 August 2023, institutmontaigne.org.
47. 'Looks Familiar?', *Contact*, August 1992, pp. 1, 5, MRC, Electrical Trades Union, 1018/ETU/P/3/1.
48. Ibid.
49. Tony Blair, Leader's Speech, Labour Party conference, Bournemouth, 28 September 1999.
50. Ibid.
51. 'How Britain Voted in 1997', IPSOS, 31 May 1997, ipsos.com.
52. Blair, *Tony Blair*, p. 61.
53. Blair, Leader's Speech, Blackpool, 1996.
54. Ibid.
55. For a thoughtful revisionist perspective on the history of the 1970s, see Lawrence Black, Hugh Pemberton and Pat Thane (eds), *Reassessing 1970s Britain* (Manchester: Manchester University Press, 2013).
56. Neil Davidson, *What Was Neoliberalism?: Studies in the Most Recent Phase of Capitalism, 1973–2008* (Chicago: Haymarket, 2023), p. 69.
57. Jon Lawrence, *Me, Me, Me?: The Search for Community in Postwar England* (Oxford: Oxford University Press, 2019), pp. 208–11.

58. Phil Wilson, 'All the Pits Are Closed: My Labour, New Labour, Twenty-First Century Labour', *Renewal* 20, nos 2–3 (2012), pp. 28–36.
59. Anthony Giddens, *The Third Way: The Renewal of Social Democracy* (London: Polity Press, 1998), p. 39.
60. David Miliband, 'Reinventing the Left', in David Miliband (ed.), *Reinventing the Left* (Cambridge: Polity Press, 1994), pp. 2–3.
61. Gordon Brown, 'The Politics of Potential: A New Agenda for Labour', in Miliband, *Reinventing the Left*, pp. 113–16.
62. Giles Radice, *Southern Discomfort* (London: Fabian Society, 1992).
63. Lawrence, *Me, Me, Me?*, pp. 72–5, 100–6.
64. Radice, *Southern Discomfort*, pp. 2–8.
65. Philip Gould, *The Unfinished Revolution: How New Labour Changed British Politics Forever*, rev. edn (London: Abacus, 2011), p. 2.
66. Ibid., pp. 3–4.
67. Ibid., pp. 22–4.
68. Blair, *Tony Blair*, p. 188.
69. David Marquand, *The Progressive Dilemma* (London: Heinemann, 1991), p. 2.
70. Peter Mandelson, *The Third Man: Life at the Heart of New Labour* (London: Harper Press, 2010), p. 80.
71. George Parker, 'A Fiscal Focus', *Financial Times*, 7 December 2009.
72. Tony Blair, Leader's Speech, Blackpool, 4 October 1994.
73. 'The BBC and Live Top Flight Football', *That 1980s Sports Blog*, 4 July 2020, that1980ssportsblog.blogspot.com.
74. 'Timeline: A History of TV Football Rights', *Guardian*, 25 February 2003.
75. Blair, Leader's Speech, Bournemouth, 1999.
76. 'Tony Blair's Conference Speech 2005', *Guardian*, 27 September 2005.
77. Gordon Brown, *Fair Is Efficient: A Socialist Agenda for Fairness* (London: Fabian Society, 1994), pp. 1–2.
78. Adam McInnes, 'Deindustrialisation and Gordon Brown's Approach to Devolution in Scotland', *Scottish Labour History* 65 (2019), p. 129.
79. Jim Tomlinson, *Managing the Economy, Managing the People: Narratives of Economic Life in Britain from Beveridge to Brexit* (Oxford: Oxford University Press, 2017), p. 105.
80. Kitty Usher, 'Labour's Record on the Economy', in Patrick Diamond and Michael Kenny (eds), *Reassessing New Labour: Market, State and Society Under Blair and Brown* (Chichester: Wiley-Blackwell, 2011), pp. 109–10.
81. Robert Joyce and Luke Sibieta, 'Labour's Record on Poverty and Inequality', *Oxford Review of Economic Policy* 29, no. 1 (2013), pp. 178–202.

82. Ruth Strachan, 'Who Killed British Manufacturing?', *Investment Monitor*, 24 November 2020, investmentmonitor.ai.
83. Steve Fothergill, Tony Gore and David Leather, *The State of the Coalfields 2024* (Sheffield: Sheffield Hallam University, 2024); Huw Beynon and Ray Hudson, *The Shadow of the Mine: Coal and the End of Industrial Britain* (London: Verso, 2021), p. 221; Andy Clark and Ewan Gibbs, 'Voices of Social Dislocation, Lost Work and Economic Restructuring: Narratives from Marginalised Localities in the "New Scotland"', *Memory Studies* 13 (2020), pp. 42–3.
84. 'Tony Blair's Speech to the IPPR and Demos'.
85. Karl Pike and Andy Hindmoor, 'Do as I Did Not as I Say: Blair, New Labour and Party Traditions', *Political Quarterly* 91 (2020), p. 152.
86. Dan Corry, 'Labour and the Economy, 1997–2010: More than a Faustian Pact', in Diamond and Kenny, *Reassessing New Labour*, pp. 123–39.
87. Ibid., p. 127.
88. Will Hutton, *The State We're In*, rev. edn (London: Vintage, 1996), pp. xix–xx.
89. Matthew Watson and Colin Hay, 'The Discourse of Globalisation and the Logic of No Alternative: Rendering the Contingent Necessary in the Political Economy of New Labour', *Policy and Politics* 31 (2003), p. 291.
90. Corry, 'Labour and the Economy', p. 131.
91. Emily Robinson, 'The Spirit of '97', *Renewal* 23, no. 3 (2015), p. 43.
92. Blair, Leader's Speech, Blackpool, 1994.
93. Joe Sim, 'The Toxic Legacy of New Labour', *Criminal Justice Matters* 102 (2015), pp. 31–2.
94. Satnam Virdee and Brendan McGeever, *Britain in Fragments: Why Things Are Falling Apart* (Manchester: Manchester University Press, 2023), pp. 102–3.
95. Lewis Minkin, *The Blair Supremacy: A Study in the Politics of Labour's Party Management* (Oxford: Oxford University Press, 2014), pp. 663–4.
96. 'Labour Issues Apology to Heckler', *BBC News*, 28 September 2005.
97. Alan Finlayson, *Making Sense of New Labour* (London: Lawrence and Wishart, 2000), p. 114.
98. Gerry Mooney and Tricia McCafferty, 'Only Looking After the Weans'? The Scottish Nursery Nurses' Strike, 2004', *Critical Social Policy* 25 (2005), pp. 223–39.
99. Ibid.
100. Alwyn W. Turner, *A Classless Society: Britain in the 1990s* (London: Aurum Press, 2014), p. 5.

101. *The Office*, series 1, episode 4, 'Training', broadcast on BBC Two, 30 July 2001.
102. 'Character Guide: Vicky Pollard', BBC Comedy: *Little Britain*, 10 October 2014, bbc.co.uk.
103. Owen Jones, *Chavs: The Demonization of the Working Class* (London: Verso, 2012), p. 2.
104. *Only Fools and Horses*, BBC One, bbc.co.uk.
105. Scott Lavery, *British Capitalism After the Crisis* (London: Palgrave, 2019), p. 5.
106. 'How Britain Voted in 1997', IPSOS, 31 May 1997, ipsos.com; 'How Britain Voted in 2005', IPSOS, 16 May 2005, ipsos.com.
107. Filip Sosenko, Glen Bramley and Arnab Bhattacharjee, 'Understanding the Post-2010 Increase in Food Bank Use in England: New Quasi-Experimental Analysis of the Role of Welfare Policy', *BMC Public Health* 22 (2022), p. 1363.

6. The White Working Class

1. Tim Samuels, *The Poles Are Coming!*, broadcast on BBC Two, 11 March 2008.
2. Ibid.
3. 'BBC Two Winter/Spring 2008', BBC, 20 November 2007, bbc.co.uk.
4. 'White working class', Ngram viewer, books.google.com; 'Working class', Ngram viewer, books.google.com.
5. Chris Haylett, 'Illegitimate Subjects? Abject Whites, Neoliberal Modernisation, and Middle- Class Multiculturalism', *Environment and Planning D: Society and Space* 19 (2001), p. 353.
6. Anoop Nayak, 'Beyond the Pales: Chavs, Youth and Social Class', in Kjartan Páll Sveinsson (ed.), *Who Cares About the White Working Class* (Runnymede Trust, 2009), p. 28.
7. Marc Isaacs, *All White in Barking*, broadcast on BBC Two, 14 March 2008.
8. Les Back, Michael Keith, Azra Khan, Kalbir Shukra and John Solomos, 'The Return of Assimilationism: Race, Multiculturalism and New Labour', *Sociological Research Online* 7 (2002); Haylett, 'Illegitimate Subjects?', p. 356.
9. Daniel Trilling, *Bloody Nasty People: The Rise of Britain's Far Right*, rev. edn (London: Verso, 2013), p. 129.
10. Robert Ford, 'Who Might Vote for the BNP? Survey Evidence on the Electoral Potential of the Extreme Right in Britain', in Roger Eatwell and Matthew Goodwin (eds), *The New Extremism in 21st Century Britain* (London: Taylor and Francis, 2010), p. 145.

11. Matthew Goodwin, *New British Fascism: The Rise of the British National Party* (Oxon: Routledge, 2011), p. 13.
12. Stephen D. Ashe, 'Whiteness, Class and the "Communicative Community"', in Stephen D. Ashe, Joel Busher, Graham Macklin and Aaron Winter (eds), *Researching the Far Right: Theory, Method and Practice* (London: Routledge, 2020), pp. 285–6.
13. James Rhodes, 'The "Trouble" with the "White Working Class": Whiteness, Class and "Groupism"', *Identities: Global Studies in Culture and Power* 19 (2012), p. 486.
14. Anthony Ince, David Featherstone, Andrew Cumbers, Danny MacKinnon and Kendra Strauss, 'British Jobs for British Workers? Negotiating Work, Nation, and Globalisation Through the Lindsey Oil Refinery Disputes', *Antipode* 47 (2015), p. 149.
15. 'Mass Walkout over Foreign Labour', BBC News, 28 January 2009, bbc.co.uk.
16. 'Deceptive Denigration of Lindsey Strike', Socialist Party, 14 April 2009, socialistparty.org.uk.
17. Dominic Sandbrook, '"Enoch Powell Speaks for Britain": The Press, the Public and the Speech', *Political Quarterly* 89 (2018), p. 392.
18. Shirin Hirsch, *In the Shadow of Enoch Powell: Race, Locality and Resistance* (Manchester: Manchester University Press, 2018), p. 53.
19. 'PM Remarks at Immigration White Paper Press Conference', UK Government, 12 May 2025, gov.uk.
20. Ashley Gething, *Sign Zone: Rivers of Blood*, broadcast on BBC Two, 8 March 2008.
21. Ibid.
22. 'Enoch Powell's "Rivers of Blood" speech, 20 April 1968', *Telegraph*, 6 November 2007.
23. Powell, 'Rivers of Blood'.
24. Security Services, Demonstration of Dockers Against the Race Relations Bill on 23 April 1968 and 24 April 1968, National Archives (hereafter TNA), KV4-480, 38.
25. Security Services, March of the Smithfield market porters to the house of commons on 24 April 1968 in support of Mr Enoch Powell MP, 25 April 1968, TNA, KV4-480, 39.
26. Ibid.
27. Fred Lindop, 'Racism and the Working Class: Strikes in Support of Enoch Powell in 1968', *Labour History Review* 66 (2001), pp. 82–9.
28. 'Comedy: Till Death Do Us Part', BBC, bbc.co.uk.
29. Hirsch, *In the Shadow of Enoch Powell*, pp. 49–63.
30. Stephen Ashe, 'The Electoral Rise and "Fall" of the British National

Party in Barking and Dagenham' (PhD thesis, University of Glasgow, 2012), pp. 123–5.

31. Barrie Clement, 'Ford Workers Angry as Blacks Are Whited Out', *Independent*, 21 February 1996.
32. Richard Hill, 'Bill Morris: A Leader and Pioneer in British Labour Rights', Black History Month 2025, 24 August 2024, blackhistorymonth.org.uk.
33. Department for Business and Trade, 'Trade Union Membership, UK, 1995 to 2024: Statistical Bulletin', 22 May 2025, gov.uk.
34. Graham Macklin, 'Modernizing the Past for the Future', in Nigel Copsey and Graham Macklin (eds), *British National Party: Contemporary Perspectives* (London: Taylor and Francis, 2011), pp. 28–9.
35. Gail Turner, 'Trico Equal Pay Strike', *Rank and File Contact*, August 1976, Modern Records Centre, University of Warwick, records of the Electrical Trades Union (ETU), MSS 387/6/CH/17.
36. Jack Saunders, *Assembling Cultures: Workplace Activism, Labour Militancy and Cultural Change in Britain's Car Factories, 1945–82* (Manchester: Manchester University Press, 2019), pp. 120–48.
37. Mark Duffield, 'Rationalization and the Politics of Segregation: Indian Workers in Britain's Foundry Industry, 1945–62', in Kenneth Lunn (ed.), *Race and Labour in Twentieth Century Britain* (London: Frank Cass, 1985), pp. 142–72.
38. Powell, 'Rivers of Blood'.
39. Roger Seifert and Andrew Hambler, 'Wearing the Turban: The 1967–1969 Sikh Bus Drivers' Dispute in Wolverhampton', *Historical Studies in Industrial Relations* 37 (2016), pp. 83–111.
40. Hirsch, *In the Shadow of Enoch Powell*, pp. 57–8.
41. Caroline Knowles, *Race, Discourse and Labourism* (London: Routledge, 1992), pp. 91–2.
42. Camilla Schofield, *Enoch Powell and the Making of Postcolonial Britain* (Cambridge: Cambridge University Press, 2013), p. 263.
43. Marc Collinson, 'A "Fertile Ground for Poisonous Doctrines"?: Understanding Far-Right Electoral Appeal in the South Pennine Textile Belt, c.1967–1979', *Contemporary British History* 34 (2020), pp. 280–2.
44. Thomas P. Linehan, 'Whatever Happened to the Labour Movement? Proletarians and the Far Right in Contemporary Britain', in Nigel Copsey and Dave Renton (eds), *British Fascism, the Labour Movement, and the State* (Basingstoke: Palgrave, 2005), p. 164.
45. Matthew J. Goodwin, Robert Ford, Bobby Duffy and Rea Robey, 'Who Votes Extreme Right in Twenty-First Century Britain?: The Social Bases of Support for the National Front and the British National Party', in

Roger Eatwell and Matthew Goodwin (eds), *The New Extremism in 21st Century Britain* (London: Taylor and Francis, 2010), p. 194.

46. Graham Macklin, *Failed Führers: A History of Britain's Extreme Right* (London: Routledge, 2020), pp. 438–44.
47. Tom Nairn, *The Break-Up of Britain: Crisis and Neo-Nationalism* (London: New Left Books, 1977), p. 282.
48. Margaret Thatcher, TV Interview for Granada World in Action, Margaret Thatcher Foundation, 27 January 1978, margaretthatcher.org.
49. Gething, *Sign Zone.*
50. Catherine Barnard, '"British Jobs for British Workers": The Lindsey Oil Refinery Dispute and the Future of Local Labour Clauses in an Integrated EU Market', *Industrial Law Journal* 38, no. 3 (2009), pp. 251–5.
51. 'Refinery Strikes Spread Across UK', BBC News, 30 January 2009, bbc.co.uk.
52. 'Refinery Staff Vote to End Strike', BBC News, 5 February 2009, bbc .co.uk.
53. 'Refinery Strikes Spread'.
54. Gary Nicks, 'We've Won Thanks to Daily Star', *Daily Star*, 6 February 2009.
55. 'Refinery Strikes Spread'.
56. HC Deb 2 February 2009, vol. 478, cc. 579–83.
57. HC Deb 23 February 2009, vol. 488, c. 106.
58. HC Deb 2 February 2009, vol. 478, cc. 585–7.
59. Vincent Keter, Government Policy on 'British Jobs for British Workers', House of Commons Library Standard Note, DN/BT/4501, 16 September 2009.
60. Andrew Bounds, 'BNP Hopes to Gain from Dispute', *Financial Times*, 17 February 2009.
61. Robert Booth, 'Mediators Called in as Wildcat Strikes Spread Across UK', *Guardian*, 31 January 2009.
62. Jonathan Guthrie, 'These Illegal Wildcat Strikers Have a Case', *Financial Times*, 4 February 2009.
63. Martin Smith, 'Economic Crisis and Job Losses: Who's to Blame?', *Socialist Review* 334, 1 March 2009, p. 10.
64. Ince et al., 'British Jobs for British Workers?', p. 140.
65. Gary Nicks, 'Great British Job Revolt Grows', *Daily Star*, 31 January 2009.
66. Gary Nicks, 'We've Won Thanks to Daily Star', *Daily Star*, 6 February 2009.
67. Steve Hughes, 'British Jobs for British Workers: Download Our Poster Now', *Daily Star*, 10 February 2009.

68. Gregor Gall, 'The Engineering Construction Strikes in Britain, 2009', *Capital and Class* 36 (2012), p. 421.
69. Bounds, 'BNP Hopes to Gain'.
70. Leigh Holmwood, 'BBC Apologises for Misleading Edit of Striking Worker', *Guardian*, 6 February 2009. 'Eyeties' is a slang but not necessarily bigoted term meaning Italians.
71. 'Ten Years Since Lindsey Strike: When Militant Action Stopped the "Race to the Bottom"', Socialist Party, 13 February 2019, socialistparty.org.uk.
72. Blaine Williams, 'Talks Restart to End the Strike Action', politics.co.uk, 3 February 2009.
73. Ince et al., 'British Jobs for British Workers?', p. 145.
74. Ibid., p. 141.
75. Macklin, *Failed Führers*, pp. 499–500.
76. Martin Fletcher, 'Far Right Mines a Rich Seam of Disaffection from Pit Closures', *The Times*, 12 May 2009, pp. 16–17.
77. Peter John, Helen Margetts, David Rowland and Stuart Weir, *The BNP: The Roots of Its Appeal* (Colchester: University of Essex, 2006), p. 7.
78. Linehan, 'Whatever Happened to the Labour Movement?', pp. 165–6.
79. Nigel Copsey and Graham Macklin, 'Introduction: Contemporary Perspectives on the British National Party', in Copsey and Macklin, *British National Party*, p. 8.
80. Goodwin, *New British Fascism*, p. 109.
81. James Bloodworth, 'Matthew Goodwin, Reform and the Politics of Resentment', *Prospect*, 16 July 2025; Matthew Goodwin, *Values, Voice and Virtue: The New British Politics* (London: Penguin, 2023), p. 39.
82. Quoted in James Rhodes, 'The Political Breakthrough of the BNP: The Case of Burnley', *British Politics* 4 (2009), p. 32.
83. Mike Makin-Waite, *On Burnley Road: Class, Race and Politics in a Northern English Town* (London: Lawrence and Wishart, 2021), p. 23.
84. Ewan Gibbs, 'Deindustrialization and Nationhood', in Tim Strangleman, Sherry Lee Linkon, Steven High, Jackie Clarke and Stefan Berger (eds), *The Routledge International Handbook of Deindustrialization Studies* (London: Routledge, 2025), pp. 138–53.
85. Ashe, 'The Electoral Rise and "Fall" of the British National Party', pp. 211–47.
86. Ian Herbert and Emily Dugan, 'Exposed: BNP's Campaign of Lies', *Independent*, 22 April 2006.
87. Ashe, 'The Electoral Rise and "Fall" of the British National Party', p. 255.
88. Jon Lawrence, *Me, Me, Me?: The Search for Community in Postwar England* (Oxford: Oxford University Press, 2019), p. 15.

89. Florence Sutcliffe-Braithwaite, *Class, Politics, and the Decline of Deference in England, 1968–2000* (Oxford: Oxford University Press, 2018), p. 86.
90. James Rhodes, "It's Not Just Them, It's Whites as Well: Whiteness, Class and BNP Support', *Sociology* 45 (2011), pp. 109–11.
91. Quoted in Makin-Waite, *On Burnley Road*, p. 97.
92. John et al., *The BNP*, pp. 13–15.
93. Trilling, *Bloody Nasty People*, pp. 121–2.
94. Karin Bottom and Colin Copus, 'The BNP in Local Government: Support for the Far-Right or for Community Politics?', in Copsey and Macklin, *British National Party*, pp. 142–3.
95. BNP, *Democracy, Freedom, Culture and Identity: British National Party General Election Manifesto 2010* (Welshpool: BNP, 2010), p. 22.
96. Ibid., p. 4.
97. Ibid., p. 35.
98. Ibid., pp. 24, 35.
99. Macklin, *Failed Führers*, p. 485.
100. Helen Pidd, 'BNP Votes to Scrap Whites-Only Policy', *Guardian*, 14 February 2010.
101. Ashe, 'The Electoral Rise and "Fall" of the British National Party', pp. 188–92.
102. Trilling, *Bloody Nasty People*, p. 181.
103. Morgan McSweeney and Jessica Studdert, *Challenging the BNP* (London: Local Government Association Labour Group, March 2010), pp. 15, 29, 37–8.
104. Patrick Maguire and Gabriel Pogrund, *Get In: The Inside Story of Labour Under Starmer* (London: Bodley Head, 2025), pp. 26, 87, 391.
105. '"Bigotgate" 10 Years On: The Full Exchange Between Gordon Brown and Gillian Duffy', *Independent*, 28 April 2020.
106. 'Gillian Duffy: "I Don't Want to Be a European"', BBC News, 25 May 2016, bbc.co.uk.
107. Jacqueline O'Reilly et al., 'Brexit: Understanding the Socio-Economic Origins and Consequences', *Socio-Economic Review* 14 (2016), p. 809.
108. James Walsh, 'A British Politician Lost Her Job over a Tweet', *Guardian*, 21 November 2014.
109. Nicola Jordan, '"White Van Dan" from Strood Is Voting Tory After Being Dragged into the Furore with Pictures Tweeted of His England Flag-Draped Home', *Kent Online*, 28 April 2015, kentonline.co.uk.
110. Dan Evans, 'Reform Won't Save Britain', *UnHerd*, 19 March 2025, unherd.com; see also Dan Evans, *A Nation of Shopkeepers: The Unstoppable Rise of the Petite Bourgeoisie* (London: Repeater, 2023).

111. 'Full text: Theresa May's Conference Speech', *Spectator*, 5 October 2016.
112. Rob Davies, 'Loan "Irregularities" Led to Collapse of Prax Lindsey Oil Refinery', *Guardian*, 20 August 2025.
113. Josiah Mortimer, '"Dancing with the Devil": Unite Condemned for Invite to Reform's Anti-Trade Union Mayor Andrea Jenkyns', *Byline Times*, 20 August 2025.

7. Essential Workers

1. Stuart Macintyre, *Little Moscows: Communism and Working-Class Militancy in Inter-War Britain* (Beckenham: Croom Helm, 1980), pp. 16–21.
2. William Gallacher, *Revolt on the Clyde* (Southampton: Camelot, 1978), p. 251; John Foster, 'Willie Gallacher – in Praise of an Agitator', *Scottish Labour History* 50 (2015), pp. 116–23.
3. Abe Moffat, *My Life with the Miners* (London: Lawrence and Wishart, 1965).
4. Miles Oglethorpe, 'Lochore, Mary Colliery', event reference: 1122932 (2006), trove.scot.
5. For a fuller discussion of Brendan's working life and the end of coal mining in Scotland, see Ewan Gibbs, *Coal Country: The Meaning and Memory of Deindustrialization in Postwar Scotland* (London: University of London Press, 2021).
6. André Gorz, *Farewell to the Working Class: An Essay on Post-Industrial Socialism*, trans. Michael Sonensche (London: Pluto, 1982), pp. 10, 38–9.
7. Gregory Burke, *Gagarin Way* (London: Faber and Faber, 2001), p. 60.
8. Danny MacKinnon and Andrew Cumbers, *An Introduction to Economic Geography: Globalization, Uneven Development and Place* (Hoboken, NJ: Pearson Education, 2007), p. 240.
9. Steve Fothergill, Tony Gore and David Leather, *The State of the Coalfields 2024: Economic and Social Conditions in the Former Coalfields of England, Scotland and Wales* (Sheffield: Sheffield Hallam University, 2024), pp. 18–19.
10. Elizabeth Hunter, 'Dunfermline: Take a Look Inside the Largest Amazon Warehouse in the UK', *Scotsman*, 23 November 2023.
11. An anonymous Amazon worker in Coventry, 'How the Amazon Wildcat Spread', *Notes from Below* 15 (7 August 2022), notesfrombelow.org.
12. *Notes from Below* 16: The Class Composition Project (21 March 2023), notesfrombelow.org.

13. 'Trade Union Organisation', *Notes from Below* 16 (21 March 2023), notesfrombelow.org.
14. Gregor Gall, *Mick Lynch: The Making of a Working-Class Hero* (Manchester: Manchester University Press, 2024), p. 98.
15. Office for National Statistics, Labour Disputes: Working Days Lost Due to Strike Action: UK (thousands), 20 March 2025, gov.uk.
16. Ken Loach, *I, Daniel Blake* (BBC Films, 2016).
17. *The Scheme*, broadcast on BBC One Scotland between 18 May 2010 and 30 May 2011, and *Benefits Street*, broadcast on Channel 4 between 6 January 2014 and 1 June 2015.
18. Alex Ritman, 'BBC Broadcast of Ken Loach's *I, Daniel Blake* Sparks Debate in UK', *Hollywood Reporter*, 7 January 2019.
19. 'The Great British Class Calculator', BBC, 3 April 2013, bbc.co.uk.
20. Mike Savage, *Social Class in the 21st Century* (London: Pelican, 2015), p. 6.
21. Ibid.
22. Ibid., p. 20.
23. Ibid., pp. 170–1.
24. Mike Savage, *The Dynamics of Working-Class Politics: The Labour Movement in Preston, 1880–1940* (Cambridge: Cambridge University Press, 1987), p. 53.
25. Savage, *Social Class in the 21st Century*, pp. 393–5.
26. Harold D. Clarke, 'What Do Willie Sutton and Tony Blair Have in Common? A Response to *The New Politics of Class* by Geoffrey Evans and James Tilley', *Political Quarterly* 88 (2017), pp. 696–7.
27. Adam McDonnell and Chris Curtis, 'How Britain Voted in the 2019 General Election', YouGov, 17 December 2019, yougov.com.
28. Geoffrey Evans and James Tilley, *The New Politics of Class: The Political Exclusion of the British Working Class* (Oxford: Oxford University Press, 2017), p. 181.
29. Rachel Reeves, 'Labour's Class Coalitions, Then and Now: A Response to *The New Politics of Class* by Geoffrey Evans and James Tilley', *Political Quarterly* 88 (2017), p. 703.
30. 'Veteran Labour Lawmaker Dennis Skinner Loses to Conservatives', Reuters, 13 December 2019, reuters.com.
31. Andrew Topping, 'MP Threatens the Return of His Boulders if Travellers Issue Isn't Resolved', *Nottingham Post*, 6 July 2020.
32. Peter Walker, 'Sunak Says No Islamophobia Issues in Tory Party Despite Anderson Remarks', *Guardian*, 26 February 2024.
33. Archie Mitchell, 'Ex-Tory Deputy Chair Lee Anderson Joins Right-Wing Populist Party Reform UK', *Independent*, 11 March 2024.
34. 'UK General Election 2024 Results', BBC News, bbc.co.uk.

35. Richard Cracknell and Carl Baker, General Election 2024: Results and Analysis, House of Commons Library Briefing No.10009, 24 September 2024, p. 17.
36. Adam McDonnell, 'How Britain Voted in the 2024 General Election', YouGov, 8 July 2024, yougov.com.
37. Chris Mason, 'Government Considers Nationalising British Steel', BBC News, 8 April 2025, bbc.co.uk.
38. Lauren Almeida, '"He's One of the Few Politicians Who Likes Crypto': My Day with the UK Tech Bros Hosting Nigel Farage', *Guardian*, 25 October 2025.
39. Sacha Hilhorst, 'Reform's Aesthetics of Industry', *Renewal* 33, no. 2 (2025), pp. 22–3.
40. Ibid., pp. 25–9.
41. Quoted in Kirsteen Paton, *Class and Everyday Life* (London: Routledge, 2023), pp. 167–8.
42. Harriet Bradley, 'Class Descriptors or Class Relations? Thoughts Towards a Critique of Savage et al.', *Sociology* 48 (2014), pp. 429–36.
43. Colin Mills, 'The Great British Class Fiasco: A Comment on Savage et al.', *Sociology* 48 (2014), p. 443.
44. Guy Standing, *The Precariat: The New Dangerous Class* (London: Bloomsbury, 2011), pp. 5–7.
45. Savage, *Social Class in the 21st Century*, pp.171, 331.
46. Phil Burton-Cartledge, 'Labour and 21st Century Class Politics', *All That Is Solid*, 13 June 2017, averypublicsociologist.blogspot.com.
47. Patrycja Rozbicka, '"Oh Jeremy Corbyn": What GE2017 Taught Us About the Link Between Music and Politics', *LSE British Politics*, 15 July 2017, blogs.lse.ac.uk.
48. 'Stormzy Praised for Heartfelt Grenfell Tower Tribute Verse', BBC News, 21 June 2017, bbc.co.uk.
49. Phil Burton-Cartledge, 'Labour and the New Working Class', *All That Is Solid*, 9 January 2020, averypublicsociologist.blogspot.com.
50. Alvaro de Miranda, 'Class and Nation in the Age of Populism: The Forward March of Labour Restarted?', *Soundings* 75 (2020), pp. 136–7.
51. For more on the project, see Hailey Maxwell, Ruth Gilbert, Suki Sangha and Ewan Gibbs, 'Scottish Workers' Stories of Life and Labour during COVID-19', *Studies in Scottish Literature* 50 (2025), pp. 120–33.
52. Jacky Yuill, 'My Experience of Being a Cleaner in a Care Home Through COVID-19', Workers' Stories Project, 12 June 2020, workersstories .org.uk. This website is no longer active, but Jacky Yuill's story will be archived as part of the Workers' Stories Project collection by the National Library of Scotland. For an online version, see the next note.

53. Jacky Yuill, 'Care Before Profit: Working as a Cleaner in a Care Home During the COVID-19 Pandemic' is archived with the Women and Workplace Struggles: Scotland 1900–2022 collection on the Open University website, open.edu.
54. Phil Butland, 'The Politics of Greta Thunberg', *Left Berlin*, 11 November 2021, theleftberlin.com.
55. Charles Read, 'Reforming the Bank of England to Tame Inflation and Boost Financial Stability', *History and Policy* paper, September 2022.
56. Office for National Statistics, Coronavirus and Key Workers in the UK, 15 May 2020, gov.uk.
57. Ewan Gibbs, 'Refusing to Be Poor Anymore?: British Trade Unionism in the 2020s', Institut Montaigne, 14 August 2023, institutmontaigne.org.
58. Gregor Gall, 'Union Busting at Amazon.com in Britain', *Indy Media*, 21 January 2004, indymedia.org.uk.
59. An anonymous Amazon worker, 'Wildcat Strike at Amazon', *Notes from Below* 15 (5 August 2022), notesfrombelow.org.
60. Ibid.
61. Callum Cant, 'Mapping the Amazon Strikes', *Notes from Below* 15 (22 August 2022), notesfrombelow.org.
62. Jamie Woodcock, *Working the Phones: Control and Resistance in Call Centres* (London: Pluto, 2017), pp. 33–44.
63. Callum Cant, *Riding for Deliveroo: Resistance in the New Economy* (London: Polity Press, 2020), pp. 144–68.
64. Department for Business and Trade, 'Trade Union Membership, UK, 1995 to 2024: Statistical Bulletin', 22 May 2025, gov.uk.
65. Taj Ali, 'England's Rugeley Amazon Warehouse Tells the Story of Postindustrial Decline', *Jacobin*, 9 May 2023, jacobin.com.
66. Andrew Kersley, 'Ambulances Called to Amazon's UK Warehouses 1,400 times in Five Years', *Guardian*, 17 August 2024.
67. Richard Partington and Heather Stewart, 'Amazon Workers in Coventry Lose Union Recognition Ballot by Handful of Votes', *Guardian*, 17 July 2024.
68. House of Commons Business and Trade Committee Oral Evidence: Make Work Pay: Employment Rights Bill, 17 December 2024, Questions 52–55. Regarding the Amazon worker who apparently got acid in his eyes, Morgan responded, 'I don't recognise that specific case. If you had details of that case, then we would write a follow-up. What I can say is that, for any incident that does take place, we conduct a thorough investigation of it.'

Conclusion

1. LBC, 'Define "Working Class": Keir Starmer Challenged by Nick Ferrari', YouTube, 23 October 2023.
2. Ibid.
3. E.P. Thompson, *The Making of the English Working Class* (Middlesex: Pelican, 1968), p. 8.
4. Bob Mason and Peter Bain, 'The Determinants of Trade Union Membership in Britain: A Survey of the Literature', *Industrial and Labor Relations Review* 46 (1993), p. 333.
5. Department for Business and Trade, Trade Union Membership, UK 1995–2023: Statistical Bulletin, 29 May 2024, p. 1.
6. Office for National Statistics, Labour Disputes: Working Days Lost Due to Strike Action; UK (thousands), 20 March 2025, gov.uk.
7. C.T.B. Smith, R. Clifton, P. Markham, S.W. Creigh and R.V. Burn, *Strikes in Britain: A Research Study of Industrial Stoppages in the United Kingdom* (London: HMSO, 1978), pp. 54–5.
8. John Goldthorpe, David Lockwood, Frank Bechhofer and Jennifer Platt, *The Affluent Worker: Industrial Attitudes and Behaviour* (Cambridge: Cambridge University Press, 1968), p. 98.
9. Lynsey Brown, Mike Welsby and David Roberts, 'Understanding Changes in Self-Employment in the UK: January 2019 to March 2022', Office for National Statistics, 6 July 2022, gov.uk.
10. Georgina Hutton, *Research Briefing: Business Statistics* (London: House of Commons Library, 2024), p. 8.
11. Dan Evans, *A Nation of Shopkeepers: The Unstoppable Rise of the Petite Bourgeoisie* (London: Repeater, 2023), pp. 231–3.
12. Nick Bano, 'The End of Landlords', *Guardian*, 19 March 2024.
13. Ministry of Housing and Local Government, English Private Landlord Survey 2024: Main Report, 5 December 2024.
14. John Boughton, *Municipal Dreams: The Rise and Fall of Council Housing* (London: Verso, 2018), p. 66.
15. Neville Kirk, *British Society and Its Three Crises: From 1960s Globalisation to the Financial Crash of 2007–8 and the Onset of Brexit in 2016* (Liverpool: Liverpool University Press, 2024), p. 16.
16. Meeting of the Scottish Parliament, 12 January 2023, Official Report, c.27.
17. Gregor Gall, *Mick Lynch: The Making of a Working-Class Hero* (Manchester: Manchester University Press, 2024), p. 98.
18. Huw Beynon, Rhys Davies and Steve Davies, 'Sources of Variation in Trade Union Membership Across the UK: The Case of Wales', *Industrial Relations Journal* 43 (2012), p. 202.

Index